the food of
INDIA

the food of
INDIA

Location photography by Jason Lowe
Recipe photography by Alan Benson
Recipes by Priya Wickramasinghe
and Carol Selva Rajah

MURDOCH BOOKS

the external boundaries of India on this map have
not been authenticated and may not be correct.

CONTENTS

FOOD JOURNEYS IN INDIA

the food of
INDIA

INDIA IS A VERY COMPLEX COUNTRY CULTURALLY, GEOGRAPHICALLY AND FROM A CULINARY POINT OF VIEW. COOKING STYLES VARY NOT ONLY FROM STATE TO STATE AND TOWN TO TOWN BUT ALSO FROM SUBURB TO SUBURB.

Modern India is one of the most diverse countries in the world. It is made up of 25 states and 7 territories and its people use 18 major (and over 1600 minor) languages and practise 7 major religions. Despite this, and its history of constant invasion and change, India has kept a strong sense of national identity and has used outside influences to its advantage.

INFLUENCES

Historically, Indian cuisine has had many influences, one of the biggest being vegetarianism, brought about by religious beliefs. Buddhism and Jainism came to India around the 6th century BC and though they faded as major religions in India, they were particularly successful in converting people to a way of life in which living beings are considered to be sacred. Hinduism predated both these religions but early Hindu texts such as the Mahabharata show that meat was not originally prohibited. Meat is still occasionally eaten by some Hindus. Over time, vegetarianism slowly pervaded Indian culture and today it is practised by many people, particularly in the South. The sacred status of the cow, a Vedic idea from before Hinduism, also remains to this day.

In 1525, the Moghul emperors arrived and brought with them their own style of cooking, architecture and living, which affirmed their religion, Islam, and its Arabic heritage. Muslims had periodically been invading India since the 10th century but this later time was the period of their greatest influence and at one stage they ruled nearly the whole subcontinent. Pork was taboo but meats such as lamb and chicken were eaten as long as they were killed according to Muslim law.

Hindu deities are on display at festival times. Old buildings in Chennai (Madras) present a range of architectural styles, all built for coolness in the heat of the day. Reading is a popular pastime in Kerala where the literacy rate officially runs at 100%. Tea is the national drink; a woman sits in her doorway in Hyderabad; vegetables, poppadoms and sweets can be bought on the streets.

A man hurls his fish onto the Sassoon Docks in Mumbai (Bombay) and poppadoms are made on the rooftops in the shadow of Delhi's Moghul architecture. Women plant rice in Kerala; Indian cooking makes great use of pulses and spices. Trading is brisk at the capital's spice market and a cow munches nonchalantly on grass in a temple. School children are laughing in Hyderabad.

Many dishes were a product of the court chefs, trained in Central Asian, Persian and Afghani culinary styles. Money was no object and imagination was boundless. The Moghuls incorporated some of their favourite foods such as almonds, cream and dried fruits into Indian cuisine and introduced cold weather fruit such as peaches, cherries and apricots to the orchards of Kashmir. The use of saffron and gold and silver leaf reflects the opulence of Moghul cuisine, especially in sweets. These influences are most apparent in northern India and in areas such as Hyderabad, the site of an ancient court, where there were Muslim settlements.

China, another ancient culture, had also long had an association with India via its maritime and overland trading routes. The karhai and wok are extremely similar in appearance, though which came first is impossible to say. Chinese-style bowls are used to serve soups and foods thought to have come from China. Some words, such as 'chiniani' meaning peach, start with 'chin'. The Chinese word for tea, 'cha', also became incorporated into the language when the British began to cultivate tea in India.

Influences from further afield can be seen in Goa and Kerala where the Portuguese established ports, in Chennai (Madras) where the British set up the East India Company, in Pondicherry, a French enclave, and in Kolkata (Calcutta), the centre of the British Raj. With the Europeans came more widespread Christianity (St Thomas had arrived in AD 52) and new styles of cooking to add to the established Muslim and Hindu ways. Foods such as potatoes, tomatoes, capsicums (peppers) and chillies, imported from the New World via Europe, were gradually incorporated into local cuisines until in some cases, as with the chilli, they became ubiquitous.

The British influence on Indian cuisine was much less than the Indian impact on British food. For example, the British encouraged the idea of frequently nibbling on tiffin, which are little snacks. Also the Indian cooks of the British Empire, urged on by their memsahibs, learned to make cakes, yeasted bread and 'curries', which were more suited to the British palate. The British developed a liking for spicy food and transported the idea back home where it was Anglicised.

INDIAN FOOD MYTHS

The type of Indian food found in the majority of Indian restaurants is based on a very successful menu formula. The original versions of these restaurants were run by Punjabis in India where they served a mixture of Punjabi cuisine, such as tandoori, and Moghul dishes such as

THE FOOD OF INDIA

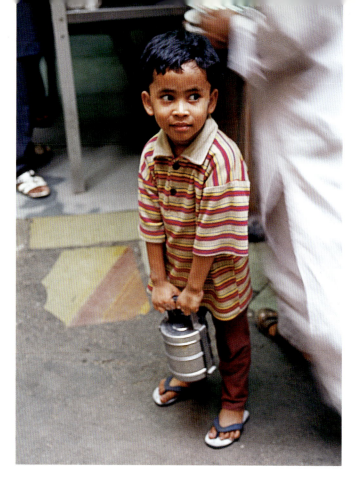

korma and biryani. As the popularity of the cuisine grew, the 'menu' was established, then replicated in new restaurants. This menu represents a tiny section of Indian cuisine.

In India, there is no such thing as a curry. The word is of English origin, based on the Tamil word 'kari' meaning black pepper, and is a term used to denote all kinds of Indian dishes, particularly those in a sauce. Dishes in India are named either for the combination of spices used (rogan josh), for the cooking method (korma, biryani, do piaza), or for their main ingredients (saag, aloo gobi). Curry powder does not exist within India, the closest equivalent being masala (spice mix). There are hundreds of masala combinations. In northern India, they tend to be dry mixtures using ground spices such as garam masala and in the southern areas, wet ones, such as coconut masala, using fresh spices. Indian food is not universally hot. Some dishes contain lots of chillies, others none at all.

EATING

Meat or vegetarian dishes are never the main part of the meal. They are always an accompaniment to rice or breads and are eaten alongside relishes, chutneys and other dishes such as dal. Yoghurt or curd is also served with meals and is particularly useful for cooling hot or spicy food. The types of dishes eaten vary according to religious group. Hindus tend to eat vegetable dishes and dals served with plain boiled rice. Muslims serve meat and seafood dishes, breads, and fried snacks such as samosas, but dal does not play such an important part. So generally, Indian meals consist of a couple of vegetable dishes (and meat or fish where appropriate), some relishes or chutneys, yoghurt, rice, breads and a dessert, usually all served at the same time. Sometimes, samosas or other deep-fried snacks are included.

Meals are often served on thalis, which are large, flat plates, made from banana leaves or metal. Though more prevalent in southern areas and in Gujarat, they are a common element of Indian cuisine, used by all strata of society. The leaf or plate is covered with either small mounds of food or metal bowls called katoris which hold the food. The food, eaten with the fingertips of your right hand, is replenished as you eat.

Paan is a collection of spices and aromatics often served at the end of the meal to freshen the breath and act as a digestive. A betel leaf is folded around pieces of betel nut, and either lime paste, red katha paste, chewing tobacco or mitha masala (spices). The whole lot is chewed before being either spat out, or in the case of mitha masala, swallowed.

Food is all encompassing in India. A small boy carries his lunch in a tiffin carrier; pickles and samosas are sold on the street and a man fishes in peace from a tank in Kolkata (Calcutta). The pace of life on the roads, whether on two wheels or more, is in direct contrast to the leisurely sale of paan, banana leaves and fish by stallholders. Kolkata's (Calcutta) New Market is busy all day.

Tandoori is popular all over the northern areas, as are Moghul-style pulaos. Delicious fruit chaat is sold on the streets alongside pistachios, amla and pomegranates. Holy cows wander the streets of Delhi as rice from around the country is unloaded at the market. The Jama Masjid (Friday mosque) is a focus for Delhi's Muslims while Hindus sell puris during Divali.

THE FOOD OF THE NORTH

The cuisines in the north of India cover a wide range of food styles, the main influences coming from the cooking of the Moghuls and Punjabs, as well as from the land, which produces a diverse range of grains. Traditionally, rice was not eaten in large quantities as the climate of the area meant it could not be easily grown. However, in Jammu and Kashmir, and in Dera Dun, rice is grown on terraces in the Himalayan foothills. Basmati, the king of rices, comes from Dera Dun and is prized throughout India.

As breads are a staple, there is a huge range to choose from. In Kashmir and Jammu, the kulcha and sheermal are Middle Eastern in style, in the Punjab and Haryana, naan are cooked in tandoors, and parathas, puris, chapatis and roti are widely eaten. Breads are usually served with dishes which have a thick sauce that is easily scooped up. Dishes with a more liquid sauce are generally served with rice.

Dairy products such as malai (cream), paneer and yoghurt appear at almost every meal in some guise or other. Butter appears in the form of ghee or makhan (white butter). Dishes are thickened and enriched with cream and in the Punjab butter is used both as a condiment and as a flavouring. Rajasthani cuisine contains many dishes cooked in buttermilk, milk or butter. This cooking style evolved because water was scarce and its use as a cooking medium had to be avoided. Northern dishes are often cooked in sealed pots in very little liquid, a method known as 'dum'.

Meat is a feature of northern cuisine. This is a reflection of Moghul influences as well as those of other communities such as the Parsis and Sikhs. Lamb is popular meat though game is also favoured in the Punjab and Rajasthan. Pulses and legumes are commonly eaten and a dal of some sort, often well spiced, will accompany every meal.

Spices in these areas tend to be based on 'hot mixes'. This means warmly flavoured spices rather than heat from chillies. Many spices are dry-roasted before being used, in order to add depth to their flavour. The most well known is garam masala which is used to temper dishes at the end of cooking.

The custom of cooking in community ovens or tandoors prevails in rural areas, especially in the Punjab. The ovens are used to cook breads and roast meats, something which is not possible in home-style kitchens, where cooking pots are set above open fires.

THE FOOD OF THE CENTRE

Central India has an eclectic mix of foods which can be roughly divided into East (Bengal), West (Gujarat and Maharashtra) and Central (Hyderabad) styles. Fish feature heavily on both coasts while Hyderabad has a cuisine with Moghul overtones and a diet rich in meat.

Fish, both coastal and those from inland waterways, appear in many Bengali, Assamese and Orissan dishes, hilsa being a particular favourite. Smaller fish are made into soupy johl or deep-fried with spices. Larger ones are covered with thick spice pastes and steamed or fried. On the opposite coast, the fish market on Mumbai's (Bombay) Sassoon Docks is the busiest in India and caters to the varied communities of Mumbai (Bombay), as well as national and international buyers. The Parsi people in Mumbai (Bombay) and Gujarat use fish for more elaborate dishes such as patra ni machi, which is traditionally served at weddings.

Spices are varied in their use. Seed spices such as cumin and coriander grow in Gujarat, as do turmeric and chillies. These are all used extensively in the mainly vegetarian cuisine of the area. In Bengal, a spice mix called panch phoron dominates and mustard seeds and mustard oil are a common combination. Hyderabad, further south, uses southern spices and aromatics, such as curry leaves and tamarind, blended with a Moghul style of cooking.

Rice is eaten as a staple across most of the Centre. Red patni rice, with its chewy texture and nutty aroma, grows in the Centre and West, especially in coastal areas, and is thought to be good for giving energy. In Hyderabad, rice is cooked with saffron and spices and transformed into biryani and pulao, or added to lentils to make khichhari, which is a favourite breakfast dish eaten with poppadoms and kheema.

Dairy-based sweets such as rossogollas, gulab jamun and sandesh are found all over Bengal but especially in the capital, Kolkata (Calcutta), where there are numerous sweet shops. Gujarat produces jaggery, a raw sugar made from sugar cane. This is eaten as a sweetmeat and is also added in small quantities to pulse and vegetable dishes.

Tea is grown all along the Brahmaputra valley in Assam, the main tea-producing area of India. It is here that the first tea gardens were established by the British in the 19th century. India's finest tea, however, is grown in Darjeeling, a hill station in the foothills of the Himalayas in West Bengal.

Children play on the streets in Kolkata (Calcutta). Pulses and vegetables are eaten across the central states. Fish are popular in Bengal and Maharashtra. Tea is grown in Assam. On the west coast in Mumbai (Bombay), people gather on Chowpatty beach at sunset to walk, talk and eat chaat. Bhajis are fried on request. In Hyderabad the selection of pickles is incomparable.

15

The southern part of India is a land abundant in fruit and vegetables. Fish is sold within hours of being caught, some coming from the Chinese fishing nets in the backwaters of Kerala. Chicken is popular as are turmeric and coconuts, while vanilla is grown for the international market. Elephants carry their own lunch to work and masks hang on a wall in Kochi (Cochin).

KAY BEES
CHICKENS
ഇറച്ചി കോഴി

THE FOOD OF THE SOUTH

The food of southern India has a lighter, fresher flavour than that of the northern parts. It is often more pungent because of its use of chillies and souring agents such as lime juice, kokum and tamarind. Freshly grated coconut is used in abundance and coconut milk is a common cooking liquid.

Along the west coast in Goa, Karnataka and Kerala, there are culinary influences from the Portuguese who lived in the area for 500 years, the Syrian Christians, and the Jews of Kochi (Cochin). Commercial coconut cultivation was encouraged by the Portuguese, tea was planted around the hill stations in the Nilgiris by the British, and coffee, which is grown across the South, a legacy of Arab merchants, is more popular than tea. The chilli, which was to have a profound effect on the cuisine of India, arrived in Kerala with the Portuguese.

The spice centre of India is Kochi (Cochin) in Kerala and it is here that the Indian Spices Board has its headquarters. Cardamom, turmeric, vanilla, pepper and ginger grow in abundance in the Cardamom Hills and are sold locally and internationally via the spice market in Kochi.

Rice is the main staple, along with pulses and legumes, and dishes are flavoured with wet (fresh) spice and herb mixtures, and coconut. Many dishes are tempered with a final seasoning (tarka), usually a combination of mustard seeds, dried chillies and curry leaves heated in oil and stirred into the dish. Pulses are eaten as dals and also ground into flours to make poppadoms and other deep-fried snacks. Appams, idlis and dosas are common across southern India and are eaten with chutneys and stew-like dishes, or in the case of the dosa, holding a spicy potato filling.

Pork and beef are sold and eaten in Goa and Kerala, supported by a high level of religious tolerance. Vindaloo and bafath are popular pork dishes with European styles of cooking using local ingredients. Lamb dishes are eaten by the Mappilas, the Muslims of the Malabar coast, descendants of Arab traders. Moghul-style recipes such as korma are cooked using southern flavours including coconut and curry leaves. In contrast, Karnataka and Tamil Nadu both have a strong vegetarian bent to their cuisine.

Both the coast and waterways of the area provide many types of fish and shellfish. In Kerala, there are Chinese fishing nets used for catching fish in the backwaters. Seafood caught off the coast is some of the best in India.

TIFFIN

Don't over-stuff the samosas or they will burst when cooked. Seal them and use a fork to press the edges together firmly.

SAMOSAS

THESE CRISP, DEEP-FRIED PASTRIES ARE THE MOST POPULAR SAVOURY SNACK IN INDIA. THIS RECIPE HAS A DELICIOUS SPICY VEGETABLE FILLING BUT IF YOU PREFER A MEAT SAMOSA, YOU CAN USE THE SINGHARA FILLING ON PAGE 46. SAMOSAS ARE USUALLY SERVED WITH CHUTNEY.

PASTRY
450 g (1 lb) maida or plain
  (all-purpose) flour
1 teaspoon salt
4 tablespoons oil or ghee

FILLING
400 g (14 oz) potatoes, cut into
  quarters
80 g (1/2 cup) peas
1 1/2 teaspoons cumin seeds
1/2 teaspoon coriander seeds
2 tablespoons oil
1/2 onion, finely chopped
1/4 teaspoon ground turmeric
1/2 teaspoon garam masala
  (page 284)
2 green chillies, chopped
3 cm (1 1/4 inch) piece of ginger,
  chopped
1 1/2 tablespoons lemon juice
2 tablespoons chopped coriander
  (cilantro) leaves

oil for deep-frying

MAKES 30

TO MAKE the pastry, sift the maida and salt into a bowl, then rub in the oil or ghee until the mixture resembles breadcrumbs. Add 185 ml (3/4 cup) warm water, a little at a time, to make a pliable dough. Turn out onto a floured surface and knead for 5 minutes, or until smooth. Cover and set aside for 15 minutes. Don't refrigerate or the oil will harden.

TO MAKE the filling, cook the potato in simmering water for 10 minutes, or until tender. Drain and cut into small cubes. Cook the peas in simmering water for 2 minutes. Drain and refresh in cold water.

PLACE a small frying pan over low heat, dry-roast the cumin seeds until aromatic, then remove. Dry-roast the coriander seeds. Grind 1/2 teaspoon of the cumin and all the coriander to a fine powder in a spice grinder or pestle and mortar.

HEAT the oil in a heavy-based saucepan over low heat and fry the onion until light brown. Stir in all the cumin, the coriander, turmeric and garam masala. Add the potato, chilli, ginger and stir for 1 minute. Mix in the lemon juice and coriander leaves and salt, to taste, then leave to cool.

ON a floured surface, roll out a third of the pastry to a 28 cm (11 inch) circle, about 3 mm (1/8 inch) thick. Cut 10 circles with an 8 cm (3 inch) cutter and spoon 1/2 tablespoon of filling onto the centre of each. Moisten the edges with water, then fold over and seal with a fork into a semicircle. Repeat to use all the filling and pastry. Cover until ready to fry.

FILL a karhai or heavy-based saucepan one-third full with oil and heat to 180°C/350°F (a cube of bread will brown in 15 seconds). Fry a few samosas at a time until lightly browned. Turn them over and brown them on the other side. Drain on a wire rack for 5 minutes before draining on paper towels. Serve warm or cold.

PORK TIKKA

ENCRUSTED IN SPICES AND MOUTHWATERINGLY TENDER ON THE INSIDE, PORK TIKKA IS A POPULAR DISH IN PUNJABI DHABAS (ROADSIDE RESTAURANTS) AND AT STREET STALLS. IT IS OFTEN SERVED WITH CHAPATIS, ROTI OR NAAN AND CHUTNEY ON THE SIDE.

MARINADE
1 onion, roughly chopped
3 garlic cloves, roughly chopped
5 cm (2 inch) piece of ginger, roughly chopped
1/2 tablespoon ground cumin
1 teaspoon ground coriander
1/2 tablespoon garam masala (page 284)
1/4 teaspoon chilli powder
1/2 pinch ground black pepper
250 ml (1 cup) thick plain yoghurt (page 280)

500 g (1 lb 2 oz) pork tenderloin, centre cut, cut into 2.5 cm (1 inch) cubes

SAUCE
1 large red onion, roughly chopped
1 garlic clove, roughly chopped
2.5 cm (1 inch) piece of ginger, roughly chopped
1 green chilli, roughly chopped
25 g (3/4 cup) coriander (cilantro) leaves

125 ml (1/2 cup) oil
1 tablespoon garam masala (page 284)

SERVES 4

TO PREPARE the marinade, finely chop the onion, garlic and ginger in a food processor or, if you don't have a processor, with a knife. Add the spices and yoghurt to the paste and mix through.

PUT the pork in a bowl, add the marinade and mix well. Cover and marinate in the fridge for 2 hours or overnight.

TO MAKE the sauce, finely chop the onion, garlic, ginger, chilli and coriander in a food processor or, if you don't have a processor, with a knife.

HEAT the oil in a heavy-based frying pan, large enough to fit the meat in a single layer, until sizzling but not smoking. Add the sauce and stir over medium heat for 2 minutes, or until softened but not brown. Increase the heat to high and add the pork with the marinade. Stir constantly for 5 minutes, then reduce the heat to medium and let the meat and its juices bubble away for 15–20 minutes, or until the liquid has completely evaporated. The meat and the dryish sauce will be a rich dark brown.

SEASON with salt, to taste, and sprinkle with the garam masala. Cook for another 2 minutes to allow the added seasoning to be absorbed.

A Punjabi dhaba in Mumbai (Bombay) sells speciality snacks.

Chapatis are cooked on a large tava at a street stall.

TANDOORI PANEER

300 g (11 oz) paneer (page 279)
2 green capsicums (peppers)
1 onion
2 firm tomatoes
310 ml (1¼ cups) thick plain
 yoghurt (page 280)
1 teaspoon ground turmeric
2 cm (³⁄₄ inch) piece of ginger, grated
4 garlic cloves, crushed
1½ tablespoons lemon juice
2 tablespoons chopped mint leaves
1 tablespoon chopped coriander
 (cilantro) leaves
2 tablespoons oil

SERVES 4

CUT the paneer into pieces measuring about 2 x 1.5 cm (³⁄₄ x ⁵⁄₈ inch). Cut the capsicums into squares, the onion into chunks and the tomatoes into cubes. Mix the yoghurt, turmeric, ginger, garlic and lemon juice, together with a little salt, in a large bowl. Stir in the herbs. Add the paneer and vegetables, cover and refrigerate for 3 hours.

PREHEAT the grill (broiler) to its highest setting. Using 8 skewers, thread onto each 5 pieces of paneer and some capsicum, onion and tomato. Brush with the oil, season with salt and grill (broil) on all sides for 3–4 minutes, or until the paneer and vegetables are cooked and slightly charred around the edges. Serve with roti (page 220) and a salad such as laccha (page 233).

NIMKI

THESE ARE SMALL, DEEP-FRIED PIECES OF DOUGH SERVED AS A SNACK. THE KALONJI GIVE THESE TIDBITS A PUNGENT, DISTINCTIVE TASTE AND AROMA. IN INDIA, THEY ARE SOLD AT SWEET SHOPS WHERE THEY ALSO SELL NUTS AND OTHER SAVOURIES SUCH AS SINGHARAS.

NIMKI

250 g (2 cups) maida or plain
 (all-purpose) flour
1 teaspoon salt
1 teaspoon kalonji (nigella seeds)
1 tablespoon ghee
oil for deep-frying

MAKES 60

SIFT the maida and salt into a bowl and add the kalonji. Rub in the ghee until the mixture resembles breadcrumbs. Add about 125 ml (½ cup) water, a little at a time, to make a pliable dough. Turn the dough out onto a floured surface and knead for 5 minutes, or until smooth, then cover and rest it for 10 minutes. Don't refrigerate the dough or the ghee will harden.

DIVIDE the dough into two portions and roll out each portion until about 3 mm (⅛ inch) thick. Cut into 1 cm (½ inch) wide strips, then into diamonds 3 cm (1¼ inches) long, by making diagonal cuts along the strips. Prick the diamonds with a fork.

FILL a karhai or heavy-based saucepan one-third full with oil and heat to about 170°C/325°F (a cube of bread will brown in 20 seconds). Fry the nimki in batches until light golden and crisp. Drain on paper towels. Serve with mint and coriander chutney (page 250).

CHUCUMBER

A VERY HEALTHY NORTH INDIAN SNACK OFTEN SERVED AS A STARTER IN RESTAURANTS, OR WITH DRINKS. MANY OF THE INGREDIENTS CAN BE INCREASED OR DECREASED ACCORDING TO PERSONAL TASTE. THE COMBINATION OF CUCUMBER AND FRESH CORIANDER (CILANTRO) IS VERY REFRESHING.

1 red onion, finely chopped
2 small cucumbers, about 200 g (7 oz), finely chopped
100 g (3¹/₂ oz) ripe tomatoes, finely chopped
3 tablespoons finely chopped coriander (cilantro)
1 red chilli, finely chopped
1 green chilli, finely chopped
1¹/₂ tablespoons lemon juice
1 teaspoon oil
125 g (³/₄ cup) unroasted peanuts, roughly chopped
1 teaspoon salt
¹/₂ teaspoon ground black pepper
1¹/₂ teaspoons chaat masala (page 284)

SERVES 4

STIR together in a bowl the onion, cucumber, tomato, coriander, chillies and lemon juice.

HEAT the oil in a heavy-based frying pan over high heat, add the peanuts and salt and fry for 1 minute. Sprinkle with the pepper and chaat masala and stir. Fry for 2 minutes. Remove from the heat and add to the onion mixture. Season with more salt, to taste, just before serving. The seasoning is added at the end to prevent the ingredients releasing too much juice before serving.

SERVE in small bowls. Chucumber can be eaten with a spoon or scooped up in pieces of roti (page 220) or poppadoms.

Chilli powder and turmeric marry well with small fish to make both spicy snacks and curries.

SPICY WHITEBAIT

AS A DELICIOUS SNACK TO GO WITH DRINKS, SMALL FISH CAUGHT IN RIVERS AND WATERWAYS IN INDIA ARE QUICKLY DEEP-FRIED AND SEASONED WITH SALT AND SPICES. THIS WORKS PARTICULARLY WELL WITH WHITEBAIT. YOU CAN VARY THE STRENGTH OF THE SEASONING ACCORDING TO TASTE.

300 g (10¹/₂ oz) whitebait
¹/₂ teaspoon chilli powder
¹/₄ teaspoon cayenne pepper
¹/₂ teaspoon ground turmeric
oil for deep-frying

SERVES 4

RINSE the whitebait and dry them thoroughly on paper towels. Mix the chilli powder, cayenne pepper and turmeric together and toss the whitebait in the seasoning until well coated.

FILL a karhai or heavy-based saucepan one-third full with oil and heat to 190°C/375°F (a cube of bread will brown in 10 seconds). Fry the fish in batches until crisp, drain on paper towels and sprinkle with salt. Serve hot and crisp.

SPICY WHITEBAIT

GOLDEN EGG CURRY

8 eggs
oil for deep-frying
2 ripe tomatoes
25 g (1 oz) ghee
1 onion, finely chopped
1 garlic clove, finely chopped
420 ml (1²/₃ cups) coconut milk
  (page 283)
1 teaspoon ground turmeric
¹/₂ teaspoon cayenne pepper
6 curry leaves

SERVES 4

PUT the eggs in a saucepan of water and bring to the boil. Boil for about 6 minutes, until medium-hard, then cool quickly in a bowl of cold water. Shell them. You can now deep-fry the eggs if you wish. Fill a karhai or heavy-based saucepan one-third full with oil and heat to about 170°C/325°F (a cube of bread will brown in 20 seconds). Fry the eggs in batches until golden and crisp. Drain on paper towels. Cut each egg in half if you prefer.

SCORE a cross in the top of each tomato. Plunge into boiling water for 20 seconds, then drain and peel away from the cross. Roughly chop the tomatoes, discarding the cores and seeds.

MELT the ghee in a karhai or heavy-based frying pan over low heat, add the onion and garlic and cook until soft and golden. Add the tomato and cook until soft. Gradually stir in the coconut milk, then the turmeric, cayenne and season with salt. Bring to the boil and simmer for 2–3 minutes, until the sauce thickens slightly. Add the eggs and heat gently for 2–3 minutes. Garnish with curry leaves.

PARSI SCRAMBLED EGGS

PARSI SCRAMBLED EGGS

WHEN THE PARSIS CAME TO INDIA FROM PERSIA, THEY BROUGHT CULINARY IDEAS WITH THEM, INCLUDING THE USE OF SAFFRON. THIS EGG RECIPE IS ALSO KNOWN AS AKOORI OR EKOORI.

2 tablespoons oil or ghee
1 red onion, finely chopped
1 garlic clove, finely chopped
2 cm (³/₄ inch) piece of ginger, grated
1 teaspoon garam masala
  (page 284)
pinch of chilli powder
4 strands saffron soaked in
  2 tablespoons hot milk
6 eggs
2 green chillies, finely chopped
4 slices of toast
chopped coriander (cilantro) leaves

SERVES 4

HEAT the oil or ghee in a heavy-based saucepan over low heat, add the onion and garlic and fry for 4–5 minutes, until soft. Add the ginger and stir for 2 minutes, or until soft. Add the garam masala, chilli powder and saffron and cook for 1 minute. Season with salt.

WHISK the eggs and add them to the saucepan. Cook over low heat, scraping the egg from the side of the pan into the centre until the mixture is soft and creamy. Remove from the heat because the eggs will continue cooking. Sprinkle the chopped chilli over the egg, then fold in. Pile onto hot toast, sprinkle with chopped coriander and serve.

BHEL PURI

BHEL PURI IS A MIXTURE OF SAVOURY MORSELS, INCLUDING CRISP PUFFED RICE, POTATOES AND GREEN MANGO, TOSSED WITH A TART TAMARIND CHUTNEY AND MINT CHUTNEY. SERVED FRESHLY MADE IN BOWLS, IT IS A FAVOURITE SNACK AT SUNSET ON CHOWPATTY BEACH IN MUMBAI (BOMBAY).

MINT CHUTNEY
50 g (1²/₃ cups) coriander (cilantro) leaves
50 g (2¹/₂ cups) mint leaves
6 garlic cloves, chopped
3 red chillies, chopped
¹/₂ red onion, chopped
3 tablespoons lemon juice

TAMARIND CHUTNEY
60 g (2¹/₄ oz) fennel seeds
440 ml (1³/₄ cups) tamarind purée (page 280)
100 g (3¹/₂ oz) ginger, sliced
300 g (1²/₃ cups) jaggery or soft brown sugar
1 teaspoon chilli powder
1 tablespoon ground cumin
1 tablespoon chaat masala (page 284)
1 teaspoon black salt

3 potatoes
1 tomato
120 g (4 oz) puffed rice
60 g (2¹/₄ oz) sev (besan flour) noodles
1 green unripe mango, sliced into thin slivers
1 onion, finely chopped
4 tablespoons finely chopped coriander (cilantro) or mint leaves
1 teaspoon chaat masala (page 284)
12 crushed puri crisps (page 219)

coriander (cilantro) leaves

SERVES 6

TO MAKE the mint chutney, blend the ingredients together in a food processor or pestle and mortar. Transfer to a saucepan and bring to the boil. Remove from the heat, leave to cool, then season with salt.

TO MAKE the tamarind chutney, place a small frying pan over low heat and dry-roast the fennel until aromatic. Mix together the tamarind, ginger, sugar and 250 ml (1 cup) water in a saucepan. Cook over low heat until the tamarind blends into the mixture and the sugar completely dissolves.

STRAIN OUT the ginger and cook the remaining mixture to a thick pulp. Add the fennel seeds, chilli powder, cumin, chaat masala and black salt. Season with salt and reduce, stirring occasionally, over medium heat until thickened to a dropping consistency (it will fall in sheets off the spoon). Leave to cool.

TO MAKE the bhel puri, cook the potatoes in boiling water for 10 minutes or until tender, then cut into small cubes. Score a cross in the top of the tomato. Plunge into boiling water for 20 seconds, then drain and peel. Roughly chop the tomato, discarding the core and seeds and reserving any juices.

PUT the puffed rice, noodles, mango, onion, chopped coriander, chaat masala and puri crisps in a large bowl and toss them together. When well mixed, stir in a little of each chutney. Vary the chutney amounts depending on the flavour you want to achieve. The tamarind chutney has a tart flavour and the mint chutney is hot. Serve in small bowls and garnish with coriander leaves.

LEFTOVER MINT chutney can be eaten with samosas (page 20) or pakoras (page 41) but cannot be stored. Store unused tamarind chutney in a jar in the fridge. It will keep for several weeks.

A bhel puri seller prepares potatoes on Chowpatty beach.

LAMB KOFTA

THESE MINIATURE MEATBALLS ARE OFTEN SERVED AS A SNACK IN HOMES AND RESTAURANTS. THEY ARE A TYPICAL EXAMPLE OF A DISH THAT MIGRATED FROM PERSIA TO INDIA. THE MEATBALLS ARE SOFT AND SUCCULENT INSIDE BECAUSE THE MIXTURE IS THOROUGHLY KNEADED BEFORE COOKING.

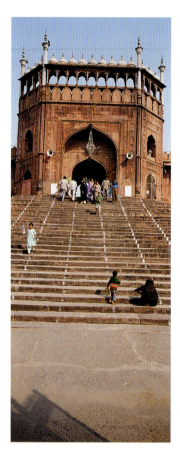

The Jama Masjid in Delhi.

1 small onion, roughly chopped
5 cm (2 inch) piece of ginger, roughly chopped
2 garlic cloves, roughly chopped
2 green chillies, seeded and roughly chopped
15 g (1/2 cup) coriander (cilantro) leaves
2 tablespoons thick plain yoghurt (page 280)
500 g (1 lb 2 oz) minced (ground) lamb
2 1/2 teaspoons ground cumin
1 1/2 teaspoons ground coriander
2 teaspoons garam masala (page 284)
1/4 teaspoon chilli powder
2 1/2 teaspoons salt
1/2 teaspoon ground black pepper
3–4 tablespoons oil

SERVES 6

BLEND the onion, ginger, garlic, chopped chilli and the coriander leaves together in a food processor until they form a paste. If you don't have a food processor, use a pestle and mortar, or finely chop everything together with a knife. Add the yoghurt to the paste and mix well.

PUT the lamb mince in a bowl, add the paste and mix by hand, kneading the ingredients into the meat until thoroughly combined. Add all the spices, and the salt and pepper, and mix again to distribute evenly. Cover and refrigerate for 1–2 hours to allow the flavours to develop and also to make the mixture firmer and therefore easier to handle.

WET YOUR hands and roll small handfuls (about a heaped tablespoon) of the mince mixture into small balls (wetting your hands prevents the mixture sticking to your hands). You should have about 30–40 meatballs.

HEAT 1 tablespoon of the oil in a large, heavy-based frying pan. When hot but not smoking, add 10 meatballs in a single layer. Brown on all sides by gently shaking the pan for 2–3 minutes. Don't be tempted to turn them over with a spoon or they may break up. Test a kofta by breaking it open. If it is cooked through, there should be no pink meat inside. If the meat is still pink, cook for another minute or two. Remove and drain on paper towels. Repeat with the remaining meatballs. Serve with cocktail sticks for picking them up. Mint and coriander chutney (page 250) is the perfect accompaniment but other chutneys are also suitable.

ALOO KI TIKKI

THESE ARE POTATO PATTIES SOLD AT STREET FOOD STALLS IN NORTHERN INDIA. THERE ARE MANY VARIATIONS, SOME OF WHICH INCLUDE MEAT, AND THEY ARE SERVED WITH A VARIETY OF CHUTNEYS SUCH AS TAMARIND OR MINT AND CORIANDER (CILANTRO). THEY ARE A GOOD STARTER OR SNACK.

500 g (1 lb 2 oz) potatoes, cut into pieces
150 g (1 cup) fresh or frozen peas
4 tablespoons oil
2 green chillies, finely chopped
1/2 red onion, finely chopped
2 cm (3/4 inch) piece of ginger, grated
1 teaspoon ground turmeric
1 teaspoon ground cumin
1 teaspoon ground coriander
1/2 teaspoon garam masala (page 284)
2 tablespoons besan flour
1 tablespoon lemon juice

MAKES 24

COOK the potatoes in boiling water for 15 minutes, or until tender enough to mash. Drain well until they are dry but still hot. Cook the peas in boiling water for 4 minutes, or until tender, then drain.

MASH the potato in a large bowl and add the peas. Put 1 tablespoon of the oil in a small saucepan and fry the chilli, onion, ginger and spices for 1 minute, or until aromatic. Add them to the potato with the besan flour and mix. Mix in the lemon juice and some salt. Divide the potato into portions the size of golf balls and shape into patties.

HEAT the remaining oil in a heavy-based frying pan (non-stick if you have one) and add the potato patties in batches. Fry them on each side until crisp and golden brown. Serve hot or cold in small dishes.

ALOO CHAAT

ALOO CHAAT

ALOO CHAAT IS A SAVOURY SNACK THAT CAN BE SERVED AS A POTATO SALAD OR A LIGHT MEAL. SALAD POTATOES OR OTHER WAXY POTATOES ARE USED BECAUSE THEY HOLD THEIR SHAPE WELL. THE TANGY FLAVOURS OF THE CHAAT MASALA AND THE TAMARIND MAKE THE SALAD QUINTESSENTIALLY INDIAN.

1 kg (2 lb 4 oz) small salad potatoes, unpeeled
80 ml (1/3 cup) tamarind purée (page 280)
4 green chillies, seeded and finely chopped
4 tablespoons chopped coriander (cilantro) leaves
2 teaspoons chaat masala (page 284)

SERVES 4

BOIL the potatoes in their skins for 15 minutes, or until just tender. Peel the potatoes and slice them into small rounds. Put them in a serving bowl.

MIX the tamarind purée with 2 tablespoons water. Mix all the other ingredients with the tamarind, then season with salt.

GENTLY toss the potato rounds with the tamarind mixture and serve as a snack or as a refreshing salad on a very hot day.

STREET FOOD is available at all hours of the night and day and ranges from a simple bag of fried peanuts or lentils sold by a wandering vendor, or pakoras fried to order, to a pani puri filled with spiced tamarind water or a more elaborate plate of dal and rice and bhaji. A delicious variety of snacks is sold not just at breakfast, lunch or dinner, but all day long.

STREET FOOD

IN INDIA, THERE ARE FOOD CARTS, TEA STALLS AND MOBILE SNACK VENDORS ON ALMOST EVERY STREET CORNER. EATING THROUGHOUT THE DAY IS A WAY OF LIFE AND THE DIVERSITY OF FRESHLY MADE SNACKS TO CHOOSE FROM IS INCREDIBLE.

Street food, part of the culture in India, came about after mass migration to the cities. It provides not just delicious food but a way of life, including an opportunity to socialize. Eating street food starts as early as breakfast time when men in suits snack on their way to work. They visit again at lunchtime when they take a quick break for a nourishing dish of rice and dal. In the evening, families and young couples stroll in parks, or on beaches, and nibble on chickpea crackers or pistachio kulfi (ice cream). At other times of the day, there is room for a refreshing glass of lassi (whipped yoghurt drink), a pani puri (deep-fried stuffed bread) or a quick sandwich made from dubble roti (sliced bread).

Some vendors have permanent fixtures for their stall or cart. Others (komcha-wallahs) carry baskets of prepared foods on their heads or around their waists, or set up karhais (cooking pots) filled with bubbling oil to deep-fry morsels, such as samosas, to order. The vendor with the longest queue is likely to have the best reputation and the tastiest snacks.

The food sold on the street varies regionally and is an indication of the cuisine that is popular with the locals. In the south, idlis (steamed rice cakes) and dosas (rice pancakes)

CHOWPATTY BEACH is the place where all of Mumbai (Bombay) gathers to eat chaat (snacks) and take in the sea air at dusk. Families, couples and groups of friends buy snacks and stroll around, while children play on the mini fairground with its hand-cranked rides. As the sun sets, the lights come on and the bustle around the stalls increases as ingredients are prepared and chaat are mixed and served.

feature heavily, as do vada (deep-fried doughnut shapes made of ground lentils or semolina). Samosas (filled pastries) are dunked into tamarind chutneys, and bondas (deep-fried balls of urad dal batter) are served with coconut chutney. In the north, you find meat kebabs wrapped in roti (bread), pakoras (fritters) and bhaji (deep-fried tidbits).

Indians love to enjoy a variety of chaat when relaxing and socializing. Chaat are little spicy nibbles made from a diverse range of foods ranging from fruit to puffed rice. The most famous chaat, bhel puri, appeals to all your tastebuds at once. Chaat sellers make up each type to a basic recipe, or to your specification. They add a selection of either chillies for heat, tamarind chutney for sourness, yoghurt for cooling and chaat masala for flavour. These are spooned onto aloo ki tikki (potato cakes), stuffed into puris (puffed fried breads), sprinkled on fruit or tossed with sev (besan flour) noodle and lentils.

KACHORIS

A SPECIALITY FROM GUJARAT, WHERE A LOT OF SEED SPICES ARE GROWN, THESE LITTLE FRIED BREADS STUFFED WITH SPICY DAL ARE SOMEWHAT TIME-CONSUMING TO MAKE BUT THE RESULT IS WELL WORTH THE EFFORT. THEY ARE PERFECT WITH A CHUTNEY FOR A VEGETARIAN STARTER.

FILLING
100 g (3½ oz) urad dal
1½ tablespoons oil
1 teaspoon cumin seeds
¼ teaspoon ground turmeric
¼ teaspoon asafoetida
3 green chillies, finely chopped
   (optional)
2 cm (¾ inch) piece of ginger,
   grated

DOUGH
200 g (7 oz) atta (chapati flour), or
   100 g (3½ oz) wholemeal flour,
   mixed with 100 g (3½ oz) maida
   or plain (all-purpose) flour
1 teaspoon kalonji (nigella seeds)
2 teaspoons oil or ghee

oil for deep-frying

MAKES 20

TO MAKE the filling, soak the dal in 500 ml (2 cups) cold water for 2 hours. Drain and chop in a food processor for a few seconds to form a coarse paste. If you don't have a food processor, grind the dal in a pestle and mortar. Heat the oil over medium heat in a saucepan, add the cumin seeds, then cover and allow the seeds to pop. Add the turmeric, asafoetida, chilli and ginger and stir until well mixed. Add the dal paste and 125 ml (½ cup) water and cook over low heat, stirring constantly until the liquid has evaporated. Add salt, to taste. Spread on a plate and leave until cold.

TO MAKE the dough, sift the atta and a little salt into a bowl and add the kalonji. Rub in the oil or ghee until the mixture resembles breadcrumbs. Add 125–170 ml (½–⅔ cup) warm water, a little at a time, to make a pliable dough. Turn out onto a floured surface and knead for 5 minutes, or until the dough is smooth. Cover and set aside for 15 minutes. Don't refrigerate or the oil will harden.

DIVIDE the dough into 20 balls. Roll one out on a floured surface to resemble a thin pancake 8–10 cm (3–4 inches) in diameter. Place 1 heaped teaspoon of the dal mixture in the centre, then fold over the dough to form into a semicircle. Pinch the edges together to seal securely. Gently roll out on a floured surface, taking care that the filling doesn't ooze out. Try to retain the semicircular shape. Repeat to use all the dough and filling.

FILL a karhai or heavy-based saucepan one-third full with oil and heat to 180°C/350°F (a cube of bread will brown in 15 seconds). Lower a kachori into the hot oil and, when it rises to the surface, gently push it down using the back of a spoon, to keep it submerged until it puffs up. Turn it over and cook until the other side is lightly browned. Drain on a wire rack and keep the cooked kachori warm while you cook the rest.

Try to keep the kachoris in their semicircular shape, folding and rolling gently so the filling doesn't ooze out. Fry until they puff up.

PRAWN PAKORAS

PAKORAS, KNOWN AS BHAJIS IN SOME PLACES, ARE VERSATILE SNACKS THAT CAN BE MADE USING PRAWNS (SHRIMP), FISH PIECES OR VEGETABLES. THE BESAN FLOUR AND POMEGRANATE SEEDS MAKE A TANGY FLAVOURSOME BATTER. MANGO CHUTNEY AND MINT CHUTNEY GO WELL WITH PAKORAS.

Deep-fry the pakoras in batches of six or eight so that the temperature of the oil remains constant. Cooking too many at once will cool the oil.

600 g (1 lb 5 oz) prawns (shrimp)
50 g (1/2 cup) besan flour
1 large red onion, finely chopped
1 teaspoon dried pomegranate
    seeds
4 green chillies, seeded and
    finely chopped
2 tablespoons finely chopped
    coriander (cilantro) leaves
pinch of bicarbonate of soda
ghee or oil for deep-frying

MAKES 30

PEEL and devein the prawns, then cut into small pieces. Put the besan flour in a bowl and add 2 tablespoons of water, or enough to make a thick batter, mixing with a fork to beat out any lumps. Add the remaining ingredients, except the oil, to the batter, season with salt and mix well.

FILL a karhai or heavy-based saucepan one-third full with ghee or oil and heat to 180°C/350°F (a cube of bread will brown in 15 seconds). Drop 1 heaped teaspoon of batter at a time into the ghee or oil and deep-fry in lots of six or eight pakoras until they are brown all over. Remove and drain on paper towels. Serve hot.

GOLL BHAJI

THESE ARE DEEP-FRIED NIBBLES ENJOYED AS TEA TIME SNACKS. THEY ARE KNOWN BY DIFFERENT NAMES IN DIFFERENT AREAS AND HAVE REGIONAL IDIOSYNCRASIES INCLUDING THEIR SHAPE AND THE TYPES OF FLOUR AND FLAVOURINGS USED IN THE BATTER. SERVE WITH A CHUTNEY.

GOLL BHAJI

90 g (1/2 cup) rice flour
50 g (1/3 cup) cashew nuts
75 g (2/3 cup) besan flour
pinch of bicarbonate of soda
10 curry leaves, chopped
4 green chillies, seeded and
    finely chopped
2 cm (3/4 inch) piece of ginger,
    finely chopped
1 red onion, finely chopped
1 tablespoon ghee
oil for deep-frying

MAKES 20

PLACE a small frying pan over low heat and dry-roast the rice flour until it turns light brown. Dry-roast the cashew nuts in the same pan until they brown, then finely chop them. Mix the rice flour with the besan flour, then add the bicarbonate of soda and a pinch of salt. Add the cashew nuts, curry leaves, green chilli, ginger, onion and ghee. Mix together well, adding a few drops of water, if necessary, to make a stiff dough. Form into 20 small balls.

FILL a karhai or heavy-based saucepan one-third full with ghee or oil and heat to 180°C/350°F (a cube of bread will brown in 15 seconds). Fry five or six balls at a time until golden brown, then drain each batch on paper towels.

Chillies on display at the spice market in Delhi.

KASHMIRI LAMB CUTLETS

THESE CUTLETS ARE SIMPLE TO MAKE AND LOOK VERY GOOD IN THIS BESAN COATING, WHICH PUFFS AROUND THE CHOPS AND GIVES THEM A CRUNCHY, GOLDEN CRUST. THE PRE-COOKING MAKES THEM VERY TENDER. THEY ARE AN IDEAL SNACK BECAUSE THE BONES MAKE THEM EASY TO PICK UP.

1 kg (2 lb 4 oz) lamb cutlets
3/4 teaspoon cumin seeds
1 teaspoon coriander seeds
3/4 teaspoon black peppercorns
500 ml (2 cups) milk
2 cinnamon sticks
10 cardamom seeds
10 cloves
2 cm (3/4 inch) piece of ginger, grated
2 onions, finely chopped
75 g (2/3 cup) besan flour
2 teaspoons chilli powder
125 ml (1/2 cup) thick plain yoghurt (page 280)
oil for deep-frying
lime quarters

SERVES 6

TRIM the lamb of any fat and scrape the bone ends clean. Place a small frying pan over low heat and dry-roast the cumin seeds until aromatic. Remove them and dry-roast the coriander seeds. Crush the coriander and cumin seeds with the peppercorns in a spice grinder or pestle and mortar. Transfer to a large, heavy-based saucepan and add the milk, cinnamon, cardamom, cloves, ginger and onion. Bring to the boil over medium heat, then add the chops to the pan and return to the boil. Reduce the heat and simmer for 30 minutes, or until the meat is tender and very little liquid remains. Remove the cutlets and drain them.

WHISK the besan flour and chilli powder into the yoghurt with 60 ml (1/4 cup) water, to make a batter.

FILL a karhai or heavy-based saucepan one-third full of oil and heat to 180°C/350°F (a cube of bread will brown in 15 seconds). Dip the cutlets in the batter, shake off any excess, then fry them in batches in the hot oil until they are crisp. Drain on paper towels and keep them warm. Serve sprinkled with a little lime juice and salt, to taste.

CHILLI LAMB CUTLETS

CHILLI LAMB CUTLETS

8 lamb cutlets
1/4 teaspoon chilli powder
1/2 teaspoon ground turmeric
1 teaspoon garam masala (page 284)
2 cm (3/4 inch) piece of ginger, grated
1 garlic clove, crushed
1 tablespoon thick plain yoghurt (page 280)
3 tablespoons lemon juice

MAKES 8

TRIM the lamb of any fat and scrape the bone ends clean. Mix together the remaining ingredients to form a paste, adding a little of the lemon juice if necessary. Rub the paste over the chops, then cover and refrigerate for 2 hours or overnight.

PREHEAT the grill (broiler) to its highest setting. Sprinkle the chops with salt on both sides and grill (broil) them on each side for 2–3 minutes, or until they are browned and sizzling. Squeeze the remaining lemon juice over them before serving.

VEGETABLE BHAJI

THESE DEEP-FRIED VEGETABLES MAKE AN EXCELLENT SNACK OR STARTER. IN INDIA, STREET VENDORS LINE THE STREETS ALL DAY, DUCKING BETWEEN BICYCLES, CARS AND PEDESTRIANS WHILE SETTING UP STALLS SELLING SUCH ITEMS. USUALLY THE BUSIER THE STALL, THE TASTIER THE SNACK.

Fry the vegetable sticks in clumps. The batter will help them stick to each other and will set around them as they cook.

100 g (3¹/₂ oz) carrots
100 g (3¹/₂ oz) snowpeas
   (mangetout)
50 g (1³/₄ oz) thin eggplants
   (aubergines)
220 g (2¹/₄ cups) besan flour
1 teaspoon chilli powder
1 teaspoon ground turmeric
¹/₄ teaspoon asafoetida
6 curry leaves
oil for deep-frying

MAKES 20

CUT the vegetables into thin sticks. Mix together the besan flour, chilli powder, turmeric, asafoetida and a pinch of salt. Add enough water to make a thick batter that will hold the vegetables together. Mix the vegetables and curry leaves into the batter.

FILL a karhai or heavy-based saucepan one-third full with oil and heat to 180°C/350°F (a cube of bread will brown in 15 seconds). Lift clumps of vegetables out of the batter and lower carefully into the oil. Fry until golden all over and cooked through, then drain on paper towels. Sprinkle with salt and serve hot with chutney or raita.

MASALA VADA

MASALA VADA

100 g (3¹/₂ oz) urad dal
120 g (4 oz) chana dal
2 green chillies, seeded and
   finely chopped
8 curry leaves, roughly chopped
¹/₂ teaspoon fennel seeds, crushed
1 red onion, finely chopped
¹/₂ teaspoon garam masala
   (page 284)
3 tablespoons grated coconut
   (page 283)
3 cm (1¹/₄ inch) piece of ginger,
   grated
4 tablespoons chopped coriander
   (cilantro) leaves
3 tablespoons rice flour or
   urad dal flour
pinch of baking powder (optional)
oil for deep-frying

MAKES 18

SOAK the dal in cold water for 4 hours, then drain. Reserve 2 tablespoons of the soaked dal and coarsely grind the remainder in a food processor or pestle and mortar. Add the reserved dal to the ground dal for texture. Add the chillies, curry leaves, fennel, onion, garam masala, coconut, ginger and coriander leaves. Mix well and season with salt. Add the flour and baking powder, if using (it gives a crisper texture), then mix until the texture is soft but the dough can be shaped (you may need to add a little water). Divide the mixture into 18 portions and form each into a ball. Slightly flatten each ball to form a patty.

FILL a karhai or heavy-based saucepan one-third full with oil and heat to 180°C/350°F (a cube of bread will brown in 15 seconds). Fry the patties in the hot oil, in batches of four or five, until golden brown and crisp. Drain well on paper towels and serve hot with a chutney.

Form a cone shape with the pastry, then fill it. Fold in the top and seal carefully so the singhara does not spring open.

SINGHARAS

SINGHARAS, THE BENGALI VERSION OF SAMOSAS, ARE LITTLE PARCELS SERVED AT EVERY INDIAN WEDDING OR FESTIVAL AS WELL AS BEING A POPULAR TIFFIN DISH. SAMOSAS ARE SEMI-CIRCULAR IN SHAPE, WHILE SINGHARAS ARE TRIANGULAR. THE VEGETABLE FILLING FROM PAGE 20 CAN BE USED.

PASTRY
250 g (2 cups) maida or plain
   (all-purpose) flour
2 tablespoons ghee

MEAT FILLING
4 ripe tomatoes
2 tablespoons ghee or oil
2 cinnamon sticks
6 cloves
1 cardamom pod
3 green chillies, chopped
1 large onion, finely chopped
3–4 curry leaves
4 garlic cloves, crushed
1 teaspoon ground turmeric
5 cm (2 inch) piece of ginger,
   grated
500 g (1 lb 2 oz) minced (ground)
   lamb
150 g (1 cup) peas
1 teaspoon garam masala
   (page 284)

oil for deep-frying

MAKES 24

TO MAKE the pastry, sift the maida and a pinch of salt into a bowl. Rub in the ghee until the mixture resembles breadcrumbs. Add 125 ml (1/2 cup) warm water, a little at a time, to make a pliable dough. Turn onto a floured surface and knead for 5 minutes on a floured surface, or until the dough is smooth. Cover and set aside for 30 minutes. Don't refrigerate or the ghee will harden.

TO MAKE the meat filling, score a cross in the top of each tomato. Plunge into boiling water for 20 seconds, drain and peel away from the cross, then roughly chop, discarding the cores and seeds and reserving any juices. Heat the ghee or oil in a karhai or large saucepan over low heat and fry the cinnamon, cloves, cardamom and chilli. Add the onion, curry leaves, garlic, turmeric and ginger and fry for 5 minutes, or until the onion is brown. Add the lamb, fry until brown, then add the tomato and cover with a tight lid. Cook gently, stirring occasionally until the lamb is tender. Add the peas, cover and cook for 5 minutes. If there is any liquid left, turn up the heat and let it evaporate. Remove the whole spices. Season with salt, to taste, and sprinkle with garam masala.

DIVIDE the dough into 12 portions, roll out each to a 12 cm (5 inch) circle, then cut each circle in half. Take one piece and form a hollow cone by folding the dough in half and sealing the two edges of the cut side together. It is easiest to wet one edge and make a small overlap. Fill three-quarters full with filling. Don't overfill. Seal the top edges, then pinch to give a fluted finish. Repeat with the remaining dough and filling.

FILL a karhai or heavy-based saucepan one-third full with oil and heat to 180°C/350°F (a cube of bread will brown in 15 seconds). Deep-fry the singharas in batches until well browned. Drain on a wire rack and keep them warm in a low oven.

Kolkata (Calcutta)

BANANA CHIPS

THESE CHIPS, ALONG WITH ROASTED FRIED PEANUTS, ARE SOLD BY INDIAN VENDORS WHO STROLL THE STREETS WITH LARGE BASKETS BALANCED ON THEIR HEADS. THEY WEAR BROADCLOTH TURBANS TO PROVIDE A FOOTHOLD FOR THE BASKET AND A PLACE TO KEEP THEIR MONEY.

10 small green bananas
oil for deep-frying
1 tablespoon salt
ground turmeric (optional)

SERVES 8

BEFORE you start, oil your hands or put on disposable gloves as a thick, sticky sap will be given off by the unripe bananas. Using a knife or mandolin, cut the bananas into 5 mm (1/4 inch) thick slices, oiling the blade if it gets sticky.

FILL a karhai or heavy-based saucepan one-third full with oil and heat to 180°C/350°F (a cube of bread will brown in 15 seconds). Put the sliced bananas directly into the hot oil in batches and stir while the chips cook. After 1 or 2 minutes, put in a teaspoon of salt (the oil will not splutter). You will need to do this for the first batch, then for every second batch.

REMOVE the banana chips when golden brown, drain on paper towels and toss them in some ground turmeric.

STORE the banana chips in an airtight container when they are completely cold. If the chips are not cooled completely, they will go soggy. The chips will keep for 2 weeks but may need refreshing after 10 days. Do this by heating them in a hot oven, or under a grill (broiler), until they are crisp.

Green bananas give off a sticky substance so wear gloves when preparing them. Use a mandolin to give nice even slices.

RASAM

THIS SOUP-LIKE DISH WAS ORIGINALLY KNOWN AS 'MULLIGA THANNI', LITERALLY TRANSLATED AS 'PEPPER WATER'. IN AN INDIAN SETTING, IT IS SERVED SPOONED OVER RICE AS PART OF THE MAIN MEAL. THE BRITISH VERSION IS CALLED MULLIGATAWNY.

Pepper, shown here in its fresh form, is indigenous to India.

3 tablespoons tamarind purée
  (page 280)
1¹/₂ tablespoons coriander seeds
2 tablespoons cumin seeds
1 tablespoon black peppercorns
1 tablespoon oil
5 garlic cloves, skins on,
  roughly pounded
1 red onion, thinly sliced
2–3 dried chillies, torn into pieces
2 stalks curry leaves
200 g (7 oz) skinless, boneless
  chicken thighs, cut into
  small pieces

SERVES 4

MIX the tamarind purée with 750 ml (3 cups) water. Place a small frying pan over low heat and dry-roast the coriander seeds until aromatic. Remove, then dry-roast the cumin seeds, followed by the black peppercorns. Grind them together using a spice grinder or a pestle and mortar.

HEAT the oil in a large, heavy-based saucepan over low heat, add the garlic and onion and fry until golden. Add the chilli and the curry leaves and fry for 2 minutes, or until they are aromatic. Add the tamarind water, the ground spices and season with salt. Bring to the boil, reduce the heat and simmer for 10 minutes.

ADD the chicken to the saucepan with 250 ml (1 cup) water and simmer for 20 minutes, gradually adding another 250 ml (1 cup) water as the soup reduces. Remove any garlic skin which has floated to the top. Season with salt, to taste. Serve with rice (page 276).

TAMATAR SHORBA

TAMATAR SHORBA

2 tablespoons oil
1 onion, finely chopped
3 Indian bay leaves (cassia leaves)
5 cm (2 inch) cinnamon stick
12 peppercorns
2 teaspoons ground cumin
2 teaspoons garam masala
  (page 284)
2 x 400 g (14 oz) tins chopped
  tomatoes
1 teaspoon sugar
250 ml (1 cup) chicken stock
coriander (cilantro) leaves

SERVES 2

HEAT the oil over low heat in a heavy-based saucepan and fry the onion, bay leaves, cinnamon and peppercorns until the onion is soft. Add the cumin, garam masala and the tomato, mashing the tomatoes with a fork to break them up. Add the sugar and stock and slowly bring to the boil. Simmer over low heat for 30 minutes.

STRAIN the soup by pushing it through a sieve, using the back of a metal spoon to push against the solids and extract as much of the liquid as possible. Discard what's left in the sieve. Reheat, then season with salt, to taste, and garnish with the coriander leaves before serving.

SAMBHAR

SAMBHAR IS OFTEN SERVED WITH DOSAS OR RICE FOR BREAKFAST OR LUNCH. DRUMSTICKS ARE A LONG, POD-LIKE VEGETABLE AND COME FRESH OR TINNED. TINNED ONES SHOULD BE ADDED AT THE END OF COOKING. TO EAT DRUMSTICKS, SCRAPE OUT THE FLESH AND DISCARD THE OUTER SHELL.

225 g (³/4 cup) toor dal (yellow lentils)
2 tablespoons coriander seeds
10 black peppercorns
¹/2 teaspoon fenugreek seeds
2 tablespoons grated coconut (page 283)
1 tablespoon roasted chana dal
6 dried chillies
2 drumsticks, cut into 5 cm (2 inch) pieces
2 carrots, cubed
1 onion, roughly chopped
125 g (4¹/2 oz) eggplants (aubergines), cubed
50 g (1³/4 oz) small okra, topped and tailed
1 tablespoon tamarind purée (page 280)
2 tablespoons oil
1 teaspoon black mustard seeds
10 curry leaves
¹/2 teaspoon ground turmeric
¹/2 teaspoon asafoetida

SERVES 6

SOAK the dal in 500 ml (2 cups) water for 2 hours. Drain the dal and put them in a saucepan with 1 litre (4 cups) of water. Bring to the boil, then skim off any scum from the surface. Cover and simmer for 2 hours, or until the dal is cooked and tender.

PLACE a small frying pan over low heat and dry-roast the coriander, peppercorns, fenugreek, coconut, chana dal and chillies, stirring constantly until the coconut is golden brown. Grind the roasted mixture to a fine powder using a pestle and mortar or a spice grinder.

BRING 750 ml (3 cups) water to the boil in a saucepan. Add the pieces of drumstick and the cubed carrot and bring back to the boil. Simmer for 10 minutes, then add the onion, eggplant and okra and more water if necessary. Simmer until the vegetables are almost cooked.

PUT the boiled dal and their liquid, the ground spices, the vegetables (with any vegetable water) and tamarind in a large saucepan and bring slowly to the boil. Reduce the heat and simmer for 30 minutes. Season with salt, to taste.

HEAT the oil in a small saucepan over medium heat, add the mustard seeds, cover and shake the pan until they start to pop. Add the curry leaves, turmeric, asafoetida and a little salt. Pour onto the simmering dal and stir until well mixed.

Eggplants (aubergines) and drumsticks are a common sight in most south Indian markets.

FISH & SEAFOOD

PATRA NI MACCHI

THIS IS A DISH FROM THE PARSI PEOPLE, DESCENDANTS OF PERSIANS WHO MIGRATED TO THE WEST COAST OF INDIA, WHICH IS TYPICALLY SERVED AT WEDDINGS. THE LITTLE PARCELS ARE QUITE AROMATIC WHEN OPENED AND LOOK VERY APPEALING. YOU CAN USE ANY FIRM, WHITE FISH FOR THE RECIPE.

500 g (1 lb 2 oz) pomfret, sole or
    leatherjacket fillets, skinned
young banana leaves
1 teaspoon ground cumin
1/2 teaspoon sugar
150 g (5 1/2 oz) grated coconut
    (page 283)
4 green chillies, seeded and
    chopped
4 tablespoons chopped coriander
    (cilantro) leaves
a few mint leaves
6 garlic cloves, chopped
1 green unripe mango, diced
3 tablespoons oil or ghee
3 tablespoons lime or lemon juice
mint leaves
whole green chillies

SERVES 4

WASH the fish fillets, pat dry and cut into 8 cm (3 inch) pieces. Cut the banana leaves into as many 23 cm (9 inch) squares as there are pieces of fish (you should have about six to eight). Soften the banana leaves by dipping them into a pan of very hot water. Wipe the pieces dry as they become pliant. If you can't get banana leaves, use foil.

GRIND the cumin, sugar, coconut, chilli, coriander, mint, garlic and green mango to a paste in a food processor, blender or pestle and mortar. Heat 1 tablespoon of the oil or ghee in a frying pan and cook the paste over low heat until aromatic. Season with salt.

PLACE the banana leaf squares on a work surface. Apply the paste liberally to both sides of each piece of fish. Sprinkle some lime or lemon juice on the fish. Place a piece of fish on each banana leaf and wrap up like a parcel, tying them firmly with kitchen string.

USING a large, heavy-based frying pan which has a lid, heat the remaining oil or ghee and shallow-fry the fish parcels together on one side. After about 5 minutes, turn the parcels over and fry for another 5 minutes. The leaves will darken and shrink. Cover the pan and cook the fish for a few more minutes.

OPEN out each fish parcel on its plate. Garnish with mint leaves and green chilli 'flowers' (do this by making slits down into the chilli from the top towards the stem so you form strips which fan out).

Wrap each piece of fish in banana leaf and then use pieces of string to tie up the parcels so they don't spring open.

MOLEE

A MOLEE IS A RICH CREAMY DISH POPULAR IN KERALA ON INDIA'S WEST COAST WHERE IT IS MADE WITH LOCAL FISH. THERE ARE MANY VERSIONS, SOME VERY HOT. THIS ONE IS FAIRLY MILD AND THEREFORE PERFECT FOR THOSE WHO DON'T LIKE FIERY FOOD. YOU CAN ADAPT IT TO YOUR TASTE.

1 tablespoon oil
1 large onion, thinly sliced
3 garlic cloves, crushed
2 small green chillies, finely chopped
2 teaspoons ground turmeric
1 teaspoon ground coriander
1 teaspoon ground cumin
4 cloves
6 curry leaves
420 ml (1²/₃ cups) coconut milk
   (page 283)
¹/₂ teaspoon salt
600 g (1 lb 5 oz) pomfret, sole or
   leatherjacket fillets, skinned
1 tablespoon chopped coriander
   (cilantro) leaves
curry leaves

SERVES 6

HEAT the oil in a karhai or deep, heavy-based frying pan, add the onion and cook for 5 minutes. Add the garlic and chilli and cook for another 5 minutes, or until the onion has softened and looks translucent. Add the turmeric, coriander, cumin and cloves and stir-fry with the onion for 2 minutes. Stir in the curry leaves, coconut milk and salt and bring to just below boiling point. Reduce the heat and simmer for 20 minutes.

CUT each fish fillet into two or three large pieces and add them to the sauce. Bring the sauce back to a simmer and cook for 5 minutes, or until the fish is cooked through and flakes easily. Check the seasoning, add more salt if necessary, then stir in the coriander leaves. Garnish with the curry leaves.

A truck waiting to be loaded with fresh fish at Sassoon Docks in Mumbai (Bombay).

BOMBAY-STYLE FISH

2 garlic cloves, crushed
3 small green chillies, seeded
   and finely chopped
¹/₂ teaspoon ground turmeric
¹/₂ teaspoon ground cloves
¹/₂ teaspoon ground cinnamon
¹/₂ teaspoon ground cayenne pepper
1 tablespoon tamarind purée
   (page 280)
170 ml (²/₃ cup) oil
800 g (1 lb 12 oz) pomfret, sole or
   leatherjacket fillets, skinned
310 ml (1¹/₄ cups) coconut cream
   (page 283)
2 tablespoons chopped coriander
   (cilantro) leaves

SERVES 4

MIX together the garlic, chilli, spices, tamarind and 125 ml (¹/₂ cup) of the oil. Place the fish fillets in a shallow dish and spoon the marinade over them. Turn the fish over, cover and refrigerate for 30 minutes.

HEAT the remaining oil in a large, heavy-based frying pan and add the fish in batches. Cook for 1 minute on each side. Return all the fish to the pan, then reduce the heat to low and add any remaining marinade and the coconut cream. Season with salt and gently cook for 3–5 minutes, or until the fish is cooked through and flakes easily. If the sauce is too runny, lift out the fish, simmer the sauce for a few minutes, then pour it over the fish. Garnish with the coriander leaves.

BOMBAY-STYLE FISH

Green unripe mangoes, often used in Indian cookery, have a firm flesh and are used to give a tart flavour to recipes.

PRAWNS WITH GREEN MANGO

250 g (9 oz) tiger prawns (shrimp)
1¹/₂ teaspoons chilli powder
1 teaspoon ground turmeric
¹/₂ teaspoon cumin seeds
¹/₂ teaspoon yellow mustard seeds
4 garlic cloves, roughly chopped
4 cm (1¹/₂ inch) piece of ginger, roughly chopped
1 red onion, roughly chopped
4 tablespoons oil
1 red onion, thinly sliced
1 green unripe mango, finely chopped

SERVES 4

PEEL and devein the prawns, leaving the tails intact. Put the chilli powder, turmeric, cumin, mustard, garlic, ginger and chopped red onion in a blender, food processor or pestle and mortar and process to form a paste. If necessary, add a little water.

HEAT the oil in a karhai or heavy-based frying pan and fry the sliced onion. When it starts to brown, add the curry paste and fry until aromatic.

ADD the prawns and 185 ml (³/₄ cup) water to the pan, cover and simmer for about 3–4 minutes, until the prawns are cooked and start to curl up. Add the mango and cook for another minute or two to thicken the curry. Season with salt.

CREAMY PRAWN CURRY

THIS COCONUT-FLAVOURED PRAWN (SHRIMP) CURRY IS A SPECIALITY OF BENGAL. TRADITIONALLY, THE PRAWNS ARE COOKED INSIDE A PARTIALLY MATURED COCONUT. CARE SHOULD BE TAKEN NOT TO OVERCOOK THE PRAWNS OR THEY WILL BECOME RUBBERY.

CREAMY PRAWN CURRY

500 g (1 lb 2 oz) tiger prawns (shrimp)
1¹/₂ tablespoons lemon juice
3 tablespoons oil
¹/₂ onion, finely chopped
¹/₂ teaspoon ground turmeric
5 cm (2 inch) cinnamon stick
4 cloves
7 cardamom pods
5 Indian bay leaves (cassia leaves)
2 cm (³/₄ inch) piece of ginger, grated
3 garlic cloves, chopped
1 teaspoon chilli powder
50 g (1³/₄ oz) creamed coconut mixed with 170 ml (²/₃ cup) water, or 170 ml (²/₃ cup) coconut milk (page 283)

SERVES 4

PEEL and devein the prawns, leaving the tails intact. Put them in a bowl, add the lemon juice, then toss together and leave them for 5 minutes. Rinse the prawns under running cold water and pat dry with paper towels.

HEAT the oil in a karhai or heavy-based frying pan and fry the onion until lightly browned. Add the turmeric, cinnamon, cloves, cardamom, bay leaves, ginger and garlic, and fry for 1 minute. Add the chilli powder, creamed coconut or coconut milk, and salt, to taste, and slowly bring to the boil. Reduce the heat and simmer for 2 minutes. Add the prawns, return to the boil, then reduce the heat and simmer for 5 minutes, or until the prawns are cooked through and the sauce is thick.

ROHU KALIA

THIS FISH DISH, IN WHICH THE FISH IS FRIED BEFORE BEING PUT INTO A SPICY YOGHURT SAUCE, IS A BENGALI SPECIALITY. FROZEN PIECES OF ROHU (A TYPE OF CARP) ARE AVAILABLE IN INDIAN FOOD SHOPS. HOWEVER, AS ROHU HAS MANY BONES, YOU MAY PREFER SALMON, HALIBUT OR COD.

850 g (1 lb 14 oz) skinless rohu, salmon, halibut or cod fillets
4–6 tablespoons mustard oil
5 cm (2 inch) cinnamon stick
5 cardamom pods
4 cloves
4 Indian bay leaves (cassia leaves)
1 onion, finely chopped
4 garlic cloves, crushed
7 cm (2³⁄₄ inch) piece of ginger, grated
¹⁄₂ teaspoon ground turmeric
1 teaspoon ground cumin
1 teaspoon chilli powder (optional)
500 ml (2 cups) thick plain yoghurt (page 280)
3 green chillies, shredded

SERVES 4

CUT the fish into fairly large chunks. Heat the oil in a karhai or heavy-based frying pan over medium heat and fry the fish a few pieces at a time until golden brown on each side. Drain on paper towels. Add more oil, if necessary, and fry the cinnamon, cardamom, cloves and bay leaves over low heat for 1 minute. Add the onion and fry for 5 minutes, or until golden. Add the garlic, ginger, turmeric, cumin and chilli powder, if using, and fry for 30 seconds.

REMOVE from the heat and stir in the yoghurt a little at a time to prevent it curdling. Return to low heat, add the chillies and bring to the boil. Season with salt. Slide in the fish and bring to the boil. Simmer for 10 minutes or until the fish flakes easily and is cooked through. Serve immediately as if you let the dish sit, the fish may give off liquid and make the sauce more runny.

Draining the browned pieces of fish on paper towels will make the final dish less oily.

FISH IN YOGHURT SAUCE

1 kg (2 lb 4 oz) skinless, firm white fish fillets such as halibut or cod
3 tablespoons oil
1 onion, chopped
4 cm (1¹⁄₂ inch) piece of ginger, finely chopped
6 garlic cloves, chopped
1 teaspoon ground cumin
2 teaspoons ground coriander
¹⁄₄ teaspoon ground turmeric
1 teaspoon garam masala (page 284)
185 ml (³⁄₄ cup) thick plain yoghurt (page 280)
4 green chillies, finely chopped
coriander (cilantro) leaves

SERVES 4

CUT each fish fillet into two pieces and very thoroughly pat them dry.

HEAT the oil in a heavy-based frying pan over low heat and fry the onion until softened and lightly browned. Add the ginger, garlic and spices and stir for 2 minutes. Add the yoghurt and green chilli and bring to the boil. Season with salt, then cover and simmer for 10 minutes. Slide in the pieces of fish and continue to simmer for 10–12 minutes, until the fish flakes easily and is cooked through. Don't overcook or the fish will give off liquid and the sauce will split.

GARNISH with coriander leaves and serve immediately. If you let the dish sit, the fish may give off liquid and make the sauce more runny.

FISH IN YOGHURT SAUCE

FISH IN BANANA LEAF

THIS TRADITIONAL WAY OF PREPARING FISH IN BENGAL OFTEN USES HILSA (ELISH), A FAVOURITE FISH OF THE AREA. MUSTARD OIL IS AN IMPORTANT INGREDIENT IN BENGALI COOKING AND GIVES A UNIQUE FLAVOUR TO DISHES, THOUGH IF UNAVAILABLE YOU CAN USE SUNFLOWER OIL INSTEAD.

Ready-cut banana leaves on sale in Chennai (Madras) market.

4 x 120 g (4 oz) pieces hilsa (elish) or blue-eye fillet, skinned
1 1/2 tablespoons lemon juice
1/2 teaspoon salt
3 tablespoons brown mustard seeds
5 cm (2 inch) piece of ginger, chopped
4 green chillies, chopped
3 teaspoons mustard oil
1/4 teaspoon ground turmeric
1 teaspoon chilli powder
4 pieces young banana leaf, or foil, cut into neat pieces big enough to wrap the fish

SERVES 4

WASH the fish and pat dry with paper towels. Mix the lemon juice and salt and rub into the fish.

GRIND the mustard seeds to a fine powder in a spice grinder or pestle and mortar. Put the mustard, ginger, chilli, mustard oil, turmeric and chilli powder in a food processor or pestle and mortar and grind to a smooth paste. Soften the banana leaves by dipping them in very hot water. Wipe dry the pieces as they become pliant.

SMEAR the fish with the paste to thoroughly coat. Grease the leaves, or foil, with oil. Place a piece of fish and some marinade in the centre of each and loosely fold into a parcel. Tie with kitchen string and put in a steamer over a saucepan of simmering water. Cover and steam for 10–12 minutes. Open a parcel to check that the fish flakes easily and is cooked. Serve still in the banana leaves.

CURRIED SQUID

CURRIED SQUID

1 kg (2 lb 4 oz) fresh squid
1 teaspoon cumin seeds
1 teaspoon coriander seeds
1 teaspoon chilli powder
1/2 teaspoon ground turmeric
2 tablespoons oil
1 onion, finely chopped
10 curry leaves
1/2 teaspoon fenugreek seeds
4 garlic cloves, crushed
7 cm (2 3/4 inch) piece of ginger, grated
4 tablespoons coconut milk powder mixed with 170 ml (2/3 cup) water
3 tablespoons lime juice

SERVES 4

PULL the squid heads and tentacles out of the bodies, along with any innards, and discard. Peel off the skins. Rinse the bodies, pulling out the clear quills, then cut the bodies into 2.5 cm (1 inch) rings.

PLACE a small frying pan over low heat and dry-roast the cumin until aromatic. Remove, then dry-roast the coriander. Grind both to a fine powder with the chilli and turmeric, using a spice grinder or pestle and mortar. Mix the spices with the squid.

HEAT the oil in a karhai or heavy-based frying pan and fry the onion until lightly browned. Add the curry leaves, fenugreek, garlic, ginger and coconut. Bring slowly to the boil. Add the squid, then stir well. Simmer for 2–3 minutes, or until cooked and tender. Stir in the lime juice, season and serve.

The fish markets at Sassoon Dock, Mumbai (Bombay).

CHILLI CRAB

THIS RECIPE COMBINES SWEET-TASTING CRAB MEAT WITH AROMATIC SPICES AND THE HEAT FROM CHILLIES. PROVIDE YOUR GUESTS WITH A CRAB CRACKER, PICKS, FINGER BOWLS AND PIECES OF ROTI TO MOP UP THE WONDERFUL JUICES. YOU CAN USE ANY KIND OF CRAB FOR THIS RECIPE.

4 x 250 g (9 oz) small live crabs
  or 2 x 500 g (1 lb 2 oz) live crabs
125 ml (1/2 cup) oil
2 garlic cloves, crushed
4 cm (1 1/2 inch) piece of ginger,
  grated
1/2 teaspoon ground cumin
1/2 teaspoon ground coriander
1/4 teaspoon ground turmeric
1/4 teaspoon cayenne pepper
1 tablespoon tamarind purée
  (page 280)
1 teaspoon sugar
2 small red chillies, finely chopped
2 tablespoons chopped coriander
  (cilantro) leaves

SERVES 4

PUT the crabs in the freezer for 2 hours to immobilize them. Using a large, heavy-bladed knife or cleaver, cut off the large front claws from each crab, then twist off the remaining claws. Turn each body over and pull off each apron piece, then pull out the spongy grey gills and discard them. Cut each crab body in half (quarters if you are using the large crabs). Crack the large front claws with the handle of a cleaver or a rolling pin. Rinse off any chips of shell under cold running water and pat dry with paper towels.

MIX half the oil with the garlic, ginger, cumin, coriander, turmeric, cayenne pepper, tamarind, sugar, chilli and a generous pinch of salt until they form a paste. Heat the remaining oil in a karhai or large, heavy-based, deep frying pan over medium heat. Add the spice paste and stir for 30 seconds, or until aromatic.

ADD the crab portions to the pan and cook, stirring for 2 minutes, making sure the spice mix gets rubbed into the cut edges of the crab. Add 60 ml (1/4 cup) water, cover and steam the crabs, tossing them a couple of times during cooking, for another 5–6 minutes, or until cooked through. The crabs will turn pink or red when they are ready and the flesh will go opaque (make sure the large front claws are well cooked). Drizzle a little of the liquid from the pan over the crabs, scatter with the coriander leaves and serve.

Pull the large front claws off the crab, pull the body open and remove the gills. Crack the larger claws with the handle of a cleaver.

Use the sharp edge of a spoon to scrape out the seeds and membrane of the bitter melon in one piece.

PRAWN CURRY WITH TAMARIND

PRAWNS WITH BITTER MELON

MOST ASIANS EAT BITTER MELON BECAUSE ITS BITTER TASTE IS ONE OF THE FIVE SOUGHT-AFTER FLAVOURS: BITTER, SWEET, SOUR, SALTY AND AROMATIC. WHEN BITTER MELON IS DEGORGED, THE BITTERNESS IS LESSENED. PALER OR YELLOWER ONES ARE LESS BITTER BUT MORE FIBROUS.

1 kg (2 lb 4 oz) bitter melon, peeled
300 g (10^1/$_2$ oz) tiger prawns
  (shrimp)
1 tablespoon oil
^{1}/$_2$ tablespoon ground turmeric
1 tablespoon ground coriander
1 tablespoon ground cumin
1 teaspoon chilli powder
4–5 green chillies
pinch of sugar
1 tablespoon ghee
4 curry leaves
^{1}/$_4$ teaspoon cumin seeds
chopped coriander (cilantro) leaves
  (optional)

SERVES 4

SLICE the bitter melon in half and scoop out any seeds and membrane. Slice into half-moon shapes 5 mm (^{1}/$_4$ inch) thick. Sprinkle with salt and degorge in a colander for 30 minutes. Rinse and drain, then dry in a tea towel. Peel and devein the prawns.

HEAT the oil in a heavy-based frying pan, add the bitter melon, stir once or twice, then cover and cook for 3–4 minutes. The bitter melon will continue to sweat out liquid. Mix the turmeric, coriander, cumin and chilli powder to a paste with a small amount of water. Add to the pan and cook over high heat until liquid is reduced to almost dry. Add the prawns and green chillies and cook, tossing until dry. Season with the sugar and a little salt.

FOR the final seasoning (tarka), heat the ghee in a small pan, fry the curry leaves and cumin for 1 minute, then pour onto the bitter melon and stir in the coriander, if using.

PRAWN CURRY WITH TAMARIND

500 g (1 lb 2 oz) tiger prawns
  (shrimp)
^{1}/$_2$ teaspoon fennel seeds
1 tablespoon oil
2 cinnamon sticks
3 cardamom pods
1 large onion, finely chopped
5 garlic cloves, crushed
2 cm (^{3}/$_4$ inch) piece of ginger,
  grated
1 stalk of curry leaves
1 teaspoon turmeric
1 teaspoon chilli powder
1^1/$_2$ tablespoons tamarind purée
  (page 280)

SERVES 4

PEEL and devein the prawns, leaving the tails intact. Place a small frying pan over low heat and dry-roast the fennel seeds until aromatic.

HEAT the oil in a karhai or heavy-based frying pan and fry the fennel seeds, cinnamon, cardamom and onion until the onion is brown. Stir in the garlic, ginger and curry leaves, then add the prawns, turmeric, chilli powder and tamarind. Toss over high heat until the prawn tails turn pink and the prawns are cooked through. Remove from the heat and season with salt, to taste.

SALMON CURRY

THERE ARE SEVERAL STAGES TO THE MAKING OF THIS GOAN-STYLE DISH AND IT TAKES A LITTLE TIME

TO PREPARE THE SPICES AND THE SAUCE. THE END RESULT IS A DRY TYPE OF CURRY WITH A FAIRLY

THICK SAUCE THAT WORKS WELL WITH THE RICH FLESH OF THE SALMON CUTLETS.

SPICE MIX
6 dried chillies
1 tablespoon cumin seeds
1 teaspoon coriander seeds
1 teaspoon mustard seeds
1/4 teaspoon garam masala
   (page 284)
1/2 teaspoon ground turmeric

3 tablespoons oil
1 onion, finely sliced
1 ripe tomato, chopped
2 onions, finely chopped
8 garlic cloves, chopped
6 green chillies, chopped
5 cm (2 inch) piece of ginger,
   grated
125 ml (1/2 cup) tamarind purée
   (page 280)
3 tablespoons coconut milk powder
   or coconut cream (page 283)
1 kg (2 lb 4 oz) salmon cutlets

SERVES 6

PREPARE the spice mix by grinding the chillies, cumin, coriander and mustard seeds to a fine powder using a spice grinder or pestle and mortar, then mixing with the garam masala and turmeric.

HEAT the oil over low heat in a heavy-based frying pan large enough to hold the pieces of fish in a single layer. Add the sliced onion and fry until golden. Add the tomato, chopped onion, garlic, green chilli and ginger and fry, stirring occasionally, for 20 minutes, or until the oil separates from the sauce.

ADD the spice mix and the tamarind to the pan and bring to the boil. Add the coconut milk powder or coconut cream and stir until well mixed. Season with salt, to taste. Add the fish and bring slowly to the boil. The sauce is not very liquid but it needs to be made very hot in order to cook the fish. Simmer for 5 minutes, then turn the pieces of fish over and simmer for another 5 minutes, or until the fish is cooked through and the sauce is thick.

Flesh being extracted from semi-dried coconuts in Kerala. The dried flesh is called copra.

MUMBAI'S (BOMBAY) Sassoon Docks are a scene of frenetic activity in the early mornings. Fishing boats moor at the jetty and unload their catch by throwing it upwards in baskets onto the quay with amazing accuracy. The seafood is then sold in the noisy, crowded market. Shoppers include restaurateurs and individuals, all with an eye for a bargain and discerning in their choices.

SEAFOOD

INDIA HAS ABOUT 7000 KILOMETRES OF COASTLINE SPLIT BETWEEN ITS EAST AND WEST COASTS. IT ALSO HAS A LARGE NETWORK OF BACKWATERS, RIVERS, TANKS (RESERVOIRS) AND PONDS, ALL OF WHICH TEEM WITH FISH AND CRUSTACEANS.

Fish dishes abound in the cuisines of Bengal, Maharashtra, Kerala and Goa. And, although seawater fish are popular in Maharashtra, Goa and Kerala on the western coast, freshwater fish are more highly prized in Bengal in the East. Everything caught is utilized. Tiny fish are eaten whole and large fish such as shark, swordfish or king mackerel are cut into fillets or cutlets. Prawns (shrimp), both seawater and freshwater, are used all over India. Crabs and lobsters are eaten on the coast or in restaurants. Bivalves, including oysters, mussels and clams (vongole), are eaten on the west coast but elsewhere are largely ignored. In areas where fresh fish are not available, dried fish such as the renowned Bombay duck are used.

Fishing itself takes place in many forms. Most fish are caught from small boats, or by individual fishermen, rather than from large commercial vessels. The Koli fishermen in Mumbai (Bombay) are known for their deep-sea fishing. They put out to sea in colourful fishing boats. In Kerala, fish are caught in Chinese fishing nets or from snake boats rowed out to sea. There are also individuals with rods and nets stationed by virtually every pond, river and tank at some stage during the day, catching fish for that day's meals.

THE BACKWATERS and seas off the coast of Kerala are a rich source of fish and seafood, not only for the local community but also for the national and international market. Despite the calm, idyllic scenes on the coast and waterways, the seafood industry is booming and when the fishermen are not out fishing, they are busy selling their catch, mending their nets or tending to their boats.

Fish is bought from wet fish stalls at markets, or direct from the dock or beach. In Kochi (Cochin) in Kerala, fish is sold by a fast-talking auctioneer from a large rectangle of blue plastic mat laid out on the shore or beach. Each batch of fish or prawns (shrimp) is tipped onto the plastic and haggled over before being scooped up and spirited away to be cleaned and cooked. At the Sassoon Docks in Mumbai (Bombay), huge quantities of seafood are unloaded onto the quay, then sold out of baskets. The scene is a colourful melee of women, fishermen, commercial buyers and private shoppers.

Fish caught locally are not only eaten in India but are also sold, fresh and frozen, to the international market. Prized fish particular to Indian cuisine, such as hilsa, rohu and pomfret, are airfreighted to be sold to Indian communities worldwide. Other seafood such as tuna and prawns (shrimp), suitable for the markets in Japan and Europe, are flown there daily.

FRESH prawns (shrimp), such as these tiny ones, are sold in Mumbai (Bombay) at the fish markets, either with their shells still on, or peeled (as they are here) and ready for use.

Cut the lobster in half down the centre and pull the two halves apart. Scrape the flesh away from the shell using a small knife.

TANDOORI LOBSTER

THERE ARE AS MANY TANDOORI RECIPES AS THERE ARE TANDOORS, BUT THIS LOBSTER RECIPE IS PARTICULARLY INTERESTING AS IT DOESN'T TAKE LONG TO COOK AND THE COLOURS OF THE SPICES AND THE LOBSTER SHELLS ARE EVOCATIVE OF CELEBRATION. YOU CAN ALSO USE LARGE PRAWNS (SHRIMP).

2 large or 4 small live lobsters
1 egg
4 cm (1½ inch) piece of ginger, grated
½ teaspoon paprika
2 teaspoons soft brown sugar
170 ml (⅔ cup) thick (double/heavy) cream
pinch of ajowan
4 garlic cloves, crushed
2 tablespoons lemon juice
2 tablespoons besan flour
2 teaspoons garam masala (page 284)
½ teaspoon ground white pepper
20 g (¾ oz) unsalted butter, melted, for basting
coriander (cilantro) leaves

SERVES 4

PLACE the lobsters in the freezer for 2 hours to immobilize them. Using a large, heavy-bladed knife or cleaver, cut the lobsters in half. Remove the flesh from the tail shells in one piece, then cut the flesh into large chunks. Clean out the head ends of the shells and wash the shells all over, scrubbing out any membrane.

BREAK the egg into a bowl, add the ginger, paprika, sugar, cream, ajowan, garlic, lemon juice, besan flour, garam masala, white pepper and a pinch of salt and whisk together. Brush the lobster pieces with the mixture, then cover and marinate in the fridge for 2 hours.

PREHEAT the oven to its highest setting. Skewer the lobster pieces on long metal skewers, keeping the pieces 2 cm (¾ inch) apart. Put the skewers on a wire rack set over a baking tray.

ROAST the lobster for 6 minutes, turning once. Baste with the butter and roast again for about 2–4 minutes, until the lobster is cooked through. Roast the shells on a separate tray until they turn red. Take the lobster pieces off the skewers and put them back in the shells, garnish with coriander leaves and serve hot.

FISH WITH KOKUM

3 x 5 cm (2 inch) pieces kokum or
   2 tablespoons tamarind purée
   (page 280)
4 ripe tomatoes
2 tablespoons oil
1 teaspoon black mustard seeds
1/2 teaspoon fenugreek seeds
3 cm (1 1/4 inch) piece of ginger,
   grated
4 green chillies, slit in half
1 garlic clove, crushed
2 onions, sliced
1 teaspoon ground turmeric
1 tablespoon ground coriander
250 ml (1 cup) coconut milk
   (page 283)
800 g (1 lb 12 oz) skinless pomfret,
   sole or leatherjacket fillets, cut into
   large chunks
1 stalk of curry leaves

SERVES 6

RINSE the kokum, remove any stones and put the kokum in a bowl with cold water for a few minutes to soften. Meanwhile, score a cross in the top of each tomato. Plunge them into boiling water for 20 seconds, then drain and peel away from the cross. Roughly chop the tomatoes, discarding the cores and seeds and reserving any juices.

REMOVE the kokum from the water and slice it into pieces.

HEAT the oil over low heat in a karhai or deep, heavy-based frying pan, add the mustard seeds and cook until they start to pop. Add the fenugreek, ginger, chilli, garlic and onion and fry until the onion is soft. Add the turmeric and coriander and fry for 2 minutes. Add the coconut milk, tomato and kokum, bring to the boil and simmer for 5 minutes. Add the fish to the liquid and simmer for 2–3 minutes or until the fish flakes easily and is cooked through. Season with salt, to taste, and add the curry leaves.

BENGALI FRIED FISH

600 g (1 lb 5 oz) rainbow trout or
   salmon cutlets
1 1/2 tablespoons lemon juice
1/2 teaspoon ground turmeric
1/2 teaspoon salt
3 green chillies, chopped
3 ripe tomatoes, chopped
5 cm (2 inch) piece of ginger,
   chopped
4 tablespoons mustard oil or oil
2 teaspoons panch phoron
   (page 284)
1/2 teaspoon garam masala
   (page 284)

SERVES 4

SPRINKLE the fish with the lemon juice and leave for 10 minutes. Wash in cold water and pat dry. Rub the fish with the combined turmeric and salt.

PUT the chilli, tomato and ginger in a food processor and chop until smooth, or finely chop together with a knife.

HEAT the oil in a heavy-based frying pan over low heat and fry the fish a few pieces at a time until brown on both sides. Drain on paper towels. Add more oil if necessary, add the panch phoron and fry for 1 minute until aromatic. Add the tomato mixture and fry for another 2 minutes. Add 185 ml (3/4 cup) water and bring slowly to the boil. Simmer for 3 minutes, add the fish, slowly return to the boil, then simmer for another 3 minutes. Sprinkle with the garam masala and season with salt, to taste.

BENGALI FRIED FISH

A fish stall at Fort Kochi
(Cochin), Kerala.

Fish is sold fresh off the boats in
the early hours of the morning all
along India's coast.

FISH TIKKA

TIKKA IS THE HINDI WORD FOR CHUNK. HERE, FISH CHUNKS ARE MARINATED IN A BLEND OF SPICES
AND YOGHURT AND COOKED. IN INDIA, A TANDOOR, A CHARCOAL-FIRED CLAY OVEN, WOULD BE USED.
HOWEVER, BARBECUING IS A GOOD SUBSTITUTE AS IT ALSO IMPARTS A SMOKY FLAVOUR.

MARINADE
500 ml (2 cups) thick plain yoghurt
    (page 280)
1/2 onion, finely chopped
2 cm (3/4 inch) piece of ginger,
    grated
4 garlic cloves, crushed
1 teaspoon ground coriander
2 tablespoons lemon juice
1 1/2 tablespoons garam masala
    (page 284)
1 teaspoon paprika
1 teaspoon chilli powder
2 tablespoons tomato paste (purée)
1 teaspoon salt

500 g (1 lb 2 oz) skinless firm white
    fish such as halibut, monkfish or
    blue-eye
2 onions, each cut into 8 chunks
2 small green or red capsicums
    (peppers), each cut into 8 chunks

50 g (1 3/4 oz) cucumber, peeled
    and diced
1 tablespoon chopped coriander
    (cilantro)
lemon wedges

SERVES 8

TO MAKE the marinade, mix half the yoghurt with
all the other marinade ingredients in a shallow
dish that is long enough and deep enough to
take the prepared skewers. You will need eight
metal skewers.

CUT the fish into about 24–32 bite-sized chunks.
On each metal skewer, thread three or four
pieces of fish and chunks of onion and capsicum,
alternating them as you go. Put the skewers in
the marinade and turn them so that all the fish
and vegetables are well coated. Cover and
marinate in the fridge for at least 1 hour, or
until you are ready to cook.

PREHEAT the barbecue or grill (broiler). Lift the
skewers out of the marinade. Cook on the
barbecue, or under a grill on a wire rack set
above a baking tray, for 5–6 minutes, turning
once, or until the fish is cooked and firm and both
the fish and the vegetables are slightly charred.

MEANWHILE, stir the cucumber and coriander
into the other half of the yoghurt. Serve the fish
with the yoghurt and lemon wedges.

POULTRY & MEAT

CHICKEN TIKKA

LOOSELY TRANSLATED TO MEAN 'CHUNKS OF CHICKEN', THIS DISH CONTAINS CHICKEN MARINATED IN A SPICY YOGHURT SAUCE, THEN COOKED IN A TANDOOR. YOU CAN USE AN OVEN OR GRILL (BROILER).

MARINADE
1/2 tablespoon paprika
1 teaspoon chilli powder
2 tablespoons garam masala
   (page 284)
1/4 teaspoon tandoori food colouring
1 1/2 tablespoons lemon juice
4 garlic cloves, roughly chopped
5 cm (2 inch) piece of ginger,
   roughly chopped
15 g (1/2 cup) coriander (cilantro)
   leaves, chopped
125 ml (1/2 cup) thick plain yoghurt
   (page 280)

500 g (1 lb 2 oz) skinless chicken
   breast fillets, cut into cubes
wedges of lemon

SERVES 4

FOR the marinade, blend all the ingredients together in a food processor until smooth, or chop the garlic, ginger and coriander leaves more finely and mix with the rest of the marinade ingredients. Season with salt, to taste.

PUT the chicken cubes in a bowl with the marinade and mix thoroughly. Cover and marinate overnight in the fridge.

HEAT the oven to 200°C (400°F/Gas 6). Thread the chicken pieces onto four metal skewers and put them on a metal rack above a baking tray. Roast, uncovered, for 15–20 minutes, or until the chicken is cooked through and browned around the edges. Serve with wedges of lemon to squeeze over the chicken.

CHICKEN TIKKA MASALA

CHICKEN TIKKA MASALA

1 tablespoon oil
1 onion, finely chopped
2 cardamom pods
2 garlic cloves, crushed
400 g (14 oz) tin chopped tomatoes
1/4 teaspoon ground cinnamon
1 tablespoon garam masala
   (page 284)
1/2 teaspoon chilli powder
1 teaspoon jaggery or
   soft brown sugar
310 ml (1 1/4 cups) cream
1 tablespoon ground almonds
1 quantity chicken tikka (above)
1 tablespoon chopped coriander
   (cilantro) leaves

SERVES 6

HEAT the oil in a karhai or heavy-based saucepan over low heat. Add the onion and cardamom pods and fry until the onion is soft and starting to brown. Add the garlic to the pan, cook for 1 minute, then add the tomato and cook until the paste is thick.

ADD the cinnamon, garam masala, chilli powder and sugar to the pan and cook for 1 minute. Stir in the cream and almonds, then add the cooked chicken tikka pieces and gently simmer for 5 minutes, or until the chicken is heated through. Garnish with the chopped coriander.

The Naya Bazaar in Delhi.

MURGH MASALA

THIS IS A MILD DISH WHICH ORIGINATED IN NORTHERN INDIA. BECAUSE OF ITS SUBTLE FLAVOUR, IT IS SUITABLE FOR SERVING AT ANY MEAL. A COMBINATION OF TOMATOES, GINGER AND SPICES GIVES FLAVOURING, AND THE YOGHURT ENRICHES THE SAUCE.

1.5 kg (3 lb 5 oz) skinless chicken thighs or chicken pieces
2 teaspoons ground cumin
2 teaspoons ground coriander
1¹/₂ teaspoons garam masala (page 284)
¹/₄ teaspoon ground turmeric
2 onions, finely chopped
4 garlic cloves, roughly chopped
5 cm (2 inch) piece of ginger, roughly chopped
2 very ripe tomatoes, chopped
3 tablespoons oil or ghee
5 cloves
8 cardamom pods
5 cm (2 inch) cinnamon stick
10 curry leaves
170 ml (²/₃ cup) thick plain yoghurt (page 280)

SERVES 4

TRIM off any excess fat or skin from the chicken. Mix the cumin, coriander, garam masala and turmeric together and rub it into the chicken.

PUT half the onion with the garlic, ginger and chopped tomato in a food processor and blend to a smooth paste. If you don't have a blender, finely chop the ingredients and mix them together.

HEAT the oil or ghee in a karhai or casserole over low heat, add the remaining onion, the cloves, cardamom, cinnamon and curry leaves and fry until the onion is golden brown. Add the tomato and onion paste and stir for 5 minutes. Season with salt, to taste. Add the spiced chicken, stir in the yoghurt and bring slowly to the boil.

REDUCE the heat, cover and simmer for 50 minutes or until the oil separates from the sauce. Stir the ingredients occasionally to prevent the chicken from sticking. If the sauce is too thin, simmer for a couple of minutes with the lid off. Season with salt, to taste.

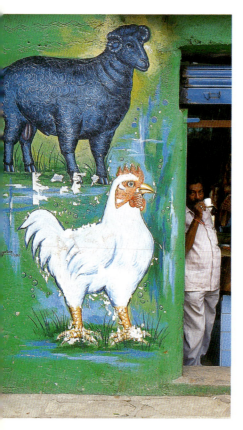

Butchers shops in Kerala advertise their wares through pictures. Lamb or goat and chicken are the most popular.

CARDAMOM CHICKEN

THIS DISH HAS A HIGHLY AROMATIC SAUCE FLAVOURED WITH CARDAMOM. THE YOGHURT MAKES THE SAUCE DELICIOUSLY CREAMY. IF YOU DON'T MAKE YOUR OWN YOGHURT, DRAIN COMMERCIAL YOGHURT OVERNIGHT. THIS MAKES THE SAUCE MUCH RICHER BY GETTING RID OF ANY EXCESS LIQUID.

1.5 kg (3 lb 5 oz) chicken or
  chicken pieces
25 cardamom pods
4 garlic cloves, crushed
3 cm (1¼ inch) piece of ginger,
  grated
310 ml (1¼ cups) thick plain
  yoghurt (page 280)
1½ teaspoons ground black
  pepper
grated rind of 1 lemon
2 tablespoons ghee or oil
420 ml (1⅔ cups) coconut milk
  (page 283)
6 green chillies, pricked all over
2 tablespoons chopped coriander
  (cilantro) leaves
3 tablespoons lemon juice

SERVES 4

IF USING a whole chicken, cut it into eight pieces by removing both legs and cutting between the joint of the drumstick and thigh. Cut down either side of the backbone and remove the backbone. Turn the chicken over and cut through the cartilage down the centre of the breastbone. Cut each breast in half, leaving the wing attached to the top half. Trim off the wing tips. Remove the skin if you prefer.

REMOVE the seeds from the cardamom pods and crush them in a spice grinder or pestle and mortar. In a blender, mix the garlic and ginger with enough of the yoghurt (about 3 tablespoons) to make a paste, or, if you prefer, mix them with a spoon. Add the cardamom, pepper and grated lemon rind. Spread this over the chicken pieces, cover, and leave in the fridge overnight.

HEAT the ghee or oil in a karhai or heavy-based frying pan over low heat and brown the chicken pieces all over. Add the remaining yoghurt and coconut milk to the pan, bring to the boil, then add the whole chillies and the coriander leaves. Simmer for 20–30 minutes or until the chicken is cooked through. Season with salt, to taste, and stir in the lemon juice.

QUAIL MASALA

QUAIL IS AN EXOTIC DISH, EVEN IN INDIA. MANY OF THE ROYAL HOUSEHOLDS TRADITIONALLY USED QUAIL IN MANY DIFFERENT WAYS. HERE IT IS INCORPORATED INTO A DRY-STYLE, STEAMED RECIPE. TENDER YOUNG CHICKEN OR SPATCHCOCK (POUSSIN) CAN BE SUCCESSFULLY USED INSTEAD.

6 x 150 g (5½ oz) quails

MARINADE
100 g (⅔ cup) blanched almonds
3 garlic cloves, crushed
3 cm (1¼ inch) piece of ginger,
    grated
½ onion, finely chopped
½ teaspoon chilli powder
½ teaspoon ground cloves
½ teaspoon ground cinnamon
1 teaspoon ground cumin
1 teaspoon garam masala
    (page 284)
2 tablespoons mint leaves,
    finely chopped
185 ml (¾ cup) thick plain yoghurt
    (page 280)
1 teaspoon jaggery or
    soft brown sugar

RICE STUFFING
60 g (¼ cup) rice
1 teaspoon amchoor powder
50 g (⅓ cup) chopped pine nuts
1½ tablespoons lemon juice

2 young banana leaves
3 tablespoons lemon juice
cucumber slices
mango or green mango slices
mint leaves

SERVES 6

CLEAN the quails by rinsing them well and wiping them dry. Prick the flesh all over so that the marinade will penetrate the meat.

TO MAKE the marinade, grind the almonds in a food processor or finely chop them with a knife, then mix them with the remaining marinade ingredients. Coat the quails evenly with the marinade, then cover and marinate for 4 hours, or overnight, in the fridge.

TO MAKE the rice stuffing, preheat the oven to 200°C (400°F/Gas 6). Cook the rice in boiling water for 15 minutes or until just tender. Drain well and allow to cool. Combine the rice, amchoor powder, pine nuts and lemon juice and season with salt. Just before cooking, fill the quails with the rice stuffing and brush some marinade on the quails. If you are making the stuffing in advance, make sure you refrigerate it until you are ready to use it.

CUT the banana leaves into neat pieces big enough to wrap a quail. Soften the leaves by dipping them into a pan of very hot water. Wipe them dry as they become pliant. If you can't get banana leaves, use foil. Brush with oil.

WRAP each quail individually in a piece of banana leaf, drizzling with any excess marinade. Tie firmly with a piece of kitchen string. Place the parcels, with the seam side up, on a rack above a baking tray and bake for 25–30 minutes. Check to see if the quails are cooked by opening one—the flesh should be slightly pink but the juices should run clear when the flesh is pierced. If necessary, cook the quails for another 5 minutes. Open the packets completely for 3 minutes at the end of cooking, to brown the quail slightly. Sprinkle a dash of lemon juice over each quail. Serve in the packets with some sliced cucumber, sliced mango and mint leaves.

To make sure none of the flavour or juices escape while the quails cook, wrap them in banana leaves as if they are little parcels.

KASHMIRI CHICKEN

THIS CHICKEN DISH, COMBINING NUTS AND SAFFRON, IS DELICATELY FLAVOURED WITH A CREAMY SAUCE. TO MAKE THE SPICES MORE AROMATIC, IT IS BEST TO DRY-ROAST THEM AS SUGGESTED IN THE RECIPE, RATHER THAN USE READY-GROUND ONES.

Saffron from Kashmir is considered to be of a very high quality and is sold in small boxes.

1.5 kg (3 lb 5 oz) chicken or chicken pieces
6 cardamom pods
1/2 teaspoon coriander seeds
1/2 teaspoon cumin seeds
2 cm (3/4 inch) cinnamon stick
8 peppercorns
6 cloves
100 g (2/3 cup) blanched almonds
75 g (1/2 cup) shelled pistachios
2 tablespoons ghee or oil
1 onion, finely chopped
4 garlic cloves, finely chopped
5 cm (2 inch) piece of ginger, finely chopped
125 ml (1/2 cup) chicken stock
250 ml (1 cup) thick plain yoghurt (page 280)
1/2 teaspoon saffron threads

SERVES 4

IF USING a whole chicken, cut it into eight pieces by removing both legs and cutting between the joint of the drumstick and thigh. Cut down either side of the backbone and remove the backbone. Turn the chicken over and cut through the cartilage down the centre of the breastbone. Remove the skin from the chicken and cut the flesh off the bones. Cut the chicken into bite-sized pieces. (You can reserve the carcass for making stock if you wish.)

REMOVE the seeds from the cardamom pods. Place a small frying pan over low heat and dry-roast the coriander seeds until aromatic. Remove and dry-roast the cumin seeds, then the piece of cinnamon stick. Grind the cardamom seeds, roasted spices, peppercorns and cloves to a fine powder using a spice grinder or pestle and mortar. Finely chop the almonds and pistachios in a food processor or spice grinder, or with a knife.

HEAT the ghee or oil in a karhai or casserole over low heat and fry the onion until golden brown. Add the garlic, ginger and chicken and fry rapidly for about 5 minutes. Add the ground spices and the chicken stock and simmer, covered tightly for 30 minutes.

STIR the ground nuts into the yoghurt. Mix the saffron with 1 teaspoon of hot water. Add the yoghurt and the saffron to the pan and bring to the boil. Simmer, uncovered, for 10 minutes. Season with salt, to taste.

SPICY GRILLED CHICKEN

THESE ARE IDEAL TO COOK ON A BARBECUE AND SERVE WITH SALADS, OR MAKE IN ADVANCE AND EAT COLD AT PICNICS. THEY ALSO MAKE A GOOD STARTER OR SNACK FOOD WHEN SERVED WITH A CHUTNEY OR RAITA. THE AROMATIC FRESHLY ROASTED SPICES ADD SPICINESS TO THE FLAVOUR.

Domestic stoves in India are usually wood-fired. Cooking pots are placed over the opening at the top and fuel is lit from below.

MARINADE
3 teaspoons coriander seeds
2 teaspoons cumin seeds
4 cm (1½ inch) cinnamon stick
1 teaspoon cardamom seeds
1 onion, roughly chopped
6–8 garlic cloves, roughly chopped
2.5 cm (1 inch) piece of ginger, roughly chopped
½ teaspoon ground cloves
½ teaspoon cayenne pepper
3 tablespoons oil
1 tablespoon tomato paste (purée)
3 tablespoons clear vinegar
1 teaspoon salt

600 g (1 lb 5 oz) skinless chicken breast fillets, cut into 1 cm (¾ inch) strips

SERVES 6

TO MAKE the marinade, place a small frying pan over low heat and dry-roast the coriander seeds until aromatic. Remove the coriander seeds and dry-roast the cumin, then the cinnamon. Grind the roasted spices and the cardamom to a fine powder using a spice grinder or pestle and mortar.

BLEND all the marinade ingredients in a blender or food processor until smooth. If you don't have a blender, finely chop the onion, garlic and ginger and pound together in a pestle and mortar, or very finely chop all the large pieces with a knife and mix with the remaining marinade ingredients. Mix the paste thoroughly with the chicken strips. Cover and marinate in the fridge overnight.

PREHEAT a chargrill pan or barbecue until very hot, or heat the grill (broiler) to its highest setting. Cook the chicken for 4 minutes on each side on the chargrill or barbecue, or spread the pieces on a baking sheet and grill (broil) for 8–10 minutes on each side, until almost black in patches.

KASHMIRI CHICKEN LIVERS

225 g (8 oz) chicken livers, trimmed of all sinew
3 tablespoons oil
2 onions, finely chopped
3 garlic cloves, chopped
1 teaspoon cumin seeds
1 teaspoon chilli powder
2 cm (¾ inch) piece of ginger, grated
½ teaspoon ground turmeric

SERVES 4

CUT the chicken livers into bite-sized pieces.

HEAT the oil in a karhai or heavy-based saucepan. Add the onion and cook until transparent but not browned. Add the garlic and cumin seeds and fry for 1 minute. Add the chilli powder, ginger and turmeric.

TURN up the heat slightly and fry the liver for 2–3 minutes. Add 250 ml (1 cup) water, bring to the boil and simmer for 10–15 minutes, or until the livers are just cooked and the sauce has thickened. Season with salt, to taste.

KASHMIRI CHICKEN LIVERS

BUTTER CHICKEN

BUTTER CHICKEN, OR MURGH MAKHNI, IS A MOGHUL DISH THAT HAS MANY VERSIONS. THE BUTTER IN THE TITLE REFERS TO GHEE, A TYPE OF CLARIFIED BUTTER. RICE IS AN IDEAL ACCOMPANIMENT AND PIECES OF ROTI OR NAAN CAN BE USED TO MOP UP THE DELICIOUS JUICES.

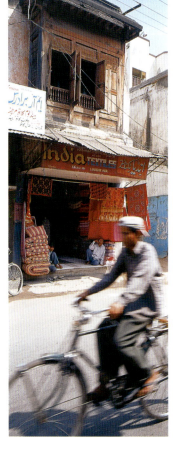

Bicycles are a common form of transport all over India.

2 cm (³/4 inch) piece of ginger, roughly chopped
3 garlic cloves, roughly chopped
80 g (1/2 cup) blanched almonds
170 ml (2/3 cup) thick plain yoghurt (page 280)
1/2 teaspoon chilli powder
1/4 teaspoon ground cloves
1/4 teaspoon ground cinnamon
1 teaspoon garam masala (page 284)
4 cardamom pods, lightly crushed
400 g (14 oz) tin chopped tomatoes
1 1/4 teaspoons salt
1 kg (2 lb 4 oz) skinless, boneless chicken thigh fillets, cut into fairly large pieces
5 tablespoons ghee or clarified butter
1 large onion, thinly sliced
6 tablespoons finely chopped coriander (cilantro) leaves
4 tablespoons thick (double/heavy) cream

SERVES 6

BLEND the ginger and garlic together to a paste in a food processor or pestle and mortar, or crush the garlic and finely grate the ginger and mix them together. Grind the almonds in a food processor or finely chop with a knife. Put the paste and almonds in a bowl with the yoghurt, chilli powder, cloves, cinnamon, garam masala, cardamom pods, tomato and salt, and blend together with a fork. Add the chicken pieces and stir to coat thoroughly. Cover and marinate for 2 hours, or overnight, in the fridge.

PREHEAT the oven to 180°C (350°F/Gas 4). Heat the ghee or clarified butter in a karhai or deep, heavy-based frying pan, add the onion and fry until softened and brown. Add the chicken mixture and fry for 2 minutes. Mix in the fresh coriander. Put the mixture into a shallow baking dish, pour in the cream and stir with a fork.

BAKE for 1 hour. If the top is browning too quickly during cooking, cover with a piece of foil. Leave to rest for 10 minutes before serving. The oil will rise to the surface. Just before serving, place the dish under a hot grill (broiler) for about 2 minutes to brown the top. Before serving, slightly tip the dish and spoon off any extra oil.

PARSI CHICKEN WITH APRICOTS

IN THIS DELICIOUS PARSI DISH FROM MUMBAI (BOMBAY), THE USE OF DRIED APRICOTS, JAGGERY AND VINEGAR GIVE A SWEET SOUR FLAVOUR. THE POTATO STRAWS MAKE AN UNUSUAL GARNISH AND ADD A CONTRASTING CRUNCHY TEXTURE TO ENHANCE THE RECIPE.

1.5 kg (3 lb 5 oz) chicken or
  chicken pieces
3 tablespoons oil
2 large onions, finely sliced
1 clove garlic, finely chopped
4 cm (1½ inch) piece of ginger,
  finely chopped
3 dried chillies
1½ teaspoons garam masala
  (page 284)
2 tablespoons tomato paste (purée)
1 teaspoon salt
2 tablespoons clear vinegar
1½ tablespoons jaggery
  or soft brown sugar
12 dried apricots

POTATO STRAWS
1 large waxy potato
1 tablespoon salt
oil for deep-frying

SERVES 4

IF USING a whole chicken, cut it into eight pieces by removing both legs and cutting between the joint of the drumstick and thigh. Cut down either side of the backbone and remove the backbone. Turn the chicken over and cut through the cartilage down the centre of the breastbone. Cut each breast in half, leaving the wing attached to the top half. Trim off the wing tips.

HEAT the oil in a karhai or casserole. Add the onion and stir over medium heat until softened and starting to brown. Stir in the garlic, ginger, dried chillies and garam masala, then add all the chicken pieces. Stir and brown the chicken for 5 minutes, taking care not to burn the onion. Add the tomato paste, salt and 250 ml (1 cup) water. Bring to the boil, then reduce the heat, cover and simmer gently for 20 minutes.

ADD the vinegar, jaggery and dried apricots to the pan, cover and simmer for another 15 minutes.

TO MAKE the potato straws, grate the potato on the largest holes of a grater, then put in a large bowl with about 1.5 litres (6 cups) water and the salt. Stir and remove some potato a handful at a time, squeezing and patting it dry on a tea towel. Fill a karhai or deep, heavy-based saucepan one-third full with oil. Heat the oil slowly to 160°C/315°F (a cube of bread will brown in 30 seconds), then add a small handful of potato. Be careful not to add too much as it will make the oil bubble and rise up the pan at first. When the potato is golden and crisp, remove it and drain on paper towels. Cook all the potato in the same way.

SERVE the chicken pieces garnished with the potato straws.

Street decorations on a busy street in Mumbai (Bombay) during the festival of Divali.

CHICKEN WITH CORIANDER AND ALMONDS

ALMONDS ARE PLENTIFUL IN NORTHERN INDIA AND ARE OFTEN COMBINED WITH CREAM IN SAVOURY DISHES AND DESSERTS. THIS DISH IS OFTEN SERVED ON SPECIAL OCCASIONS WITH PUNJABI BREADS SUCH AS CHAPATIS OR NAAN. ALOO GOBI OR INDIAN-STYLE CABBAGE ARE IDEAL ACCOMPANIMENTS.

1.5 kg (3 lb 5 oz) chicken or
   chicken pieces
50 g ($^1/_3$ cup) blanched almonds
2 onions, roughly chopped
4 garlic cloves, roughly chopped
2 green chillies, roughly chopped
5 cm (2 inch) piece of ginger,
   roughly chopped
7 tablespoons oil or ghee
2 Indian bay leaves (cassia leaves)
1$^1/_2$ tablespoons ground coriander
1 tablespoon ground cumin
$^1/_4$ teaspoon chilli powder
$^1/_4$ teaspoon ground turmeric
$^1/_4$ teaspoon paprika
2 teaspoons salt
1 teaspoon ground black pepper
4 tablespoons finely chopped
   coriander (cilantro) leaves
170 ml ($^2/_3$ cup) cream or thick
   (double/heavy) cream for
   thicker sauce

SERVES 4

IF USING a whole chicken, cut it into eight pieces by removing both legs and cutting between the joint of the drumstick and thigh. Cut down either side of the backbone and remove the backbone. Turn the chicken over and cut through the cartilage down the centre of the breastbone. Cut each breast in half, leaving the wing attached to the top half. Trim off the wing tips.

GRIND the almonds in a food processor or finely chop with a knife.

BLEND the onion, garlic, chilli and ginger together in a food processor until finely chopped, but not puréed. If you don't have a food processor, finely chop them together with a knife.

HEAT the oil or ghee in a karhai or casserole over medium heat, add the onion mixture and bay leaves and stir until lightly browned. Add the chicken to the pan and fry, turning constantly for 10 minutes, or until golden on all sides.

ADD the coriander, cumin, chilli powder, turmeric, paprika, salt and pepper to the pan and stir with the chicken for 3 minutes until well absorbed into the meat. Add 125 ml ($^1/_2$ cup) water, stirring the chicken for another 5 minutes over medium heat. The water will have reduced to a rich, thick sauce. Add another 125 ml ($^1/_2$ cup) water and bring to the boil. Reduce the heat, cover and simmer for 20 minutes. Add three-quarters of the coriander to the chicken and stir.

BLEND the almonds with 125 ml ($^1/_2$ cup) of the cream in a blender to form a smooth paste. If you don't have a blender, just mix the cream with the ground nuts. Add to the chicken, stir well and cook until heated through. Stir in the remaining cream before serving, to create a creamy, even sauce. Sprinkle with the remaining coriander.

TANDOORI CHICKEN

TRADITIONALLY COOKED IN A TANDOOR (CLAY OVEN), THIS IS PERHAPS THE MOST POPULAR CHICKEN DISH FROM NORTHERN INDIA, WHERE IT IS SERVED WITH NAAN AND LACCHA. YOU CAN NEVER GET EXACTLY THE SAME RESULTS AT HOME BUT THIS IS A VERY GOOD APPROXIMATION.

1.5 kg (3 lb 5 oz) chicken or skinless chicken thighs and drumsticks

MARINADE
2 teaspoons coriander seeds
1 teaspoon cumin seeds
1 onion, roughly chopped
3 garlic cloves, roughly chopped
5 cm (2 inch) piece of ginger, roughly chopped
250 ml (1 cup) thick plain yoghurt (page 280)
grated rind of 1 lemon
3 tablespoons lemon juice
2 tablespoons clear vinegar
1 teaspoon paprika
2 teaspoons garam masala (page 284)
1/2 teaspoon tandoori food colouring (optional)

2 tablespoons ghee
onion rings
lemon wedges

SERVES 4

REMOVE the skin from the chicken and cut the chicken in half. Using a sharp knife, make 2.5 cm (1 inch) long diagonal incisions on each limb and breast, taking care not to cut through to the bone. If using thighs and drumsticks, trim away any excess fat and make an incision in each piece.

TO MAKE the marinade, place a frying pan over low heat and dry-roast the coriander seeds until aromatic. Remove and dry-roast the cumin seeds. Grind the roasted seeds to a fine powder using a spice grinder or pestle and mortar. In a food processor, blend all the marinade ingredients to form a smooth paste. Season with salt, to taste. If you don't have a food processor, chop the onion, garlic and ginger more finely and mix with the rest of the ingredients in a bowl.

MARINATE the chicken in the spicy yoghurt marinade for at least 8 hours, or overnight. Turn the chicken occasionally in the marinade to ensure that all sides are soaked.

HEAT the oven to 200°C (400°F/Gas 6). Place the chicken on a wire rack on a baking tray. Cover with foil and roast on the top shelf for 45–50 minutes or until cooked through (test by inserting a skewer into a thigh—the juices should run clear). Baste the chicken with the marinade once during cooking. Remove the foil 15 minutes before the end of cooking, to brown the tandoori mixture. Preheat the grill (broiler) to its highest setting.

PRIOR to serving, while the chicken is still on the rack, heat the ghee, pour it over the chicken halves and cook under the grill (broiler) for 5 minutes to blacken the edges of the chicken like a tandoor.

SERVE the chicken garnished with onion rings and lemon wedges. The chicken pieces can also be grilled (broiled), barbecued or spit-roasted.

Newly made yoghurt is left to set in porous earthenware bowls, which help to drain and thicken it.

SPICY ROAST CHICKEN IN BANANA LEAVES

IN THIS RECIPE, THE CHICKEN IS WRAPPED IN BANANA LEAVES BEFORE IT IS ROASTED. THIS CREATES A DISTINCTIVE AROMA AND FLAVOUR. ENCLOSING IT IN BANANA LEAVES ALSO KEEPS THE CHICKEN MOIST AND SUCCULENT WHILE IT COOKS. FOR A SPECIAL OCCASION, SERVE IT WITH PLAIN PULAO.

2 kg (4 lb 8 oz) chicken
3 tablespoons lemon juice
1 tablespoon oil
2 large onions, roughly chopped
4 garlic cloves, crushed
4 cm (1 1/2 inch) piece of ginger,
   roughly chopped
3 tablespoons ground almonds
1/2 teaspoon chilli powder
1 teaspoon ground turmeric
2 teaspoons garam masala
   (page 284)
3 coriander (cilantro) roots,
   chopped
4 tablespoons chopped coriander
   (cilantro) leaves
3–4 young banana leaves

SERVES 6

TRIM off any excess fat from the chicken. Pat the chicken completely dry with paper towels and prick all over with a skewer so the marinade can penetrate the flesh. Rub the lemon juice and 1 teaspoon of salt all over the skin and inside the cavity of the chicken.

HEAT the oil in a heavy-based frying pan over low heat, add the onion and cook until the onion starts to brown. Add the garlic and ginger and cook for 2 minutes, or until soft. Add the almonds, chilli powder, turmeric and garam masala and cook for 1 minute. Allow the onion mixture to cool completely.

PLACE the cooled mixture in a food processor or a pestle and mortar, along with the coriander roots and leaves. Grind to a smooth paste and rub the paste thoroughly all over the chicken and inside the cavity. Cover and refrigerate for 6 hours or overnight.

PREHEAT the oven to 200°C (400°F/Gas 6). Soften the banana leaves by dipping them into a pan of very hot water. Wipe the pieces dry as they become pliant. Tie the legs of the chicken together to keep them in place.

WRAP the chicken in the banana leaves, making sure that it is well covered. Tie a piece of kitchen string around the chicken like a parcel. If you can't buy banana leaves, wrap the chicken in a large sheet of foil instead. Place the chicken in a roasting tin and bake for 1 1/2 hours. Unwrap the banana leaves or the foil from around the top of the chicken, baste the chicken with some of the juices and return it to the oven for 10 minutes, or until well browned. Check that the chicken is cooked by pulling away one leg—the juices should run clear. Rest the chicken for 10 minutes before carving.

Banana leaves on sale in Kolkata's (Calcutta) New Market.

NAYA BAZAAR is Delhi's spice market. Here in a labyrinth of alleyways and staircases, chillies, turmeric, ginger and seed spices are sold in bulk. Porters stagger backwards and forwards, weighed down by huge sacks that are heaved on and off large scales. The covered buildings around the edges of the bazaar hold the godowns and offices of the traders and all available space is used to display wares.

SPICES

SPICES BECAME IMPORTANT ITEMS OF COMMERCE EARLY IN THE EVOLUTION OF TRADE. THEY WERE SMALL, EASILY TRANSPORTED AND OFTEN WORTH THEIR WEIGHT IN GOLD.

India was essentially 'discovered' by Vasco da Gama in May 1498 as he searched for the 'Indies', the origin of the spices which were arriving in Europe via Arab traders. It is said that he came ashore and shouted "for Christ and for spices". The discovery of the spice coast of India had a profound effect on the European spice trade as it broke the stranglehold of the Arabs and cut out the middlemen.

Cloves and nutmeg from the East Indies were taken by Muslim traders from Malacca to southern India where black pepper and cinnamon (from Kerala and Sri Lanka) were added to the cargo. The whole lot was then sold onwards to Europe from the spice ports on the west coast of India. The use of maritime trading routes meant that war, religious differences and other disruptions to the overland routes did not upset the flow of spices to Europe. This kept their prices relatively constant and affordable. The next logical step was to grow spices like cloves and nutmeg in southern India which had only previously been available from the Moluccas.

Kochi (Cochin) in Kerala became a bustling spice port in 1341 after a flood in the area created a natural harbour. The area around Mattancherry is still busy with major trading and carts of spices trundle back and forth between the wholesale dealers and their godowns (warehouses) all day.

CARDAMOMS are the world's third most expensive spice. They are native to south India and here are shown growing in the hills around Kumily in Kerala. The seed pods are picked by hand just before they ripen and split. They are dried for 24 hours before being polished to remove the flower husks. Cardamoms are graded by size. They are sorted by passing them through sieves and then picked over by hand.

Amongst the spices of India, pepper, cardamom, nutmeg, mace, ginger, vanilla and turmeric are grown in Kerala and Tamil Nadu, seed spices such as coriander, cumin, dill and fennel are found in Gujarat and Rajasthan, and chillies grow in every state and union territory in India. Saffron is cultivated in Kashmir, mustard in Andhra Pradesh and fenugreek in Uttar Pradesh.

Spices have a strong association with Indian food of all types and Indian cuisine is probably the most highly spiced in the world. In the North, spices are often dry-roasted and ground before use, warming mixtures such as garam masala are used as a seasoning and chillies are not always important. In the South, spices are ground with coconut or fresh herbs to make a wet paste and a seasoning (tarka) of mustard seeds, curry leaves and dried chilli, all fried in oil, may be stirred into the dish at the end of cooking.

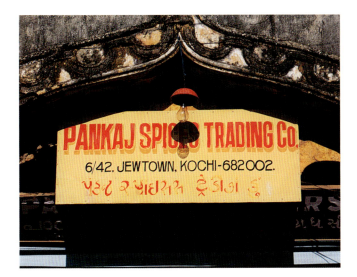

JEW TOWN, the centre of India's spice trade, is built on a plot of land given to the Jewish community by the Raja of Kochi (Cochin) in the 16th century.

ROGAN JOSH

THERE ARE MANY CURRY PASTES AVAILABLE FOR MAKING THIS CLASSIC. HOWEVER, NOTHING COMPARES
WITH A VERSION MADE WITH FRESHLY GROUND SPICES. THE COLOUR COMES FROM THE CHILLI POWDER
AND PAPRIKA. IN KASHMIR, RED COCKSCOMB FLOWERS ARE TRADITIONALLY USED FOR COLOUR.

8 garlic cloves, crushed

6 cm (2¹/₂ inch) piece of ginger, grated

2 teaspoons ground cumin

1 teaspoon Kashmiri chilli powder

2 teaspoons paprika

2 teaspoons ground coriander

1 kg (2 lb 4 oz) boneless leg or shoulder of lamb, cut into 3 cm (1¹/₄ inch) cubes

5 tablespoons ghee or oil

1 onion, finely chopped

6 cardamom pods

4 cloves

2 Indian bay leaves (cassia leaves)

8 cm (3 inch) cinnamon stick

185 ml (³/₄ cup) thick plain yoghurt (page 280)

4 strands saffron, mixed with 2 tablespoons milk

¹/₄ teaspoon garam masala (page 284)

SERVES 6

MIX the garlic, ginger, cumin, chilli powder, paprika and coriander in a large bowl. Add the meat and stir thoroughly to coat the meat cubes well. Cover and marinate for at least 2 hours, or overnight, in the fridge.

HEAT the ghee or oil in a karhai or casserole over low heat. Add the onion and cook for about 10 minutes, or until the onion is lightly browned. Remove from the pan.

ADD the cardamom pods, cloves, bay leaves and cinnamon to the pan and fry for 1 minute. Increase the heat to high, add the meat and onion, then mix well and fry for 2 minutes. Stir well, then reduce the heat to low, cover and cook for 15 minutes. Uncover and fry for another 3 minutes, or until the meat is quite dry. Add 125 ml (¹/₂ cup) water, cover and cook for 5–7 minutes, until the water has evaporated and the oil separates out and floats on the surface. Fry the meat for another 1–2 minutes, then add 250 ml (1 cup) water. Cover and cook for 40–50 minutes, gently simmering until the meat is tender. The liquid will reduce quite a bit.

STIR in the yoghurt when the meat is almost tender, taking care not to allow the meat to catch on the base of the pan. Add the saffron and milk. Stir the mixture a few times to mix in the saffron. Season with salt, to taste. Remove from the heat and sprinkle with the garam masala.

The poppy seeds used in Indian cuisine are white rather than black. They are used to thicken kormas and are usually ground, then mixed into a wet paste.

A shop selling freshly made yoghurt in Hyderabad.

LAMB KORMA

THIS MILD DISH, WHICH COMES IN MANY GUISES, NEEDS TO BE COOKED VERY SLOWLY TO LET THE SUBTLE FLAVOURS EMERGE. THIS VERSION USES WHITE POPPY SEEDS AND CASHEW NUTS TO THICKEN THE SAUCE AND YOGHURT TO MAKE IT CREAMY.

1 kg (2 lb 4 oz) boneless leg or shoulder of lamb, cut into 2.5 cm (1 inch) cubes
2 tablespoons thick plain yoghurt (page 280)
1 tablespoon coriander seeds
2 teaspoons cumin seeds
5 cardamom pods
2 onions
2 tablespoons grated coconut (page 283)
1 tablespoon white poppy seeds (khus khus)
3 green chillies, roughly chopped
4 garlic cloves, crushed
5 cm (2 inch) piece of ginger, grated
25 g (1 oz) cashew nuts
6 cloves
1/4 teaspoon ground cinnamon
2 tablespoons oil

SERVES 4

PUT the meat in a bowl, add the yoghurt and mix to coat thoroughly.

PLACE a small frying pan over low heat and dry-roast the coriander seeds until aromatic. Remove and dry-roast the cumin seeds. Grind the roasted mixture to a fine powder using a spice grinder or pestle and mortar. Remove the seeds from the cardamom pods and grind them.

ROUGHLY chop one onion and finely slice the other. Put just the roughly chopped onion with the ground spices, coconut, poppy seeds, chilli, garlic, ginger, cashew nuts, cloves and cinnamon in a blender, add 170 ml (2/3 cup) water and process to a smooth paste. If you don't have a blender, crush everything together in a pestle and mortar, or finely chop with a knife, before adding the water.

HEAT the oil in a karhai or casserole over medium heat. Add the finely sliced onion and fry until lightly browned. Pour the blended mixture into the pan, season with salt and cook over low heat for 1 minute, or until the liquid evaporates and the sauce thickens. Add the lamb with the yoghurt and slowly bring to the boil. Cover tightly and simmer for 1 1/2 hours, or until the meat is very tender. Stir the meat occasionally to prevent it from sticking to the pan. If the water has evaporated during the cooking time, add another 125 ml (1/2 cup) of water to make a sauce. The sauce should be quite thick.

MOGHUL-STYLE LAMB

FOR THIS DISH, THE LAMB IS MARINATED, PREFERABLY OVERNIGHT, BEFORE IT IS COOKED. THIS ENSURES THAT THE MEAT IS TENDER AND FULL OF FLAVOUR. THE CREAM IS ADDED TO TEMPER THE STRONG COMBINATION OF SPICES.

6 garlic cloves, roughly chopped
4 cm (1 1/2 inch) piece of ginger, roughly chopped
50 g (1/3 cup) blanched almonds
2 onions, thinly sliced
750 g (1 lb 10 oz) boneless leg or shoulder of lamb, cut into 2.5 cm (1 inch) cubes
2 teaspoons coriander seeds
40 g (1 1/2 oz) ghee
7 cardamom pods
5 cloves
1 cinnamon stick
1 teaspoon salt
310 ml (1 1/4 cups) cream
1/2 teaspoon cayenne pepper
1/2 teaspoon garam masala (page 284)
flaked toasted almonds

SERVES 4

BLEND the garlic, ginger, almonds and 50 g (1 3/4 oz) of the onion in a blender or food processor. If you don't have a blender, finely chop them with a knife or grind together in a pestle and mortar. Add a little water if necessary to make a smooth paste, then put in a bowl with the lamb and mix thoroughly to coat the meat. Cover and marinate in the fridge for 2 hours, or overnight.

PLACE a small frying pan over low heat, dry-roast the coriander seeds until aromatic, then grind to a fine powder using a spice grinder or pestle and mortar.

HEAT the ghee in a karhai or casserole. Add the cardamom pods, cloves and cinnamon stick and, after a few seconds, add the remaining onion and fry until it is soft and starting to brown. Transfer the onion to a plate.

FRY the meat and the marinade in the pan until the mixture is quite dry and has started to brown a little. Add 170 ml (2/3 cup) hot water to the pan, cover tightly and cook over low heat for 30 minutes, stirring occasionally.

ADD the ground coriander, salt, cream, cayenne pepper and cooked onion to the pan, cover and simmer for another 30 minutes, or until the lamb is tender. Stir occasionally to prevent the lamb from sticking to the pan. Remove the cardamom pods, cloves and cinnamon stick, then stir in the garam masala. Sprinkle with flaked almonds.

The remains of an ancient college built in 1354 in Haus Khas village, Delhi.

In Hyderabad, kheema matar is served for breakfast with poppadoms and chutney.

KHEEMA MATAR

DURING THE WINTER MONTHS, WHEN PEAS ARE IN SEASON IN NORTHERN INDIA, THIS DRY-STYLE LAMB CURRY IS OFTEN SERVED WITH UBIQUITOUS VEGETABLE DISHES SUCH AS ALOO GOBI AND ALOO METHI. LEAVE OUT THE CHILLIES FOR A MILD VERSION.

2 onions, roughly chopped
4 garlic cloves, roughly chopped
5 cm (2 inch) piece of ginger, roughly chopped
4 green chillies
170 ml (^{2}/$_3$ cup) oil
2 Indian bay leaves (cassia leaves)
500 g (1 lb 2 oz) minced (ground) lamb
pinch of asafoetida
2 tablespoons tomato paste (purée)
^{1}/$_4$ teaspoon ground turmeric
^{1}/$_2$ teaspoon chilli powder
2 tablespoons ground coriander
2 tablespoons ground cumin
2 tablespoons thick plain yoghurt (page 280)
3 teaspoons salt
1 teaspoon ground black pepper
235 g (1^1/$_2$ cups) fresh or frozen peas
^{1}/$_4$ teaspoon garam masala (page 284)
5 tablespoons finely chopped coriander (cilantro)

SERVES 4

PUT the onion, garlic, ginger and two of the chillies in a food processor and process until very finely chopped. If you don't have a food processor, finely chop the ingredients or grind them together in a pestle and mortar.

HEAT the oil in a karhai or heavy-based frying pan over medium heat, add the onion mixture and bay leaves and fry for 3–4 minutes, or until golden brown. Add the lamb and fry for 15 minutes, stirring occasionally to prevent the meat sticking. Break up any lumps of meat with the back of a fork. During this time, the flavours of the onion, garlic, ginger and chilli will infuse into the meat. Add the asafoetida and tomato paste, stir and lower the heat to a simmer.

ADD the turmeric, chilli powder, coriander and cumin and stir for 1 minute. Add the yoghurt, salt and pepper and continue frying for 5 minutes. Add 185 ml (^{3}/$_4$ cup) water, a little at a time, stirring after each addition until it is well absorbed. Add the peas and the two remaining whole chillies, stir well, then cover and simmer for 20 minutes, or until the peas are cooked through. If using frozen peas, cook the lamb and chillies for 20 minutes and add the peas 5 minutes before the end of cooking. Add the garam masala and chopped coriander and stir for 1 minute before serving.

A hand-painted film poster in Chennai (Madras).

LAMB MADRAS

TRADITIONALLY IN INDIA, HOGGET (SHEEP) OR GOAT MEAT IS OFTEN THE ONLY MEAT AVAILABLE. AS GOAT CAN BE TOUGH WHEN COOKED THIS WAY, WE HAVE USED LAMB. IT IS COOKED SLOWLY SO THE SAUCES ARE ABSORBED AND THE CURRY MATURES TO A FULL FLAVOUR. BEEF CAN ALSO BE USED.

Fresh, aromatic curry leaves are bought from market vendors on a daily basis.

1 kg (2 lb 4 oz) boneless leg or shoulder of lamb, cut into 2.5 cm (1 inch) cubes
1½ teaspoons ground turmeric
2 tablespoons coriander seeds
2 teaspoons cumin seeds
10 dried chillies
12 curry leaves
10 garlic cloves, roughly chopped
5 cm (2 inch) piece of ginger, roughly chopped
1 teaspoon fennel seeds
1 tablespoon tamarind purée (page 280)
4 tablespoons oil or ghee
3 large onions, sliced
625 ml (2½ cups) coconut milk (page 283)
8 cm (3 inch) cinnamon stick
6 cardamom pods
curry leaves

SERVES 6

RUB the cubed lamb with the ground turmeric. Place a small frying pan over low heat and dry-roast the coriander seeds until aromatic. Remove and dry-roast the cumin seeds, then repeat with the chillies. Grind them all to a powder in a pestle and mortar or spice grinder. Add six curry leaves, the garlic and ginger and grind to a paste.

DRY-ROAST the fennel seeds in the pan until they brown and start to pop. Dissolve the tamarind in 125 ml (½ cup) hot water.

HEAT the oil or ghee in a karhai or casserole over low heat and fry the onion for 5–10 minutes until soft. Add the chilli paste and cook for a few minutes or until aromatic. Add the meat and toss well to mix with the paste. Add 500 ml (2 cups) of the coconut milk and 60 ml (¼ cup) water. Bring to the boil and simmer over medium heat for 10 minutes, or until the liquid has reduced.

WHEN the liquid has reduced, add the remaining coconut milk, the cinnamon stick, cardamom pods and whole fennel seeds. Season with salt and pepper. Cover and cook, partially covered over medium heat, for 1 hour or until the meat is tender, stirring occasionally. When the meat is tender, add the tamarind and check the seasoning. Stir until the oil separates out from the meat, then spoon it off or blot with paper towels before removing the pan from the heat.

STIR well and add the remaining six curry leaves. Garnish with more curry leaves.

Enclose the egg completely by shaping the meat around it with your hands. Gently smooth over the join and neaten the shape.

An egg stall at Kolkata's (Calcutta) New Market, formerly known as Hogg Market.

NARGISI KOFTA

NARGISI KOFTA ARE SO NAMED BECAUSE, WHEN SLICED OPEN, THEY LOOK LIKE THE ALMOND-SHAPED FLOWER OF THE NARCISSUS. THEY ARE SHAPED BY HAND, THEN FRIED AND DIPPED INTO A SPICY SAUCE TO BE SERVED AS A MAIN MEAL. MAKE THEM WITHOUT THE SAUCE AS A SNACK.

KOFTAS
10 small eggs
1 onion, finely chopped
4 garlic cloves, crushed
1 teaspoon salt
1/2 teaspoon ground turmeric
1 teaspoon garam masala
   (page 284)
1 teaspoon chilli powder
550 g (1 lb 4 oz) minced (ground)
   lamb
3 tablespoons rice flour
oil for deep-frying

SAUCE
2 large ripe tomatoes
1 tablespoon oil
1 onion, finely sliced
2 garlic cloves, chopped
2 cm (3/4 inch) piece of ginger,
   grated
1 teaspoon ground turmeric
1 teaspoon salt
1/2 teaspoon chilli powder (optional)
1/2 teaspoon sugar
1 teaspoon garam masala
   (page 284)
125 ml (1/2 cup) thick plain yoghurt
   (page 280)

SERVES 4

TO MAKE the koftas, cook eight of the eggs in boiling water for 10 minutes to hard-boil, then cool them immediately in cold water to prevent grey rings around the yolks. When cold, peel them.

MIX the onion, garlic, salt, turmeric, garam masala and chilli powder in a large bowl. Add the lamb and knead the mixture well. Beat one of the remaining eggs in a bowl and knead it into the lamb until completely amalgamated.

DIVIDE the meat mixture into eight portions and shape each portion into a ball. Flatten a ball into a pancake on the palm of your hand and place a hard-boiled egg in the centre. Wrap the mixture around the egg, smoothing the outside of the kofta and distributing the meat evenly to make a smooth shape. Make the rest in the same way, then dust with rice flour.

FILL a karhai or deep, heavy-based saucepan one-third full with oil and heat to 180°C/350°F (a cube of bread will brown in 15 seconds). Beat the remaining egg with a little water. Dip each kofta in the beaten egg, shake off any excess, then deep-fry one at a time until golden. Drain on paper towels. Discard the oil.

TO MAKE the sauce, score a cross in the top of each tomato, then plunge into boiling water for 20 seconds. Drain, peel away from the cross, then finely chop the tomatoes, discarding the cores and seeds and reserving any juices. Heat the oil in the karhai and fry the onion, garlic and ginger for 5 minutes. Stir in the turmeric, salt, chilli powder, sugar and garam masala, then add the tomato. Simmer for a few minutes, then stir in the yoghurt and 125 ml (1/2 cup) hot water. Season, simmer for 3 minutes, then add the koftas and simmer gently for 5 minutes on each side, or until warmed through. Cut in half and serve with the sauce.

SAAG GOSHT

THIS IS A RICHLY FLAVOURED, TRADITIONAL DISH FROM THE NORTHERN PART OF INDIA. IT IS COOKED UNTIL THE SAUCE IS VERY THICK. IT CAN BE SERVED WITH EITHER RICE OR BREADS. IF YOU CAN'T BUY FRESH SPINACH, YOU CAN USE DEFROSTED, DRAINED, FROZEN SPINACH INSTEAD.

Amaranth is a green or red leafy vegetable used in India instead of spinach. It is interchangeable with spinach in all saag recipes.

2 teaspoons coriander seeds
1½ teaspoons cumin seeds
3 tablespoons oil
1 kg (2 lb 4 oz) boneless leg or shoulder of lamb, cut into 2.5 cm (1 inch) cubes
4 onions, finely chopped
6 cloves
6 cardamom pods
10 cm (4 inch) cinnamon stick
10 black peppercorns
4 Indian bay leaves (cassia leaves)
3 teaspoons garam masala (page 284)
¼ teaspoon ground turmeric
1 teaspoon paprika
8 cm (3 inch) piece of ginger, grated
4 garlic cloves, crushed
185 ml (¾ cup) thick plain yoghurt (page 280)
450 g (1 lb) English spinach or amaranth leaves, roughly chopped

SERVES 6

PLACE a small frying pan over low heat and dry-roast the coriander seeds until aromatic. Remove them and dry-roast the cumin seeds. Grind the roasted seeds to a fine powder using a spice grinder or pestle and mortar.

HEAT the oil in a karhai or casserole over low heat and fry a few pieces of meat at a time until browned. Remove from the pan. Add more oil to the pan and fry the onion, cloves, cardamom pods, cinnamon stick, peppercorns and bay leaves until the onion is lightly browned. Add the cumin and coriander, garam masala, turmeric and paprika and fry for 30 seconds. Add the meat, ginger, garlic, yoghurt and 420 ml (1⅔ cups) water and bring to the boil. Reduce the heat to a simmer, cover and cook for 1½–2 hours, or until the meat is very tender. At this stage, most of the water should have evaporated. If it hasn't, remove the lid, increase the heat and fry until the moisture has evaporated. Season with salt, to taste.

COOK the spinach briefly in a little simmering water until it is just wilted, then refresh in cold water. Drain thoroughly, then finely chop. Squeeze out any extra water by putting the spinach between two plates and pushing them together.

ADD the spinach to the lamb and cook for 3 minutes, or until the spinach and lamb are well mixed and any extra liquid has evaporated.

LAMB KEBAB

5 garlic cloves, roughly chopped
5 cm (2 inch) piece of ginger,
    roughly chopped
3 green chillies, roughly chopped
1 onion, roughly chopped
3 tablespoons thick plain yoghurt
    (page 280)
3 tablespoons coriander (cilantro)
    leaves
1/2 teaspoon ground black pepper
500 g (1 lb 2 oz) minced (ground)
    lamb
red onion rings
lemon wedges

SERVES 4

COMBINE the garlic, ginger, chilli, onion, yoghurt and coriander leaves in a food processor to form a thick smooth paste. If you don't have a processor, chop the vegetables more finely and use a pestle and mortar. Add the pepper, season with salt, then mix in the lamb. If you are using a pestle and mortar, mix the lamb with the paste in a bowl. Divide the meat into 16 portions, about 2 tablespoons each. Shape each portion into an oval patty, cover and chill for 20 minutes.

HEAT the grill (broiler) to high. Using four metal skewers, thread four meatballs onto each. Grill (broil) for 7 minutes, or until brown. Turn and cook the other side until browned and cooked through. Serve with onion rings and lemon wedges.

DO PIAZA

DO PIAZA

DO PIAZA LITERALLY MEANS 'ONIONS TWICE'. THIS CAN BE INTERPRETED AS DOUBLE THE QUANTITY OF ONIONS AS FOR MEAT, OR ONIONS USED IN TWO DIFFERENT FORMS AS IN THIS VERSION.

11/2 teaspoons cumin seeds
21/2 teaspoons coriander seeds
4 garlic cloves, roughly chopped
8 cm (3 inch) piece of ginger,
    roughly chopped
400 g (14 oz) onions, finely
    chopped
3 tablespoons oil
1 kg (2 lb 4 oz) boneless leg of
    lamb, cut into 3 cm (11/2 inch)
    cubes
2 teaspoons garam masala
    (page 284)
1 teaspoon ground turmeric

SERVES 4

PLACE a small frying pan over low heat and dry-roast the cumin seeds until aromatic. Remove, then dry-roast the coriander seeds. Grind the roasted mixture to a fine powder using a spice grinder or pestle and mortar. In a food processor or with a knife, finely chop together the garlic, ginger and two-thirds of the onion.

HEAT the oil in a karhai or casserole and fry the remaining onion until golden brown. Add the lamb and cook until the meat is brown all over. Stir in the cumin and coriander, garam masala and turmeric. Add the onion, ginger and garlic mixture and 250 ml (1 cup) water and bring slowly to the boil. Cover tightly, reduce the heat to a simmer and cook for 1 hour, or until the meat is very tender. If the liquid evaporates quickly, add 125 ml (1/2 cup) hot water. When the meat is cooked, it should have a thick coating sauce. If the sauce is too thin, simmer for a few minutes with the lid off. Season with salt, to taste.

DHANSAK

A FLAVOURSOME PARSI DISH THAT IS SERVED AT SPECIAL OCCASIONS, THIS VERSION HAS EVOLVED FROM A LAVISH RECIPE THAT USED EVEN MORE TYPES OF DAL. THE COMBINATION OF VARIOUS TYPES OF DAL GIVES A VARIED TEXTURE BUT YOU CAN USE JUST MASOOR OR TOOR.

100 g (3½ oz) toor dal (yellow
  lentils)
25 g (1 oz) moong dal
25 g (1 oz) chickpeas
50 g (1¾ oz) masoor dal
  (red lentils)
1 eggplant (aubergine), unpeeled
150 g (5½ oz) pumpkin, unpeeled
150 g (5½ oz) amaranth or English
  spinach leaves
2 tomatoes
2 green chillies
2 tablespoons ghee or oil
1 onion, finely chopped
3 garlic cloves, crushed
2 cm (¾ inch) piece of ginger,
  grated
1 kg (2 lb 4 oz) boneless leg or
  shoulder of lamb, cut into 3 cm
  (1¼ inch) cubes
2 cm (¾ inch) cinnamon stick
5 cardamom pods, bruised
3 cloves
1 tablesoon ground coriander
1 teaspoon ground turmeric
1 teaspoon chilli powder,
  or to taste
3 tablespoons lime juice

SERVES 6

SOAK the toor dal, moong dal and chickpeas in plenty of water for about 2 hours. Drain well.

PUT all four types of pulse in a saucepan, add about 1 litre (4 cups) of water, cover and bring to the boil. Uncover and simmer for 15 minutes, skimming off any scum that forms on the surface, and stirring occasionally to make sure all the pulses are cooking at the same rate and are soft. Lightly mash the soft pulses to a similar texture.

COOK the eggplant and pumpkin in boiling water for 10–15 minutes, or until soft. Scoop out the pumpkin flesh and cut it into pieces. Peel the eggplant carefully (it may be very pulpy) and cut it into small pieces. Cut the amaranth or spinach into 5 cm (2 inch) lengths, halve the tomatoes and split the chillies lengthwise, removing any seeds.

HEAT the ghee or oil in a karhai or casserole and fry the onion, garlic and ginger for 5 minutes, or until lightly brown and softened. Add the lamb and brown for about 10 minutes, or until aromatic. Add the cinnamon, cardamom pods, cloves, coriander, turmeric and chilli powder and fry for 5 minutes to allow the flavours to develop. Add 170 ml (⅔ cup) water, cover and simmer for 40 minutes, or until the lamb is tender.

ADD the mashed lentils and all the cooked and raw vegetables to the pan. Season with the lime juice and salt and pepper. Simmer for 15 minutes (if the sauce is too thick, add a little water). Stir well, then check the seasoning. The dhansak should be flavoursome, aromatic, tart and spicy.

ALOO GOSHT

THIS MILD, SUBTLY FLAVOURED NORTH INDIAN DISH COMBINES TENDER LAMB WITH CHUNKS OF POTATO. ADDING THE BONES, WITH THE MARROW STILL IN THEM, RESULTS IN A MUCH TASTIER GRAVY, WHILE STARCH FROM THE POTATOES HELPS TO THICKEN THE SAUCE.

1.5 kg (3 lb 5 oz) leg of lamb on the bone
350 g (12 oz) waxy potatoes
1¹/₂ teaspoons coriander seeds
1¹/₂ teaspoons cumin seeds
2 tablespoons oil
1 onion, chopped
2 Indian bay leaves (cassia leaves)
¹/₄ teaspoon ground turmeric
2 teaspoons garam masala (page 284)
400 g (14 oz) tin chopped tomatoes
3 green chillies, chopped
4 garlic cloves, crushed
3 cm (1¹/₄ inch) piece of ginger, grated
1 tablespoon tomato paste (purée)

SERVES 6

TRIM away any excess fat from the lamb, remove the bone and cut the lamb into 3 cm (1¹/₄ inch) cubes. Reserve the bones with their marrow.

CUT each potato into large chunks and put in a bowl of cold water.

PLACE a small frying pan over low heat and dry-roast the coriander seeds until aromatic. Remove them, then dry-roast the cumin seeds. Grind the roasted spices to a fine powder using a spice grinder or pestle and mortar.

HEAT the oil in a karhai or casserole over low heat. Add the onion and bay leaves and fry over low heat until lightly browned. Stir in the coriander and cumin mixture, turmeric and 1 teaspoon of garam masala. Add the tomato, chilli, garlic and ginger and fry until the oil separates out of the sauce. Stir in the tomato paste, then 250 ml (1 cup) water. Add the lamb and bone and mix well. Bring to the boil, cover tightly, reduce the heat and simmer for 1 hour.

ADD the potato chunks to the pan and cook for another hour, occasionally shaking the pan to prevent the meat from sticking. If all the liquid has evaporated, add 125 ml (¹/₂ cup) hot water. When the meat is cooked, the sauce should be fairly thick. Season with salt, to taste.

REMOVE the bone before serving. Serve sprinkled with the remaining garam masala.

KOFTA IN TOMATO AND YOGHURT SAUCE

EVERY NATION SEEMS TO HAVE A VERSION OF KOFTA, RANGING FROM MEATBALLS AND CROQUETTES TO RISSOLES AND DUMPLINGS. THIS RECIPE IS THE NORTH INDIAN WAY OF PREPARING THEM. THE RICH TOMATO AND YOGHURT SAUCE IS PERFECT WHEN SERVED WITH NAAN BREAD.

Cardamom pods are harvested by hand. They grow on small stalks at the base of the plant.

KOFTA

1 onion

500 g (1 lb 2 oz) minced (ground) lamb

2 cm (³/4 inch) piece of ginger, grated

3 garlic cloves, finely chopped

2 green chillies, seeded and finely chopped

1/2 teaspoon salt

1 egg

TOMATO AND YOGHURT SAUCE

2 teaspoons coriander seeds

2 teaspoons cumin seeds

3 tablespoons oil

10 cm (4 inch) cinnamon stick

6 cloves

6 cardamom pods

1 onion, finely chopped

1/2 teaspoon ground turmeric

1 teaspoon paprika

1 teaspoon garam masala (page 284)

1/2 teaspoon salt

200 g (7 oz) tin chopped tomatoes

170 ml (²/3 cup) thick plain yoghurt (page 280)

coriander (cilantro) leaves

SERVES 4

TO MAKE the kofta, grate the onion, put it in a sieve and use a spoon to press out as much of the liquid as possible. Put it in a bowl and combine with the lamb, ginger, garlic, green chilli, salt and the egg. Mix thoroughly, then divide into 20 equal portions and shape each into a ball. Cover with plastic wrap and refrigerate for about 2 hours. Alternatively, the meatballs can be put in the freezer while the sauce is being prepared, then they will be sufficiently firm enough to stay in shape when they are added to the sauce.

TO MAKE the sauce, place a small frying pan over low heat and dry-roast the coriander seeds until aromatic. Remove, then dry-roast the cumin seeds. Grind the roasted mixture to a fine powder using a spice grinder or pestle and mortar.

HEAT the oil in a karhai or heavy-based frying pan over low heat. Add the cinnamon stick, cloves, cardamom pods and onion and fry until the onion is golden. Add all the ground spices and the salt and fry for about 30 seconds. Stir in the tomato, then remove from the heat and slowly stir in the yoghurt. Return the pan to the heat, slide in the chilled meatballs and bring to the boil. Simmer, uncovered, for 1 hour, over very low heat. It may be necessary to shake the pan from time to time to prevent the meatballs from sticking. If during cooking the sauce dries out, add 125 ml (1/2 cup) water as required and continue to cook for the full hour. Remove any whole spices before serving and serve garnished with coriander leaves.

Keep whole spices in a special, lidded spice container so they are easily accessible.

Methi is sold in small bundles in Indian markets.

METHI GOSHT

IN INDIA, METHI IS THE NAME FOR FENUGREEK. IN NORTHERN INDIA, METHI LEAVES ARE OFTEN COMBINED WITH LAMB (GOSHT) AND SERVED AS A DELICACY. METHI PRODUCES A DISTINCTIVE AROMATIC FLAVOUR IN THIS DISH. SERVE WITH INDIAN BREADS OR RICE.

2 onions, roughly chopped
4 garlic cloves, roughly chopped
8 cm (3 inch) piece of ginger, roughly chopped
3 green chillies (seed them for less heat)
125 ml (1/2 cup) oil
2 Indian bay leaves (cassia leaves)
1 kg (2 lb 4 oz) boneless lamb leg or shoulder, cut into 2.5 cm (1 inch) cubes
1 tablespoon ground cumin
2 tablespoons ground coriander
1/2 teaspoon garam masala (page 284)
1/2 teaspoon chilli powder
2 teaspoons salt
1/2 teaspoon ground black pepper
4 bunches of fresh methi leaves, finely chopped (about 200 g/7 oz)

SERVES 4

BLEND the onion, garlic, ginger and chillies together in a blender or food processor until finely chopped. If you don't have a blender, finely chop them together with a knife or crush them in a pestle and mortar.

HEAT the oil in a karhai or large casserole over medium heat and add the chopped mixture and the bay leaves. Cook for 3 minutes, or until golden and just starting to catch on the base of the pan. Add the cubed lamb in batches, stirring for about 20 minutes, until it is all browned. The juices of the meat will start to run clear and the oil will separate out. You need to keep stirring or the meat will catch on the base of the pan.

ADD all the spices, and the salt and pepper, and fry for 3 minutes, or until all pieces of the lamb are thoroughly coated. Add 185 ml (3/4 cup) water, bring to the boil, then reduce the heat, cover and simmer for 45 minutes, adding a little more water if necessary. The sauce should be dryish rather than sloppy. Gently stir in the methi and cook for another 15 minutes, or until the oil separates from the lamb and the sauce has turned a rich olive green.

MEMSAHIB'S LAMB RAAN

THIS DISH LOOKS VERY IMPRESSIVE EVEN THOUGH IT CAN BE MADE WITHOUT MUCH FUSS. IT IS EXCELLENT FOR DINNER OR A SPECIAL LUNCH, BUT IT DOES NEED TO BE MARINATED OVERNIGHT SO THE FLAVOURS CAN PERMEATE THE LAMB. SERVE IT WITH A COUPLE OF VEGETABLE DISHES AND SOME RICE.

1.7 kg (3 lb 12 oz) leg of lamb

MARINADE
1 teaspoon cardamom seeds
1 onion, roughly chopped
4 garlic cloves, roughly chopped
2 cm (3/4 inch) piece of ginger,
   roughly chopped
3 green chillies, seeded
2 teaspoons ground cumin
1/2 teaspoon ground cloves
1 1/2 tablespoons lemon juice
250 ml (1 cup) thick plain yoghurt
   (page 280)

ALMOND COATING
3 tablespoons blanched almonds
1 tablespoon jaggery or
   soft brown sugar
125 ml (1/2 cup) thick plain yoghurt
   (page 280)
1/2 teaspoon red food colouring
   (optional)

coriander (cilantro) leaves (optional)

SERVES 6

TRIM the excess fat from the lamb and stab the meat all over with a sharp skewer so that the marinade will penetrate.

TO MAKE the marinade, grind the cardamom seeds to a fine powder using a spice grinder or pestle and mortar. Chop the onion, garlic and ginger to a paste with the green chillies in a blender or food processor. If you don't have a processor, finely chop them with a knife, then grind to a paste in a pestle and mortar. Mix in the ground cardamom seeds, cumin and cloves. Add the lemon juice and yoghurt and mix well.

COAT the lamb thickly all over, using half the marinade. Cover with plastic wrap and marinate in the fridge overnight. Cover the remaining marinade and refrigerate it.

TO MAKE the almond coating, preheat the oven to 190°C (375°F/Gas 5). Finely chop the almonds in a food processor or with a knife. Mix the reserved marinade with the ground almonds, jaggery, yoghurt and food colouring, if using. Uncover the lamb and coat it all over with the mixture, especially on the top and sides. Transfer the lamb to a shallow roasting tin and cover loosely with oiled foil. Bake for 1 hour, then remove the foil and bake for another 30 minutes, or until the lamb is cooked and the coating set and browned. Test the meat nearest to the bone to see whether it is cooked—a skewer should come out very hot.

CAREFULLY press on any yoghurt and almond coating that has dropped off during cooking, so that the finished product looks neat.

CARVE the meat at the table for full effect. Garnish with coriander if you like. Top each serving with a little of the almond coating.

The High Court in Kolkata (Calcutta), built in 1872 and copied from the Staadhaus in Ypres, Belgium.

MOGHUL LAMB WITH TURNIPS

THIS DISH FROM THE PUNJAB REGION WOULD HAVE BEEN SERVED IN THE ROYAL PALACES OF THE MOGHULS WHEN THEY WERE THE RULERS OF INDIA. EVEN TODAY, THIS RECIPE IS USUALLY RESERVED FOR SPECIAL OCCASIONS AND SERVED WITH PUNJABI BREADS SUCH AS CHAPATIS OR NAAN.

2 onions, roughly chopped
4 garlic cloves, roughly chopped
5 cm (2 inch) piece of ginger, roughly chopped
2 green chillies
170 ml (²/₃ cup) oil
2 Indian bay leaves (cassia leaves)
1 kg (2 lb 4 oz) boneless lamb leg or shoulder, cut into 2.5 cm (1 inch) cubes
pinch of asafoetida
1 teaspoon chilli powder
2 tablespoons ground coriander
2 tablespoons ground cumin
¹/₄ teaspoon ground turmeric
¹/₂ teaspoon garam masala (page 284)
1 tablespoon tomato paste (purée)
2 tablespoons thick plain yoghurt (page 280)
1 tablespoon salt
1 teaspoon ground black pepper
450 g (1 lb) baby turnips, large ones halved

SERVES 4

PUT the onion, garlic, ginger and chillies in a food processor and chop them to form a paste. If you don't have a food processor, chop everything finely or grind them in a pestle and mortar.

HEAT the oil in a karhai or casserole and add the onion mixture with the bay leaves. Fry over high heat for 5 minutes, then reduce the heat to medium and fry for another 2 minutes. Don't let the onions turn more than golden brown. Add the meat and stir until all the pieces are thoroughly coated with the onion mixture. Fry for 15 minutes, stirring constantly. This is a very important part of the cooking process as the longer you fry the meat, the more flavour it will absorb. It is ready when the oil starts to separate out from the meat.

ADD the asafoetida, chilli powder, coriander, cumin, turmeric and garam masala and stir in well. Cook for 1–2 minutes, then add the tomato paste and yoghurt. Fry for another minute and add the salt and pepper. Pour in 500 ml (2 cups) water a little at a time, stirring into the mixture after each addition. This will ensure that the dish retains the heat throughout and will be constantly bubbling until you have a rich, thick sauce. Cover the pan and simmer for 30 minutes.

ADD the turnips to the pan and continue simmering for another 45 minutes, or until both the lamb and turnips have completely softened and the oil has separated from the sauce and turned bright orange.

Columns at Delhi's Jama Masjid, built in the 17th century.

LAMB KALIA

IN INDIA, MUTTON IS USED MORE OFTEN THAN LAMB AND BECAUSE IT CAN BE TOUGH IT REQUIRES LONG HOURS OF TENDERIZING. IN THIS RECIPE, LAMB HAS BEEN USED INSTEAD, SO THE MARINATING TIME IS NOT AS LONG. THE GINGER AND THE YOGHURT BOTH ACT AS TENDERIZERS.

2 1/2 teaspoons cumin seeds
125 ml (1/2 cup) thick plain yoghurt
   (page 280)
2 teaspoons clear vinegar
1 teaspoon salt
1 tablespoon ginger juice
   (page 280)
3 teaspoons chilli powder
1 teaspoon ground turmeric
1 kg (2 lb 4 oz) lamb leg or chump,
   cut into 2.5 cm (1 inch) cubes
2 potatoes, cut into 2.5 cm (1 inch)
   cubes
oil for deep-frying
3 cm (1 1/4 inch) cinnamon stick
2 cardamom pods, crushed
4 garlic cloves, crushed
1/2 teaspoon sugar
4 onions, sliced
2 Indian bay leaves (cassia leaves)
1 tablespoon tomato paste (purée)

SERVES 6

PLACE a small frying pan over low heat and dry-roast 2 teaspoons of the cumin seeds until aromatic. Grind the roasted cumin seeds to a fine powder using a spice grinder or pestle and mortar.

COMBINE the ground cumin with the yoghurt, vinegar, salt, ginger juice, chilli powder and 1/2 teaspoon of the turmeric in a large bowl. Add the lamb and coat well. Cover and marinate for at least 2 hours in the fridge.

COAT the potato with the remaining 1/2 teaspoon of turmeric. Fill a karhai or casserole one-third full with oil and heat to 180°C/350°F (a cube of bread will brown in 15 seconds). Fry the potato cubes until they are golden brown, then remove and drain on paper towels. Let the oil cool a little, then pour out all but 2 tablespoons.

PLACE the pan back over medium heat and fry the remaining cumin seeds until they start to pop. Add the cinnamon stick, cardamom pods, garlic, sugar and onion and fry until golden.

ADD the meat to the pan and fry until the meat is browned (you may need to add a bit more of the oil). Add the bay leaves, tomato paste and 250 ml (1 cup) water and reduce the heat. Cover and simmer for 1 hour, or until the lamb is tender. If the sauce is still a little thin when the lamb is cooked, simmer with the lid off until it thickens. Toss the potato through the meat before serving.

Removing the seeds from the chillies will make the dish slightly milder. Gently stir the spices to evenly roast them.

The Indian version of the pestle and mortar. The base is the *sil* and the crushing stone the *nora*.

MANGALOREAN PORK BAFATH

MANGALOREAN FOOD IS SOUTH INDIAN WITH MANY OTHER INFLUENCES, INCLUDING PORTUGUESE. THIS RECIPE IS MILDLY SWEET BECAUSE OF THE KASHMIRI CHILLIES. THE PORK HAS OILS THAT ALMOST ROAST THE SPICES WITHIN THE MEAT WITH A BEAUTIFUL, AROMATIC RESULT.

20 red Kashmiri chillies, seeded
2 teaspoons coriander seeds
1 teaspoon cumin seeds
1/2 teaspoon ground turmeric
10 black peppercorns
2 tablespoons tamarind purée (page 280)
1.5 kg (3 lb 5 oz) boneless pork leg or shoulder, cut into 3 cm (1¼ inch) cubes
1 tablespoon oil
2 onions, cut into 3 cm (1¼ inch) pieces
2 cm (3/4 inch) piece of ginger, finely chopped
6 green chillies, slit lengthwise into halves
8 cloves
2 cm (3/4 inch) cinnamon stick, pounded roughly
1 tablespoon dark vinegar
3 garlic cloves, finely chopped
1 green chilli, extra, seeded, finely sliced lengthwise

SERVES 6

PLACE a small frying pan over low heat and dry-roast the chillies, coriander seeds, cumin seeds, ground turmeric and peppercorns until aromatic. Grind the roasted mixture to a fine powder using a spice grinder or pestle and mortar.

MIX all the roasted, ground ingredients with the tamarind and meat. Cover and marinate in the fridge for 2 hours.

HEAT the oil in a karhai or casserole over high heat, add the meat mixture in batches and brown all over. Return all the meat to the pan, then add the onion, ginger, chilli, cloves and cinnamon. Stir thoroughly to mix with the pork. Reduce the heat to low and cook for about 20 minutes, until the meat juices appear and mix with the spice, creating a thick sauce.

ADD the vinegar, garlic and 250 ml (1 cup) water and cook for 1–1¼ hours, until the pork is very tender. Season with salt, to taste. Cook until the oil separates from the spice mixture, which indicates the meat is ready. You can skim off the oil or blot it from the surface with paper towels if you prefer. Garnish with the chilli before serving.

PORK WITH CAPSICUM AND POTATOES

THIS IS A FAVOURITE IN SIMLA IN THE NORTH OF INDIA. THE 'POTATO OF THE MOUNTAIN' AND THE GREEN CAPSICUM ARE COOKED WITH PORK. THIS DISH IS IDEAL SERVED WITH ANY INDIAN BREADS SUCH AS PARATHAS, PURIS OR CHAPATIS.

125 ml (1/2 cup) oil
1 large onion, chopped
4 garlic cloves, crushed
8 cm (3 inch) piece of ginger, chopped
2 Indian bay leaves (cassia leaves)
600 g (1 lb 5 oz) pork sparerib chops, bones removed, meat cut into 2 cm (3/4 inch) cubes
pinch of asafoetida
1 teaspoon chilli powder
1/2 teaspoon ground turmeric
1 1/2 tablespoons ground cumin
1 1/2 tablespoons ground coriander
1/2 teaspoon garam masala (page 284)
1 1/2 tablespoons lemon juice
4 dried chillies
1 teaspoon kalonji (nigella seeds)
1 teaspoon yellow mustard seeds
2 tomatoes, finely chopped
4 green chillies
2 teaspoons paprika
2 red capsicums (peppers), cut into 2.5 cm (1 inch) pieces
2 green capsicums (peppers), cut into 2.5 cm (1 inch) pieces
1 tablespoon salt
1 teaspoon ground black pepper
500 g (1 lb 2 oz) potatoes, cut into 3 cm (1 1/4 inch) cubes
10 curry leaves
1 teaspoon garam masala (page 284), extra

SERVES 6

The spice market in Delhi houses offices and dwellings on its upper floors.

HEAT 80 ml (1/3 cup) of the oil in a karhai or casserole over medium heat. Add half of each of the onion, garlic and ginger, along with the bay leaves and fry for about 2 minutes, until the onion is soft. Increase the heat to high, add the meat and asafoetida and fry for 2 minutes, stirring until all the meat is brown. Reduce the heat to medium and cook for 10 minutes. Remove from the heat, lift out the meat with a spatula and place in a large bowl.

ADD the chilli powder, turmeric, 1 1/4 tablespoons cumin, 2 teaspoons coriander and the garam masala to the meat, stirring in while the meat is still warm. Stir in the lemon juice.

HEAT the remaining oil in the same pan over medium heat and fry the remaining onion, garlic and ginger for a few minutes until the onion is soft. Add the dried chillies, kalonji, yellow mustard seeds and the remaining coriander and cumin. Fry for 2 minutes, or until the seeds start to pop. Add the chopped tomato and fry for 1 minute. Reduce the heat to simmering and cook for 5 minutes, or until the liquid from the tomato has reduced.

STIR in the green chillies and the paprika. Add the meat and stir over medium heat for 2 minutes, or until all the sauce has been absorbed by the meat. Add the red and green capsicum, then reduce the heat to simmering and cover the pan. The capsicum will release its own water so no extra water is necessary. Cook for 10 minutes, then add the salt, pepper and cubed potato. Add 125 ml (1/2 cup) water, cover and simmer for 1 hour, stirring occasionally. Add the curry leaves and cook for another 15 minutes. The meat and potato should be very tender, but if not, cook for another 15 minutes. Add the extra garam masala and season with salt, to taste.

Fenugreek is a spice used to impart a 'curry' flavour.

PORK VINDALOO

VINDALOO IS NOTORIOUS FOR BEING HOT AND SPICY. THE NAME IS PORTUGUESE FOR 'VINEGAR AND GARLIC'. VINDALOO WAS INVENTED BY THE PORTUGUESE IN GOA. THE VINEGAR IS MADE FROM COCONUT (CLEAR) AND MOLASSES (DARK) BUT WHITE AND BALSAMIC CAN BE USED INSTEAD.

1 kg (2 lb 4 oz) leg of pork on the bone
6 cardamom pods
1 teaspoon black peppercorns
4 dried chillies
1 teaspoon cloves
10 cm (4 inch) cinnamon stick, roughly broken
1 teaspoon cumin seeds
1/2 teaspoon ground turmeric
1/2 teaspoon coriander seeds
1/4 teaspoon fenugreek seeds
4 tablespoons clear vinegar
1 tablespoon dark vinegar
4 tablespoons oil
2 onions, finely sliced
10 garlic cloves, finely sliced
5 cm (2 inch) piece of ginger, cut into matchsticks
3 ripe tomatoes, roughly chopped
4 green chillies, chopped
1 teaspoon jaggery or soft brown sugar

SERVES 4

TRIM away any excess fat from the pork, remove the bone and cut the pork into 2.5 cm (1 inch) cubes. Reserve the bone.

SPLIT open the cardamom pods and remove the seeds. Finely grind the cardamom seeds, peppercorns, dried chillies, cloves, cinnamon stick, cumin seeds, turmeric, coriander seeds and fenugreek seeds in a spice grinder or pestle and mortar.

IN a large bowl, mix the ground spices together with the vinegars. Add the pork and mix thoroughly to coat well. Cover and marinate in the fridge for 3 hours.

HEAT the oil in a karhai or casserole over low heat and fry the onion until lightly browned. Add the garlic, ginger, tomato and chilli and stir well. Add the pork, increase the heat to high and fry for 3–5 minutes, or until browned. Add 250 ml (1 cup) water and any of the marinade liquid left in the bowl, reduce the heat and bring slowly back to the boil. Add the jaggery and the pork bone. Cover tightly and simmer for about 1 1/2 hours, stirring occasionally until the meat is very tender. Discard the bone. Season with salt, to taste.

FRIED BEEF KERALA

oil for deep-frying
1 potato, cut into small cubes
500 g (1 lb 2 oz) rump steak,
 thinly sliced
3 garlic cloves, crushed
1 teaspoon ground black pepper
1 tablespoon ginger juice (page 280)
2 tablespoons oil, extra
2 onions, sliced in rings
60 ml (1/4 cup) beef stock
2 tablespoons tomato paste (purée)
1/2 tablespoon soy sauce
1 teaspoon chilli powder
3 tablespoons lemon juice
3 tomatoes, chopped
80 g (1/2 cup) fresh or frozen peas
coriander (cilantro) leaves (optional)

SERVES 4

FILL a deep, heavy-based saucepan one-third full with oil and heat to 180°C/350°F (a cube of bread will brown in 15 seconds). Deep-fry the potato cubes until golden brown. Drain on paper towels.

PUT the steak in a bowl, add the garlic, pepper and ginger juice and toss well. Heat the oil and fry the beef quickly in batches over high heat. Keep each batch warm as you remove it. Reduce the heat, fry the onion until golden, then remove.

PUT the stock, tomato paste, soy sauce, chilli powder and lemon juice in the pan and cook over medium heat until reduced. Add the fried onion, cook for 3 minutes, add the chopped tomato and the peas, then stir well and cook for 1 minute. Add the beef and potato and toss well until heated through. Garnish with coriander leaves if you like.

Rice growing in paddy fields near Kochi (Cochin), Kerala.

GOAN BEEF CURRY

8 cardamom pods
1 teaspoon fennel seeds
8 cloves
10 cm (4 inch) cinnamon stick
1/2 teaspoon fenugreek seeds
1/2 teaspoon ground black pepper
3 teaspoons coriander seeds
3 teaspoons cumin seeds
125 ml (1/2 cup) oil
2 onions, finely chopped
6 garlic cloves, finely chopped
10 cm (4 inch) piece of ginger, grated
1 kg (2 lb 4 oz) braising or stewing
 steak, cut into 2.5 cm (1 inch)
 cubes
1/2 teaspoon ground turmeric
2 teaspoons chilli powder
100 g (3 1/2 oz) creamed coconut,
 dissolved in 310 ml (1 1/4 cups)
 water, or 310 ml (1 1/4 cups)
 coconut milk (page 283)

SERVES 6

REMOVE the seeds from the cardamom pods and grind them in a spice grinder or pestle and mortar with the fennel seeds, cloves, cinnamon stick, fenugreek seeds, black pepper and the coriander and cumin seeds, until they form a fine powder.

HEAT the oil in a karhai, heavy-based frying pan or casserole over medium heat and fry the onion, garlic and ginger until lightly browned. Add the meat and fry until brown all over. Add all the spices and fry for 1 minute. Add the creamed coconut and bring slowly to the boil. Cover, reduce the heat and simmer for about 1 hour, or until the meat is tender.

IF the liquid evaporates during cooking, add about 185 ml (3/4 cup) boiling water and stir to make a thick sauce. If the sauce is still too liquid at the end of the cooking time, simmer with the lid off until it evaporates. Season with salt, to taste.

GOAN BEEF CURRY

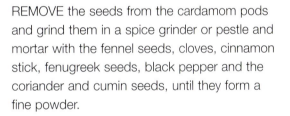

VEGETABLES

ALOO GOBI

3 tablespoons oil
1/2 teaspoon black mustard seeds
1/2 onion, finely chopped
200 g (7 oz) potatoes, cut into cubes
1/4 teaspoon ground turmeric
1 teaspoon ground cumin
1 teaspoon ground coriander
1 1/2 teaspoons garam masala
 (page 284)
4 ripe tomatoes, chopped
1 large cauliflower (about 1.25 kg/
 2 lb 12 oz), cut into florets
2 cm (3/4 inch) piece of ginger
1 teaspoon sugar

SERVES 4

HEAT the oil in a karhai or deep, heavy-based frying pan over low heat. Add the mustard seeds, cover the pan and wait for the seeds to pop. Add the onion and potato and fry until lightly browned.

ADD the turmeric, cumin, coriander and garam masala to the pan and fry for a couple of seconds. Add the tomato and stir until the spices are well mixed. Add the cauliflower florets and stir until well mixed. Stir in the ginger, sugar and 125 ml (1/2 cup) water, increase the heat to medium and bring to the boil. Reduce the heat, cover and simmer for 15 minutes, or until the vegetables are tender. Season with salt, to taste.

UNCOVER the pan and if the sauce is too runny, simmer it for another 1–2 minutes before serving.

Snake gourds are exceptionally long vegetables which grow hanging down from raised vines.

SNAKE GOURD WITH YOGHURT

THIS IS A VERSATILE RECIPE THAT CAN BE MADE USING SNAKE GOURD, BITTER MELON OR EGGPLANT (AUBERGINE). SNAKE GOURDS ARE LONG AND THIN, SOMETIMES CURLY, VEGETABLES THAT GROW ON VINES. GROWERS SOMETIMES TIE A WEIGHT TO THE VEGETABLE TO STRAIGHTEN IT AS IT GROWS.

250 g (9 oz) snake gourd
1 teaspoon ground turmeric
1 tablespoon oil
1/2 teaspoon black mustard seeds
1/2 teaspoon whole urad dal
2 dried chillies, cut in half
4 stalks of curry leaves
1 1/2 red onions, finely chopped
250 ml (1 cup) thick plain yoghurt
 (page 280)

SERVES 4

PEEL the snake gourd, slice in half horizontally and then slice diagonally into pieces about 1 cm (1/2 inch) thick. Add the turmeric and a pinch of salt and rub into the pieces of gourd. Put the gourd in a sieve to allow any liquid to drain off.

HEAT the oil in a karhai or heavy-based frying pan over low heat. Add the mustard and urad dal and when the mustard seeds pop, add the chilli and curry leaves and one-third of the onion. Cook until the onion is browned and softened. Add the snake gourd and toss over medium heat for about 10 minutes, or until the mixture looks dry and the gourd is tender. Remove from the heat.

COMBINE the yoghurt and the remaining onion in a bowl and stir well. Fold the fried snake gourd into the yoghurt just before serving and season with salt, to taste.

SNAKE GOURD WITH YOGHURT

SPICY EGGPLANT

THIS IS A WONDERFUL DISH IN WHICH EGGPLANT (AUBERGINE) IS COOKED WITH PICKLING STYLE SPICES. THE EGGPLANT CAN BE SERVED AS PART OF AN INDIAN FEAST OR AS A SPICY ACCOMPANIMENT. IT IS ALSO GOOD AS A VEGETARIAN MAIN DISH WITH RICE AND SOME YOGHURT.

Drain the fried eggplant (aubergine) to get rid of any excess oil.

800 g (1 lb 12 oz) eggplants (aubergines), cut into wedges 5 cm (2 inches) long
400 g (14 oz) ripe tomatoes or 400 g (14 oz) tin chopped tomatoes
2.5 cm (1 inch) piece of ginger, grated
6 garlic cloves, crushed
310 ml (1 1/4 cups) oil
1 teaspoon fennel seeds
1/2 teaspoon kalonji (nigella seeds)
1 tablespoon ground coriander
1/4 teaspoon ground turmeric
1/2 teaspoon cayenne pepper
1 teaspoon salt

SERVES 6

PUT the eggplant pieces in a colander, sprinkle them with salt and leave them for 30 minutes to allow any bitter juices to run out. Rinse, squeeze out any excess water, then pat dry with paper towels. If using fresh tomatoes, score a cross in the top of each and plunge into boiling water for 20 seconds. Drain and peel away from the cross. Roughly chop the tomatoes, discarding the cores and seeds and reserving any juices.

PUREE the ginger and garlic with one-third of the tomato in a blender or food processor. If you don't have a blender, finely chop the tomatoes and mix with the ginger and garlic.

HEAT 125 ml (1/2 cup) of the oil in a large, deep, heavy-based frying pan and when hot, add as many eggplant pieces as you can fit in a single layer. Cook over medium heat until brown on both sides, then transfer to a sieve over a bowl so that the excess oil can drain off. Add the remaining oil to the pan as needed and cook the rest of the eggplant in batches.

REHEAT the oil that's left in the pan and add the fennel seeds and kalonji. Cover and allow to pop for a few seconds. Add the tomato and ginger mixture and the remaining ingredients, except the eggplant. Cook, stirring regularly for 5–6 minutes, until the mixture becomes thick and fairly smooth (be careful as it may spit at you). Carefully add the cooked eggplant so the pieces stay whole, cover the pan and cook gently for about 10 minutes.

STORE the eggplant in the sauce in the fridge. Pour off any excess oil before serving. The eggplant can either be served cold or gently warmed through.

BHINDI MASALA

BHINDI, WHICH IS MORE COMMONLY KNOWN AS OKRA OR LADIES' FINGERS, IS FOUND IN ABUNDANCE THROUGHOUT INDIA. WHEN BUYING BHINDI, BE CAREFUL TO ENSURE THAT THEY ARE A BRIGHT GREEN COLOUR, LOOK CRISP AND FIRM, AND THAT THEY YIELD SLIGHTLY AT THE NARROW END.

500 g (1 lb 2 oz) okra, about 5 cm
   (2 inches) long
3 green chillies
3 tablespoons oil
1 teaspoon black mustard seeds
1 red onion, finely chopped
1 teaspoon ground cumin
1 teaspoon ground coriander
2 teaspoons garam masala
   (page 284)
1 teaspoon ground turmeric
4 garlic cloves, finely chopped

SERVES 4

WASH the okra and pat dry with paper towels. Trim the tops and tails. Ignore any sticky, glutinous liquid that appears because this will disappear as the okra cooks.

CUT the chillies in half lengthwise, leaving them attached at the stalk, and scrape out any seeds. Heat the oil in a karhai or deep, heavy-based frying pan, add the mustard seeds and onion and cook until the seeds pop and the onion is light brown. Add the cumin, coriander, garam masala and turmeric and cook until the popping stops.

ADD the garlic, okra and the chilli to the pan, fry for 5 minutes, stir and cook for 2 minutes. Add 60 ml (1/4 cup) water, 1 tablespoon at a time, and stir to make a sauce. Season with salt, to taste. Simmer for about 15 minutes, until the okra is cooked through and the sauce is thick and dry.

BHINDI BHAJI

BHINDI BHAJI

450 g (1 lb) okra
2 tablespoons oil
1 small onion, finely chopped
1/2 teaspoon ground cumin
1/2 teaspoon ground coriander
1/2 teaspoon chilli powder (optional)
1/4 teaspoon ground turmeric
150 g (51/2 oz) tinned chopped
   tomatoes

SERVES 4

WASH the okra and pat dry with paper towels. Trim the ends and cut into 2.5 cm (1 inch) pieces. Ignore any sticky, glutinous liquid that appears because this will disappear as the okra cooks.

HEAT the oil in a karhai or deep, heavy-based frying pan over medium heat and fry the onion until lightly browned. Add the spices and tomato and fry for 1 minute until well mixed, squashing the tomato to break it up.

ADD the okra and stir until well coated. Bring to the boil, cover and simmer for 5–8 minutes, until the okra is cooked through and no longer slimy. If there is any excess liquid, simmer, uncovered, until the liquid evaporates. Season with salt, to taste.

STUFFED CAPSICUMS

STUFFING VEGETABLES IS A COOKING METHOD USED FOR SPECIAL OCCASIONS. THESE STUFFED CAPSICUMS (PEPPERS) ARE SIMMERED IN A COCONUT-FLAVOURED SAUCE. THE CAPSICUMS SHOULD BE THE SMALL VARIETY USUALLY USED IN INDIA. RED OR YELLOW ONES CAN ALSO BE USED.

Make sure that the stuffing fills the capsicums (peppers) adequately, but don't pack it in too firmly or it may spill out as it cooks.

400 g (14 oz) potatoes, quartered
6 small green capsicums (peppers)
2 tablespoons oil
2 onions, finely chopped
2 teaspoons ground cumin
2 teaspoons ground coriander
1/2 teaspoon ground turmeric
1/2 teaspoon chilli powder

SAUCE
1/2 onion, finely chopped
6 cloves
6 cardamom pods
2 garlic cloves, finely chopped
2 cm (3/4 inch) piece of ginger,
   finely chopped
1 cinnamon stick
1 teaspoon ground coriander
1 teaspoon ground cumin
1/4 teaspoon ground turmeric
1/2 teaspoon chilli powder
50 g (13/4 oz) creamed coconut,
   mixed with 250 ml (1 cup) water,
   or 250 ml (1 cup) coconut cream
   (page 283)

SERVES 6

COOK the potato in a saucepan of simmering water for 15 minutes, or until tender, then drain and cut into small cubes. Bring a large saucepan of water to the boil, add the capsicums and blanch for 5 minutes. Refresh the capsicums in cold water, cut round the stem and remove both it and the seeds. Drain well upside-down.

HEAT the oil in a small frying pan and cook the onion over medium heat until soft but not browned. Add the cumin, coriander, turmeric and chilli and mix thoroughly. Mix in the potato and season with salt. Remove from the heat and leave until cool. Divide into six portions and fill each capsicum.

TO MAKE the sauce, combine all the ingredients in a deep, heavy-based frying pan and bring slowly to the boil. Reduce the heat to low, cover and simmer for 20 minutes. Season with salt, to taste. Add the stuffed capsicums to the pan, arranging them so that they stand upright in a single layer, and cook for another 5 minutes, or until the sauce is thick. Serve the capsicums with a little sauce spooned over the top.

SHEBU BHAJI

DILL IS A HERB THAT CAN BE USED IN ABUNDANCE, AS IT IS IN THIS DISH, WITHOUT BEING OVERPOWERING. IT HAS A MILD BUT VERY DISTINCTIVE FLAVOUR. INDIAN DILL IS SIMILAR TO EUROPEAN DILL AND THEY ARE INTERCHANGEABLE IN THIS RECIPE.

200 g (7 oz) potatoes
200 g (7 oz) dill
2 tablespoons oil
2 garlic cloves, chopped
1/4 teaspoon ground turmeric
1 teaspoon black mustard seeds
pinch of asafoetida
1 dried chilli

SERVES 2

CUT the potatoes into 2.5 cm (1 inch) cubes and cook in a saucepan of simmering water for 15 minutes or until just tender. Drain well.

WASH the dill in several changes of water and trim off the tough stalks. Roughly chop the dill.

HEAT the oil in a heavy-based saucepan, add the garlic and fry for 30 seconds over low heat. Add the turmeric, mustard seeds, asafoetida and the whole chilli, cover and briefly allow the seeds to pop. Stir in the potato until well mixed. Add the dill, cover and cook over low heat for 5 minutes. The dill contains sufficient moisture to cook without the addition of any water. Season with salt, to taste.

MOOLI BHAJI

THE ASIAN RADISH, OR MOOLI AS IT IS ALSO KNOWN, IS MUCH MILDER IN FLAVOUR THAN ITS WESTERN COUNTERPART. IT LOOKS LIKE A HUGE, WHITE CARROT AND HAS A CRISP, JUICY FLESH. BHAJI IS THE NAME GIVEN TO MANY VEGETABLE DISHES AND LOOSELY IT MEANS FRIED VEGETABLES.

500 g (1 lb 2 oz) mooli
25 g (1 oz) grated coconut
   (page 283)
2 tablespoons oil
1/4 teaspoon black mustard seeds
1 onion, chopped
1/4 teaspoon ground turmeric
pinch of asafoetida
1 green chilli, finely chopped

SERVES 4

CUT the mooli into batons. Heat a frying pan over low heat and dry-roast the coconut, stirring constantly until it browns lightly.

HEAT the oil in a karhai or heavy-based saucepan over low heat. Add the mustard seeds, cover and allow to pop briefly. Add the onion and cook until lightly browned. Stir in the turmeric, asafoetida, chilli and the mooli until well mixed. Add 125 ml (1/2 cup) water and simmer for 5–7 minutes, until the mooli is cooked through and tender. Season with salt, to taste. Garnish with the coconut.

MOOLI BHAJI

SPICED BANANA FLOWER

ALL PARTS OF THE BANANA PLANT ARE USED IN DIFFERENT WAYS: THE LEAVES AS AN AROMATIC FOOD WRAPPER AND AS A 'PLATE' FOR INDIAN MEALS; AND THE FRUIT, FLOWER, AND TENDER INNER RINGS OF THE STEM ARE EATEN. WEAR PLASTIC GLOVES TO STOP THE SAP STAINING YOUR HANDS.

1 banana flower
1/2 lemon
200 g (7 oz) prawns (shrimp)
25 g (1 oz) grated coconut
  (page 283)
1 tablespoon oil
125 ml (1/2 cup) lime juice
1 red chilli, finely chopped
2 tablespoons jaggery or
  soft brown sugar
1 tablespoon grated lime rind,
  or lime leaves
mint leaves

SERVES 4

Peel off the leaves and immature bananas until you reach the core, then chop off the end. Soak the quarters of core in salted water.

PEEL off one leaf at a time from the banana flower. Remove the yellow, stick-like immature bananas and discard both them and the leaves until you reach the white inner core. Chop off the top end and discard it. Chop what is left into quarters and soak it in a bowl of water with 1 teaspoon salt for 1 hour. Drain the banana flower, transfer to a saucepan, cover with fresh water and add the juice from the half lemon. Bring to the boil and cook for 15–20 minutes, or until soft. The banana flower will darken in colour as it cooks. Drain and slice into julienne strips. Peel and devein the prawns and cut each in half.

PLACE a heavy-based frying pan over low heat and dry-roast the coconut, stirring constantly until the coconut is golden brown. Finely grind in a pestle and mortar or in a spice grinder.

HEAT the oil in the frying pan and fry the prawns until they are pink and cooked through. Mix the prawns with the lime juice, chilli, jaggery and lime rind. Season with salt, to taste, then leave to cool.

JUST before serving, add the banana hearts and coconut to the prawns and toss well. Serve cold, garnished with the mint leaves.

CABBAGE WITH SPLIT PEAS

THE COMBINATION OF SPLIT PEAS AND CABBAGE GIVES THIS DISH AN UNUSUAL TEXTURE. THE MUSTARD SEEDS CRACKLE WHEN FRIED AND DEVELOP A NUTTY SWEETNESS IN THE PROCESS. THE SPLIT PEAS ARE SOAKED WELL IN ADVANCE TO SOFTEN THEM AND REDUCE THE COOKING TIME.

125 g (4^1/$_2$ oz) split peas
450 g (1 lb) green cabbage
3 tablespoons oil
^{1}/$_4$ teaspoon black mustard seeds
2 teaspoons cumin seeds
8 curry leaves
2 dried chillies
pinch of asafoetida
^{1}/$_4$ teaspoon ground turmeric
coriander (cilantro) leaves (optional)

SERVES 4

SOAK the split peas in 750 ml (3 cups) boiling water for 2 hours. Drain thoroughly.

SHRED the cabbage. Heat the oil in a karhai or deep, heavy-based frying pan over low heat. Add the mustard and cumin seeds, cover and allow to pop briefly. Add the curry leaves, dried chillies and split peas and fry for 5 minutes, stirring often. Add the asafoetida, turmeric and cabbage and fry over low heat until the cabbage is cooked through and tender. Season with salt, to taste. Serve garnished with coriander leaves if you wish.

PUNJABI CABBAGE

PUNJABI CABBAGE

ONE OF NORTHERN INDIA'S FAVOURITE VEGETABLE DISHES, SERVED WITH OTHER VEGETARIAN OR MAIN MEAT DISHES, AND OF COURSE BREADS SUCH AS PARATHAS, PHULKAS OR CHAPATIS. IT IS AN EXCELLENT DISH TO SERVE WITH CHICKEN OR A CURRY SUCH AS KHEEMA MATAR.

^{1}/$_2$ onion, roughly chopped
1 garlic clove, roughly chopped
2.5 cm (1 inch) piece of ginger, chopped
2 green chillies, seeded and chopped
4 tablespoons oil
1 teaspoon cumin seeds
1 teaspoon ground turmeric
500 g (1 lb 2 oz) green cabbage, finely shredded
1 teaspoon salt
^{1}/$_2$ teaspoon ground black pepper
2 teaspoons ground cumin
1 teaspoon ground coriander
^{1}/$_4$ teaspoon chilli powder
1 tablespoon unsalted butter

SERVES 4

PUT the onion, garlic, ginger and chilli in a food processor and chop until finely chopped but not a paste, or chop together with a knife.

HEAT the oil in a karhai or heavy-based frying pan over low heat and fry the onion mixture until softened but not browned. Add the cumin seeds and turmeric to the pan and stir for 1 minute. Mix in the cabbage, stirring thoroughly until all the leaves are coated in the yellow paste. Add the salt, pepper, ground cumin, coriander and chilli powder. Stir to coat the cabbage, then cook for 10 minutes with the pan partially covered, stirring occasionally until the cabbage is soft. If the cabbage becomes too dry and starts sticking to the pan, add 1–2 tablespoons water. Stir in the butter and season with salt, to taste.

MATAR PANEER

IN THE NORTH OF INDIA, DAIRY PRODUCTS SUCH AS PANEER ARE SERVED REGULARLY. THIS VERSION OF MATAR PANEER IS DRY BUT IT COMES IN VARIOUS GUISES. IF YOU DON'T WANT TO MAKE YOUR OWN PANEER, YOU CAN OFTEN BUY IT FROM INDIAN FOOD SHOPS OR SUPERMARKETS.

225 g (8 oz) or 1/2 quantity paneer
   (page 279)
2 tablespoons ghee
50 g (1³/4 oz) onion, chopped
200 g (1¹/3 cups) peas
1/2 teaspoon sugar
5 cm (2 inch) piece of ginger, grated
2–3 green chillies, finely chopped
1 spring onion (scallion), finely
   chopped
1/2 teaspoon garam masala
   (page 284)
1 tablespoon chopped coriander
   (cilantro) leaves

SERVES 4

CUT the paneer into 2 cm (³/4 inch) cubes. Heat the ghee in a karhai or heavy-based frying pan over medium heat and carefully fry the paneer until golden on all sides. Remove from the pan.

FRY the onion lightly in the same ghee, until softened and lightly golden. Remove the onion from the pan. Add 5 tablespoons hot water and a pinch of salt to the ghee and simmer for 1 minute. Add the peas and sugar, cover and cook for 5–6 minutes, until the peas are nearly cooked.

ADD the fried onion, paneer, ginger, chilli and spring onion to the pan and cook for 2–3 minutes. Add the garam masala and coriander leaves. Season with salt, to taste.

Fry the cubes of paneer until they are golden brown. Make sure the oil is hot enough, otherwise they may stick to the pan.

SAAG PANEER

LEAFY GREENS ARE USED IN MANY INNOVATIVE RECIPES FROM THE NORTH TO THE SOUTH OF INDIA. IN THIS RECIPE, SPINACH, TOMATOES AND PANEER ARE USED IN A MORE TEXTURED DISH THAN THE SMOOTH PUREED VERSIONS SERVED IN MANY NORTHERN INDIAN RESTAURANTS.

500 g (1 bunch) English spinach
   leaves
1/2 teaspoon ground cumin
1/2 teaspoon ground coriander
1/2 teaspoon fenugreek seeds
1 tablespoon oil
1 red onion, thinly sliced
5 garlic cloves, chopped
200 g (7 oz) tin chopped tomatoes
2 cm (³/4 inch) piece of ginger,
   grated
1 teaspoon garam masala (page 284)
225 g (8 oz) or 1/2 quantity paneer
   (page 279), cubed

SERVES 4

BLANCH the spinach leaves in boiling water for 2 minutes, then refresh in cold water, drain and very finely chop. Place a small frying pan over low heat and dry-roast the cumin until aromatic. Remove, dry-roast the coriander, then the fenugreek.

HEAT the oil in a karhai or heavy-based frying pan over low heat and fry the onion, garlic, cumin, coriander and fenugreek until brown and aromatic. Stir in the tomato, ginger and garam masala and bring to the boil. Add the spinach and cook until the liquid has reduced. Fold in the paneer, trying to keep it in whole pieces. Stir gently until heated through. Season with salt, to taste.

SAAG PANEER

Using a pair of tongs, hold the eggplant (aubergine) in the gas flame until it is charred all over. The skin should peel away easily.

SMOKY SPICED EGGPLANT

WHEN EGGPLANTS (AUBERGINES) ARE IN SEASON IN INDIA, THEY ARE OFTEN PLACED ON THE DYING EMBERS OF A CHARCOAL FIRE AND LEFT TO SMOKE OVERNIGHT, READY TO BE FRIED AND BLENDED WITH SPICES THE FOLLOWING MORNING. SERVE THIS DISH WITH BREADS OR AS A COLD RELISH.

600 g (1 lb 5 oz) eggplants (aubergines)
1 red onion, chopped
1 garlic clove, chopped
2.5 cm (1 inch) piece of ginger, chopped
1 green chilli, chopped
80 ml (1/3 cup) oil
1/4 teaspoon chilli powder
1/2 teaspoon garam masala (page 284)
2 teaspoons ground cumin
2 teaspoons ground coriander
2 teaspoons salt
1/2 teaspoon ground black pepper
2 ripe tomatoes, chopped
3–4 tablespoons coriander (cilantro) leaves, finely chopped

SERVES 4

SCORCH the eggplants by holding them over a medium gas flame, or heating them under a grill (broiler) or on an electric hotplate. Keep turning them until the skin is blackened on all sides. Set aside until cool, then peel off the charred skin. Roughly chop the flesh. Don't worry if black specks remain on the flesh because they add to the smoky flavour.

COMBINE the onion, garlic, ginger and chilli in a blender and process until chopped together but not a paste. Alternatively, chop finely with a knife and mix in a bowl.

HEAT the oil in a deep, heavy-based frying pan over medium heat, add the onion mixture and cook until slightly browned. Add all the spices, and the salt and pepper, and stir for 1 minute. Add the chopped tomato and simmer until the liquid has reduced. Put the eggplants in the pan and mash them with a wooden spoon, stirring around with the spices. Simmer for 10 minutes, or until the eggplants are soft.

STIR in the chopped coriander leaves and season with salt, to taste.

GAJAR MATAR

IN NORTHERN INDIA, PEAS (MATAR) FROM SIMLA, IN HIMACHAL PRADESH, ARE FAMOUS FOR THEIR SWEET FLAVOUR. THEY ARE OFTEN SERVED WITH CARROTS IN WINTER WHEN BOTH VEGETABLES ARE IN SEASON. GAJAR MATAR IS A STAPLE VEGETABLE DISH THAT GOES WELL WITH ALL INDIAN MEALS.

1 small onion, roughly chopped
1 garlic clove, roughly chopped
2.5 cm (1 inch) piece of ginger, chopped
125 ml (1/2 cup) oil
1 teaspoon cumin seeds
1 1/2 teaspoons ground turmeric
325 g (11 1/2 oz) carrots, diced
1 teaspoon ground cumin
1 teaspoon ground coriander
250 g (1 2/3 cups) peas
3 teaspoons salt
1/4 teaspoon sugar
1/4 teaspoon chilli powder
4 teaspoons pomegranate seeds (optional)
1/2 teaspoon garam masala (page 284)

SERVES 6

PUT the onion, garlic and ginger in a food processor and blend until finely chopped, or chop them with a knife and mix together.

HEAT the oil in a karhai or frying pan, then add the onion mixture and stir over high heat for 2 minutes, or until softened. Reduce the heat to medium and add the cumin seeds and turmeric. When the seeds are sizzling, add the carrot and stir for 2 minutes. Add the ground cumin and coriander and fry for 2 minutes. Stir in the peas and then the salt, sugar and chilli powder. Add 2 tablespoons of water if using frozen peas, or 4 tablespoons if using fresh peas. Reduce the heat to a simmer, add the pomegranate seeds, if using, and stir before partially covering the pan. Simmer for 15 minutes, or until the carrot and peas are tender. Stir in the garam masala.

SAAG BHAJI

SAAG BHAJI

200 g (7 oz) small turnips, finely chopped
1 kg (2 lb 4 oz) mixed English spinach and amaranth leaves, finely shredded
1/2 teaspoon chilli powder
1 tablespoon ghee or oil
2 cm (3/4 inch) piece of ginger, grated
1 onion, finely chopped
1 1/2 tablespoons lemon juice

SERVES 4

BRING 125 ml (1/2 cup) water to the boil in a large heavy-based saucepan over medium heat. Add the turnip, cook for 1–2 minutes, then add the spinach and amaranth. Stir in the chilli powder and a pinch of salt and cook for 2–3 minutes, or until almost all the water has evaporated. Mash the mixture well and remove from the heat.

HEAT the ghee or oil in a heavy-based saucepan over low heat and fry the ginger and onion for 2–3 minutes. Add the mashed vegetables, mix well and keep tossing until everything is well mixed. Season with salt, to taste. Serve warm with a dash of lemon juice.

Bangla Sahib Gurudwara, Delhi.

Methi leaves add a distinctive flavour to dishes they are used in. Fresh ones can be found in Indian food shops.

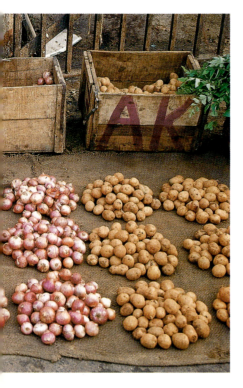

METHI ALOO

THE SCENTED AROMA AND DISTINCTIVE FLAVOUR OF METHI (FRESH FENUGREEK), WHETHER COOKED WITH MEAT OR VEGETABLES, TRANSFORMS ANY DISH. METHI ALOO CAN BE SERVED WITH MOST INDIAN MAIN MEALS. METHI CAN BE BOUGHT FROM SHOPS THAT SPECIALIZE IN INDIAN FOODS.

1 small onion, roughly chopped
2 garlic cloves, roughly chopped
2.5 cm (1 inch) piece of ginger, roughly chopped
4 tablespoons oil
$1/4$ teaspoon ground turmeric
600 g (1 lb 5 oz) potatoes, cut into cubes
2 green chillies, seeded and finely chopped
$1/4$ teaspoon chilli powder
$1/2$ teaspoon ground cumin
$1/2$ teaspoon ground coriander
3 teaspoons salt
$1/2$ teaspoon ground black pepper
2 bunches of methi (about 140 g/5 oz of methi leaves), roughly chopped
unsalted butter (optional)

SERVES 4

COMBINE the onion, garlic and ginger in a food processor and chop together, but not to a paste, or chop with a knife and mix together.

HEAT the oil in a karhai or heavy-based frying pan over medium heat and fry the onion mixture until softened. Stir in the turmeric. Add the potato and chilli and fry for 5 minutes. Add the chilli powder, cumin, coriander, salt and pepper and stir for another minute.

ADD 2 tablespoons water to the pan, cover, reduce the heat and simmer. As the potato cooks, it might start sticking to the pan, so after 10 minutes, add 2 more tablespoons of water if necessary. At no stage during the cooking time should the potato be allowed to brown.

AFTER another 10 minutes, stir in the methi and cook over low heat for 15 minutes, or until the potato is soft (the type of potato you use will determine the length of cooking time). Season with salt, to taste. Serve with a knob of unsalted butter melted on top if you like.

STUFFED OKRA

STUFFED OKRA IS SERVED AS A DELICACY IN NORTHERN INDIAN HOMES. ONE HAS TO PREPARE THIS

DISH WITH A LITTLE LOVE AND A LOT OF PATIENCE BUT ALL EFFORTS ARE REWARDED WHEN THE FINAL

DISH IS PRESENTED AT THE TABLE. IT IS DELICIOUS SERVED WITH INDIAN BREADS.

1 red onion, roughly chopped
4 garlic cloves, roughly chopped
10 cm (4 inch) piece of ginger,
  grated
5 teaspoons ground cumin
1 tablespoon ground coriander
2 teaspoons ground turmeric
1 teaspoon chilli powder
2 teaspoons garam masala
  (page 284)
1 teaspoon ground black pepper
1 tablespoon salt
550 g (1 lb 4 oz) okra
125 ml (1/2 cup) oil
pinch of asafoetida

SERVES 6

COMBINE the onion, garlic and ginger in a food processor and blend them to form a paste, or chop them all finely and pound them together in a pestle and mortar. Transfer to a bowl and add 4 teaspoons of the cumin, the coriander, 1¼ teaspoons of the turmeric, the chilli powder and garam masala and mix well. Stir in the pepper and 3 teaspoons of the salt.

CUT off the bottoms of the okra, then use a knife to make a slit lengthwise in each of them, stopping just short of the tail end. Using your hands or a small knife, put a little of the spice mixture into the insides of the okra. Some of it will ooze out but don't worry. This process will take a little time but the end result is delicious. Carefully cut all the okra into 1 cm (1/2 inch) pieces, or if you prefer, you can leave them whole.

HEAT the oil in a karhai or large, wide, heavy-based frying pan over low heat. Add the asafoetida and remaining turmeric to the pan and stir it around so that the oil absorbs the flavour. Add the okra and stir so it is coated in the flavoured oil. Add 2 tablespoons water. Cover and cook for 10 minutes, shaking the pan occasionally to prevent the okra sticking to the pan (add 2 more tablespoons of water if necessary).

ADD the remaining salt and remaining ground cumin to the pan. Shake the pan, then simmer the mixture for 5–10 minutes, until the okra is quite soft. The okra will retain a slight crunch on the outside because of its unique texture.

Stuffing the okra adds an extra dimension to the flavour. Use a small knife to help you slide the stuffing into each piece.

A vegetable shop in Kerala.

CAULIFLOWER WITH MUSTARD

THIS IS A LOVELY DISH USING CAULIFLOWER AND MANY SPICES. IN INDIA, THE VARIATIONS OF THIS DISH ALL PUT THE EMPHASIS ON QUITE DIFFERENT SPICE COMBINATIONS. THIS MUSTARDY ONE GOES WELL WITH RICE AND PIECES OF ROTI BUT IS ALSO A GOOD ACCOMPANIMENT TO MEAT DISHES.

2 teaspoons yellow mustard seeds
2 teaspoons black mustard seeds
1 teaspoon ground turmeric
1 teaspoon tamarind purée
  (page 280)
2–3 tablespoons mustard oil or oil
2 garlic cloves, finely chopped
1/2 onion, finely chopped
600 g (1 lb 5 oz) cauliflower, broken
  into small florets
3 mild green chillies, seeded
  and finely chopped
2 teaspoons kalonji (nigella seeds)

SERVES 4

GRIND the mustard seeds together to a fine powder in a spice grinder or pestle and mortar. Mix with the turmeric, tamarind purée and 125 ml (1/2 cup) water to form a smooth, quite liquid paste.

HEAT 2 tablespoons oil in a karhai or large, heavy-based saucepan over medium heat until almost smoking. Reduce the heat to low, add the garlic and onion and fry until golden. Cook the cauliflower in batches, adding more oil if necessary, and fry until lightly browned. Add the chilli and fry for 1 minute, or until tinged with brown around the edges.

RETURN all the cauliflower to the pan, sprinkle it with the mustard mixture and kalonji and stir well. Increase the heat to medium and bring to the boil, even though there's not much sauce. Reduce the heat to low, cover and cook until the cauliflower is nearly tender and the seasoning is dry. You may have to sprinkle a little more water on the cauliflower as it cooks to stop it sticking to the pan. If there is still excess liquid when the cauliflower is cooked, simmer with the lid off until it dries out. Season with salt, to taste, and remove from the heat.

AVIAL

THIS MIXED VEGETABLE CURRY IS FROM SOUTHERN INDIA WHERE DISHES OFTEN HAVE MORE SAUCE
TO SERVE WITH RICE WHICH IS A STAPLE THERE. DESPITE THE CHILLIES, THIS IS QUITE A MILD DISH
AS THE COCONUT AND YOGHURT SAUCE TONES DOWN THE HEAT.

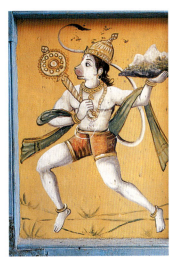

A depiction of a Hindu deity
painted on a door in Hyderabad.

1/2 teaspoon ground turmeric
200 g (7 oz) carrots, cut into batons
200 g (7 oz) sweet potato, cut into
  batons
200 g (7 oz) green beans, topped
  and tailed and cut in half
50 g (1 3/4 oz) grated coconut
  (page 283)
5 cm (2 inch) piece of ginger, grated
3 green chillies, finely chopped
1 1/2 teaspoons ground cumin
420 ml (1 2/3 cups) thick plain
  yoghurt (page 280)
1 tablespoon oil
10 curry leaves

SERVES 4

BRING 500 ml (2 cups) water to the boil in a
saucepan, add the turmeric and carrot, reduce
the heat and simmer for 5 minutes. Add the sweet
potato and the beans, return to the boil, then
reduce the heat and simmer for 5 minutes, or until
the vegetables are almost cooked.

PUT the coconut, ginger and chilli in a blender or
pestle and mortar, with a little water, and blend or
grind to a paste. Add to the vegetables with the
cumin and some salt and simmer for 2 minutes.
Stir in the yoghurt and heat through.

FOR the final seasoning (tarka), heat the oil over
low heat in a small saucepan. Add the curry
leaves and allow to crisp. Pour the hot oil and
the leaves over the vegetables.

CAULIFLOWER BHAJI

CAULIFLOWER BHAJI

1 teaspoon cumin seeds
3–4 tablespoons oil
1/4 teaspoon black mustard seeds
250 g (9 oz) potatoes, cut into
  small cubes
750 g (1 lb 10 oz) cauliflower,
  broken into florets
1/2 teaspoon ground cumin
1/2 teaspoon ground coriander
1/4 teaspoon ground turmeric
1/2 teaspoon garam masala
  (page 284)
2 garlic cloves, finely chopped
2 green chillies, seeded and
  finely chopped
5 curry leaves

SERVES 4

PLACE a small frying pan over low heat and
dry-roast 1/4 teaspoon of the cumin seeds until
aromatic. Grind the roasted seeds to a fine
powder using a pestle and mortar.

HEAT the oil over low heat in a karhai or heavy-
based saucepan. Add the mustard seeds and
remaining cumin seeds, cover and allow to pop
for a couple of seconds. Uncover, add the diced
potato and fry for 1 minute, stirring occasionally
to prevent the potato from sticking to the pan.
Add the cauliflower, all the remaining spices,
garlic, chilli and curry leaves and stir until well
mixed. Add 60 ml (1/4 cup) water and bring to the
boil. Cover and simmer for 5–7 minutes, or until
the cauliflower is cooked and tender. Season with
salt, to taste.

SPINACH KOFTA IN YOGHURT SAUCE

THIS IS A TYPICAL GUJARATI DISH AND IS MORE SUBSTANTIAL THAN SOME VEGETARIAN DISHES. YOU CAN EAT THE YOGHURT SAUCE AND THE SPINACH KOFTA AS SEPARATE DISHES BUT THEY GO VERY WELL TOGETHER AS IN THIS RECIPE.

YOGHURT SAUCE
375 ml (1½ cups) thick plain
    yoghurt (page 280)
4 tablespoons besan flour
1 tablespoon oil
2 teaspoons black mustard seeds
1 teaspoon fenugreek seeds
6 curry leaves
1 large onion, finely chopped
3 garlic cloves, crushed
1 teaspoon ground turmeric
½ teaspoon chilli powder

SPINACH KOFTAS
1 bunch English spinach (about
    450 g/1 lb), leaves picked off the
    stems, or 500 g (1 lb 2 oz) frozen
    spinach, thawed and drained
170 g (1½ cups) besan flour
1 red onion, finely chopped
1 ripe tomato, finely diced
2 garlic cloves, crushed
1 teaspoon ground cumin
2 tablespoons coriander (cilantro)
    leaves

oil for deep-frying
coriander (cilantro) leaves (optional)

SERVES 6

TO MAKE the yoghurt sauce, in a large bowl, whisk the yoghurt, besan flour and 750 ml (3 cups) water to a smooth paste. Heat the oil in a heavy-based saucepan or deep frying pan over low heat. Add the mustard and fenugreek seeds and the curry leaves, cover and allow the seeds to pop for 1 minute. Add the onion and cook for 5 minutes, or until soft and starting to brown. Add the garlic and stir for 1 minute, or until soft. Add the turmeric and chilli powder and stir for 30 seconds. Add the yoghurt mixture, bring to the boil and simmer over low heat for 10 minutes. Season with salt, to taste.

TO MAKE the spinach koftas, blanch the spinach in boiling water for 1 minute and refresh in cold water. Drain, squeeze out any extra water by putting the spinach between two plates and pushing them together. Finely chop the spinach. Combine with the remaining kofta ingredients and up to 60 ml (¼ cup) of water, a little at a time, adding enough to make the mixture soft but not sloppy. If it becomes too sloppy, add more besan flour. Season with salt, to taste. (To test the seasoning, fry a small amount of the mixture and taste it.) Shape the mixture into balls by rolling it in dampened hands, using 1 tablespoon of mixture for each.

FILL a karhai or heavy-based saucepan one-third full with oil and heat to 180°C/350°F (a cube of bread will brown in 15 seconds). Lower the koftas into the oil in batches and fry until golden and crisp. Don't overcrowd the pan. Remove the koftas as they cook, shake off any excess oil and add them to the yoghurt sauce.

GENTLY reheat the yoghurt sauce and sprinkle with the coriander leaves if using.

PULSES

Asafoetida is used as a pungent seasoning in many dishes. It is also used in dishes made with pulses because it helps dissipate the gasses they create. Powdered versions like this often contain rice flour and turmeric as well.

Pulses are on sale all over India, in their uncooked form and also fried as snacks.

CHANA MASALA

CHANA MASALA IS SERVED UP BY TRAVELLING VENDORS, IN BAZAARS OR ON THE STREETS OF INDIA, AND EATEN WITH PURIS. IT IS ENJOYED BY EVERYBODY AT ALL TIMES OF THE DAY AS A SNACK OR A LIGHT MEAL AND MAKES A GOOD ACCOMPANIMENT TO ANY INDIAN MEAL.

250 g (9 oz) chickpeas
1 large onion, roughly chopped
2 garlic cloves, roughly chopped
5 cm (2 inch) piece of ginger, roughly chopped
1 green chilli, chopped
170 ml ($^2/_3$ cup) oil
1 tablespoon ground cumin
1 tablespoon ground coriander
1 teaspoon chilli powder
pinch of asafoetida
2 tablespoons thick plain yoghurt (page 280)
$2^1/_4$ tablespoons garam masala (page 284)
2 teaspoons tamarind purée (page 280)
$^1/_2$ lemon
3 green chillies, extra
$^1/_4$ teaspoon ground black pepper
3 teaspoons salt
2 teaspoons chaat masala (page 284)
$^1/_2$ red onion, sliced into thin rings
2 cm ($^3/_4$ inch) piece of ginger, cut into thin strips
coriander (cilantro) leaves, roughly chopped (optional)

SERVES 6

SOAK the chickpeas overnight in 2 litres (8 cups) of water. Drain, then put the chickpeas in a large saucepan with another 2 litres (8 cups) water. Bring to the boil, spooning off any scum from the surface, then simmer over low heat for 1–1$^1/_2$ hours, until soft. It is important the chickpeas are soft at this stage as they won't soften once the sauce has been added. Drain, reserving the cooking liquid.

BLEND the onion, garlic, ginger and chopped chilli to a paste in a food processor or very finely chop them together with a knife.

HEAT the oil in a heavy-based saucepan over medium heat and fry the onion mixture until golden brown. Add the cumin, coriander, chilli powder and asafoetida, then stir for 1 minute. Add the yoghurt and stir for another minute. Stir in 2 tablespoons of the garam masala and pour in 1.25 litres (5 cups) of the reserved cooking liquid, a little at a time, stirring after each addition. Bring to the boil, then reduce the heat to simmering point.

ADD the tamarind purée, lemon, whole chillies, chickpeas, pepper and the salt. Partially cover the pan, simmer for 30 minutes, then remove the lemon. Cook for another 30 minutes, or until all the liquid has reduced, leaving the softened chickpeas coated in a rich dark brown sauce.

ADD the chaat masala and remaining garam masala and stir in the raw onion rings, ginger and coriander leaves if using.

A Hindu shrine.

Test to see if the toor dal are cooked by gently squeezing them between your thumb and index finger. They should be soft.

TOOR DAL

IN SOME PARTS OF INDIA IT IS COMMON TO COMBINE A SWEET AND SOUR TASTE, PARTICULARLY IN LENTIL CURRIES SUCH AS THIS ONE. PLAN IN ADVANCE WHEN YOU WANT TO MAKE THIS DISH AS THE DAL HAS TO BE SOAKED BEFORE YOU COOK IT.

500 g (1 lb 2 oz) toor dal (yellow lentils)
5 x 5 cm (2 inch) pieces of kokum
2 teaspoons coriander seeds
2 teaspoons cumin seeds
2 tablespoons oil
2 teaspoons black mustard seeds
10 curry leaves
7 cloves
10 cm (4 inch) cinnamon stick
5 green chillies, finely chopped
1/2 teaspoon ground turmeric
400 g (14 oz) tin chopped tomatoes
20 g (1/2 oz) jaggery or 10 g (1/4 oz) molasses
coriander (cilantro) leaves

SERVES 8

SOAK the lentils in cold water for 2 hours. Rinse the kokum, remove any stones and put the kokum in a bowl with cold water for a few minutes to soften. Drain the lentils and put them in a heavy-based saucepan with 1 litre (4 cups) of water and the pieces of kokum. Bring slowly to the boil, then simmer for about 40 minutes, or until the lentils feel soft when pressed between the thumb and index finger.

PLACE a small frying pan over low heat and dry-roast the coriander seeds until aromatic. Remove and dry-roast the cumin seeds. Grind the roasted seeds to a fine powder using a spice grinder or pestle and mortar.

FOR the final seasoning (tarka), heat the oil in a small pan over low heat. Add the mustard seeds and allow to pop. Add the curry leaves, cloves, cinnamon, chilli, turmeric and the roasted spice mix and cook for 1 minute. Add the tomato and cook for 2–3 minutes until the tomato is soft and can be broken up easily and incorporated into the sauce. Add the jaggery, then pour the spicy mixture into the simmering lentils and cook for another 10 minutes. Season with salt, to taste. Garnish with coriander leaves.

When the beans are soaked sufficiently, they will be creamy in colour and plump.

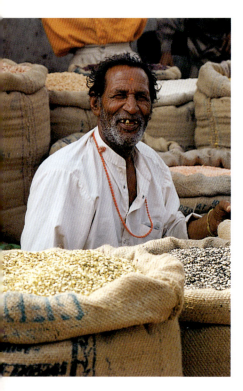

BLACK-EYED BEANS WITH MUSHROOMS

BLACK-EYED BEANS OR LOBHIA ARE SOMETIMES CALLED BLACK-EYED PEAS. THE EARTHY FLAVOUR OF THE LOBHIA COMBINED WITH MUSHROOMS AND TOMATOES MAKES THIS AN EXCELLENT VEGETARIAN MAIN COURSE. THE DISH IS ALSO SUITABLE FOR SERVING ON THE SIDE WITH MEAT OR VEGETABLES.

200 g (7 oz) black-eyed beans
400 g (14 oz) ripe tomatoes
    or 400 g (14 oz) tin chopped
    tomatoes
125 ml (1/2 cup) oil
1 teaspoon cumin seeds
3 cm (11/4 inch) cinnamon stick
150 g (51/2 oz) onion, chopped
4 garlic cloves, finely chopped
250 g (9 oz) mushrooms, sliced
2 teaspoons ground coriander
1 teaspoon ground cumin
1/2 teaspoon ground turmeric
1/4 teaspoon cayenne pepper
2 tablespoons chopped coriander
    (cilantro) leaves

SERVES 6

PUT the black-eyed beans in a large saucepan with 1 litre (4 cups) of water and bring to the boil. Cover and simmer for 2 minutes. Remove from the heat and leave to stand for 1 hour. Alternatively, if you prefer, you can soak the black-eyed beans overnight in the cold water.

SCORE a cross in the top of each ripe tomato. Plunge into boiling water for 20 seconds, then drain and peel away from the cross. Roughly chop the tomatoes, discarding the cores and seeds and reserving any juices.

BRING the black-eyed beans back to the boil, then simmer for 20–30 minutes, until tender. Drain well.

MEANWHILE, heat the oil in a karhai or deep, heavy-based frying pan or saucepan. Add the cumin seeds and cinnamon stick, let them sizzle for 10 seconds, then add the onion and garlic. Stir over medium heat until soft and starting to brown. Add the mushrooms and fry for 2–3 minutes. Add the tomato, ground coriander, cumin, turmeric and cayenne pepper. Cover and cook over low heat for 10 minutes.

COMBINE the black-eyed beans with the tomato and mushroom mixture and season with salt, to taste. Stir in the coriander leaves and simmer, uncovered, for 30 minutes.

SWEET AND SOUR CHICKPEAS

500 g (2¼ cups) chickpeas
2 tablespoons oil or ghee
2 large red onions, thinly sliced
2 cm (¾ inch) piece of ginger, finely
 chopped
2 teaspoons sugar
2 teaspoons ground coriander
2 teaspoons ground cumin
pinch of chilli powder (optional)
1 teaspoon garam masala (page 284)
3 tablespoons tamarind purée
 (page 280)
4 ripe tomatoes, chopped
4 tablespoons coriander (cilantro) or
 mint leaves, finely chopped

SERVES 6

SOAK the chickpeas overnight in 2 litres (8 cups) water. Drain, then put the chickpeas in a large saucepan with 2 litres (8 cups) water. Bring to the boil, spooning off any scum from the surface. Cover and simmer over low heat for 1–1½ hours, until soft. It is important they are soft at this stage as they won't soften once the sauce is added. Drain.

HEAT the oil in a karhai or heavy-based frying pan. Fry the onion until soft and brown, then stir in the ginger. Add the chickpeas, sugar, coriander, cumin, chilli powder, garam masala and a pinch of salt. Stir, then add the tamarind and tomato and simmer for 2–3 minutes. Add 500 ml (2 cups) water, bring to the boil and cook until the sauce has thickened. Stir in the coriander leaves. Serve with rotis (page 220).

CHOLE CHAAT

THIS IS A NORTH INDIAN WAY OF COOKING CHICKPEAS. IT IS USUALLY EATEN AT THE START OF A MEAL,

OR SERVED AS A SIDE DISH. YOU CAN USE TWO 400 G (14 OZ) TINS OF CHICKPEAS IF YOU PREFER. DRAIN

THEM, MASH A CUPFUL AND ADD THEM TO THE ONION AND SPICES WITH 400 ML (14 FL OZ) WATER.

220 g (1 cup) chickpeas
2 tablespoons oil
½ onion, chopped
1 teaspoon ground coriander
1 teaspoon ground cumin
¼ teaspoon ground turmeric
1 teaspoon garam masala
 (page 284)
2 cm (¾ inch) piece of ginger,
 grated
2 red chillies, finely chopped
200 g (7 oz) tin chopped tomatoes,
 drained

SERVES 4

SOAK the chickpeas overnight in 2 litres (8 cups) water. Drain, then put the chickpeas in a large saucepan with 2 litres (8 cups) water. Bring to the boil, spooning off any scum from the surface, then simmer over low heat for 1–1½ hours, until soft. It is important the chickpeas are soft at this stage as they won't soften any more once the sauce has been added. Drain, reserving the cooking liquid. Remove 6 tablespoons of the chickpeas and thoroughly mash them with a fork.

HEAT the oil in a heavy-based saucepan over low heat and cook the onion until golden brown. Add the coriander, cumin, turmeric and garam masala and fry for 1 minute. Add the ginger, chilli, tomato and salt, to taste, and stir until well mixed. Add the chickpeas and their cooking liquid, and the mashed chickpeas. Bring to the boil, reduce the heat and simmer, uncovered, for 5 minutes.

CHOLE CHAAT

The dal used for this recipe can be split but not skinned as shown here, or split and skinned.

DAL SAAG

URAD DAL

THIS TYPE OF LENTIL IS USED IN THE SOUTH TO MAKE DOSAS AND IDLIS, BUT IN BENGAL, GUJARAT AND RAJASTHAN IT IS EATEN REGULARLY AS A LENTIL STEW. IT IS USUALLY COOKED WITH GINGER, ASAFOETIDA AND FENNEL SEEDS, AN AROMATIC COMBINATION OF SPICES.

250 g (9 oz) unskinned urad dal
$1/4$ teaspoon ground turmeric
4 ripe tomatoes, chopped
1 small onion, roughly chopped
2 tablespoons oil
$1/2$ teaspoon cumin seeds
1 teaspoon fennel seeds
5 cm (2 inch) piece of ginger, grated
2 dried chillies, broken into pieces
pinch of asafoetida
coriander (cilantro) leaves

SERVES 4

PUT the dal in a heavy-based saucepan and add 1 litre (4 cups) water, the turmeric, chopped tomato and onion. Bring to the boil, then reduce the heat, cover and simmer for about 40 minutes, or until the dal is cooked and feels soft when pressed between the thumb and index finger.

FOR the final seasoning (tarka), heat the oil in a small saucepan, add the cumin and fennel seeds and allow to pop. Add the ginger, chilli and asafoetida and fry over low heat for 30 seconds. Pour into the hot dal and simmer for another 5 minutes. Season with salt, to taste. Garnish with coriander leaves before serving.

DAL SAAG

COMBINING VEGETABLES WITH LENTILS IS POPULAR THROUGHOUT INDIA. TAKE CARE NOT TO OVERCOOK THIS DISH AFTER ADDING THE SPINACH, OTHERWISE YOU WILL LOSE ITS LOVELY, RICH GREEN COLOUR.

225 g (8 oz) moong dal
2–3 tablespoons oil
1 teaspoon black mustard seeds
8 curry leaves
$1/4$ teaspoon asafoetida
$1/4$ teaspoon ground turmeric
1 teaspoon ground cumin
1 teaspoon ground coriander
3 cm ($1 1/4$ inch) piece of ginger, grated
2 green chillies, seeded and cut into 1 cm ($1/2$ inch) pieces
100 g ($3 1/2$ oz) English spinach leaves, roughly chopped
5 spring onions (scallions), finely chopped

SERVES 4

PUT the moong dal in a heavy-based saucepan, add 750 ml (3 cups) water and bring to the boil. Reduce the heat and simmer for 30 minutes, or until the moong dal are soft and breaking up. The moong dal tend to soak up most of the liquid so you may need to add a little more.

FOR the final seasoning (tarka), heat the oil in a saucepan, add the mustard seeds, cover and allow to pop. Stir in the curry leaves, asafoetida, turmeric, cumin, coriander, ginger and chilli, then pour into the cooked dal.

STIR in the spinach and spring onion and cook for about 2 minutes, or until the spinach is just cooked. Season with salt, to taste.

KALI DAL

DAL, WHICH IS BOTH THE NAME OF THE LENTILS, AND IN THIS CASE THE DISH, IS PART OF THE STAPLE DIET IN INDIA. THIS IS A SUMPTUOUS VERSION OF A SIMPLE DISH SERVED WITH ROTIS IN SIKH GURUDWARAS (TEMPLES). KALI MEANS BLACK AND THE GRAM IN THIS DISH HAVE A BLACK SKIN.

A huge range of pulses and legumes are sold in the markets of India. These are eaten on a daily basis, often made into dal.

250 g (9 oz) whole black gram (sabat urad)
1 onion, roughly chopped
2 garlic cloves, roughly chopped
5 cm (2 inch) piece of ginger, roughly chopped
1 green chilli, roughly chopped
125 ml (1/2 cup) oil
2 tablespoons ground cumin
1 tablespoon ground coriander
2 teaspoons salt
1/4 teaspoon chilli powder
3 tablespoons garam masala (page 284)
125 ml (1/2 cup) cream

SERVES 6

PUT the whole black gram in a large, heavy-based saucepan, add 2 litres (8 cups) water and bring to the boil. Reduce the heat and simmer for 1 hour, or until the dal feels soft when pressed between the thumb and index finger. Most of the dal will split to reveal the creamy insides. Drain, reserving the cooking liquid.

BLEND the onion, garlic, ginger and chilli together in a food processor to form a paste, or finely chop them together with a knife. Heat the oil in a frying pan and fry the onion mixture over high heat, stirring constantly, until golden brown. Add the cumin and coriander and fry for 2 minutes. Add the dal and stir in the salt, chilli powder and garam masala. Pour 310 ml (1 1/4 cups) of the reserved dal liquid into the pan, bring to the boil, then reduce the heat and simmer for 10 minutes. Just before serving, stir in the cream and simmer for another 2 minutes to heat through.

MASALA RAJMA

225 g (8 oz) kidney beans
3 tablespoons oil
1/2 onion, finely chopped
2 Indian bay leaves (cassia leaves)
5 cm (2 inch) cinnamon stick
2 garlic cloves, finely chopped
1/4 teaspoon ground turmeric
1/2 teaspoon ground coriander
1/2 teaspoon ground cumin
1/2 teaspoon garam masala (page 284)
3 dried chillies
2 cm (3/4 inch) piece of ginger, grated

SERVES 4

SOAK the kidney beans overnight in 1.25 litres (5 cups) water in a large saucepan. Drain, return the beans to the saucepan with 1.25 litres (5 cups) water and bring to the boil. Boil for 15 minutes, then reduce the heat and simmer for 1 hour, or until the beans are tender. Drain, reserving the liquid.

HEAT the oil in a heavy-based saucepan over low heat. Add the onion, bay leaves, cinnamon and garlic and cook until the onion is lightly browned. Add the turmeric, coriander, cumin, garam masala, chillies and ginger and stir well. Add the beans with enough of their liquid to make a sauce. Bring to the boil and cook for 5 minutes, stirring constantly. Season with salt, to taste. If you wish, remove the chillies before serving.

MASALA RAJMA

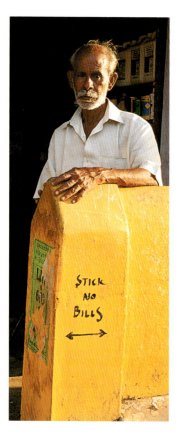

PARIPPU

A DISH THAT INCLUDES LENTILS OF SOME SORT IS A MUST AS PART OF ANY INDIAN MEAL. THIS RECIPE IS FROM THE SOUTH AND IS FLAVOURED WITH COCONUT AS WELL AS A TARKA OF FRIED ONION, CUMIN SEEDS, MUSTARD SEEDS AND CURRY LEAVES WHICH IS MIXED IN TOWARDS THE END OF COOKING.

225 g (8 oz) masoor dal (red lentils)
1 onion, roughly chopped
1 ripe tomato, roughly chopped
50 g (1³/₄ oz) creamed coconut,
   mixed with 250 ml (1 cup) water,
   or 250 ml (1 cup) coconut milk
   (page 283)
2 green chillies, chopped
¹/₄ teaspoon ground turmeric
¹/₂ teaspoon ground cumin
¹/₂ teaspoon ground coriander
2 tablespoons oil
1 teaspoon cumin seeds
¹/₂ teaspoon black mustard seeds
1 onion, very finely chopped
10 curry leaves

SERVES 4

PUT the lentils in a heavy-based saucepan with 500 ml (2 cups) water. Add the roughly chopped onion, tomato, creamed coconut or coconut milk, green chilli, turmeric, ground cumin and coriander, and bring to the boil. Simmer and cook, stirring occasionally, until the lentils are cooked to a soft mush (masoor dal does not hold its shape when it cooks). This will take about 25 minutes. If all the water has evaporated before the lentils are cooked, add 125 ml (¹/₂ cup) boiling water.

FOR the final seasoning (tarka), heat the oil in a small saucepan over low heat. Add the cumin seeds and mustard seeds, cover and allow the seeds to pop. Add the finely chopped onion and curry leaves and fry over low heat until the onion is golden brown. Pour the seasoned onions into the simmering lentils. Season with salt, to taste, and cook for another 5 minutes.

A woman binds curry leaves into neat bundles in the market.

RICE & GRAINS

PULAO

PULAO OR PILAF CAN BE PLAIN OR A FESTIVE, ELABORATE DISH WITH FRUIT, NUTS AND SPICES AS HERE. RICE DISHES THAT REFLECT THESE FLAVOURS CAN BE FOUND AS FAR AFIELD AS SOUTHERN RUSSIA, PERSIA AND MOROCCO, A LEGACY OF DISHES TRAVELLING WITH CONQUERORS AND TRADERS.

A woman sorts through her rice by tossing it in the air to get rid of any chaff. In India rice often has to be picked over before use.

500 g (2½ cups) basmati rice
1 teaspoon cumin seeds
4 tablespoons ghee or oil
2 tablespoons chopped almonds
2 tablespoons raisins or sultanas
2 onions, finely sliced
2 cinnamon sticks
5 cardamom pods
1 teaspoon sugar
1 tablespoon ginger juice
 (page 280)
15 saffron threads, soaked in
 1 tablespoon warm milk
2 Indian bay leaves (cassia leaves)
250 ml (1 cup) coconut milk
 (page 283)
2 tablespoons fresh or frozen peas
rosewater (optional)

SERVES 6

WASH the rice in a sieve under cold, running water until the water from the rice runs clear. Drain the rice and put in a saucepan, cover with water and soak for 30 minutes. Drain.

PLACE a small frying pan over low heat and dry-roast the cumin seeds until aromatic.

HEAT the ghee or oil in a karhai or heavy-based frying pan and fry the almonds and raisins until browned. Remove from the pan, fry the onion in the same ghee until dark golden brown, then remove from the pan.

ADD the rice, roasted cumin seeds, cinnamon, cardamom, sugar, ginger juice, saffron and salt to the pan and fry for 2 minutes, or until aromatic.

ADD the bay leaves and coconut milk to the pan, then add enough water to come about 5 cm (2 inches) above the rice. Bring to the boil, cover and cook over medium heat for 8 minutes, or until most of the water has evaporated.

ADD the peas to the pan and stir well. Reduce the heat to very low and cook until the rice is cooked through. Stir in the fried almonds, raisins and onion, reserving some for garnishing. Drizzle with a few drops of rosewater if you would like a more perfumed dish.

UPAMA

2 tablespoons chana dal
4 tablespoons ghee or oil
75 g (1/2 cup) cashew nuts
1 teaspoon black mustard seeds
15 curry leaves
1/2 onion, finely chopped
140 g (1 1/2 cups) coarse semolina
lime juice

SERVES 4

SOAK the dal in plenty of water for 3 hours. Drain, then put in a saucepan with 500 ml (2 cups) water. Bring to the boil and cook for 2 minutes. Drain the dal, then dry in a tea towel. Brush a little of the ghee onto the cashew nuts and toast them in a frying pan over low heat until they are golden.

HEAT the remaining ghee in a heavy-based frying pan and add the mustard seeds and dal. Cook until the seeds start to pop, add the curry leaves and onion and cook until the onion softens. Add the semolina. Toss everything together and when the semolina is hot and the grains are brown and coated in oil, sprinkle with 500 ml (2 cups) boiling water, 125 ml (1/2 cup) at a time, tossing and stirring after each addition, until absorbed. Season with salt. Sprinkle with lime juice and cashews.

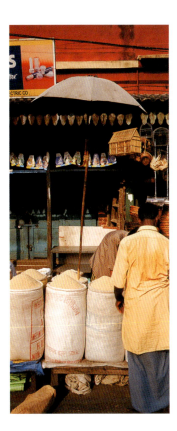

KHICHHARI

KHICHHARI OR KITCHERI IS THE PRECURSOR TO KEDGEREE, A DISH TAKEN UP WITH MUCH ENTHUSIASM BY THE BRITISH IN INDIA. THERE ARE MANY RECIPES FOR KHICHHARI AND THE LENTILS CAN BE YELLOW AS HERE OR MOONG DAL. EAT IT WITH YOGHURT OR CHUTNEYS AND BREADS.

60 g (1/4 cup) toor dal (yellow lentils)
300 g (1 1/2 cups) basmati rice
3 tablespoons ghee
1 teaspoon cumin seeds
6 cloves
1/2 cinnamon stick
2 onions, finely chopped
2 garlic cloves, finely chopped
2 cm (3/4 inch) piece of ginger, finely chopped
1 teaspoon garam masala (page 284)
3 tablespoons lemon juice
1 teaspoon salt

SERVES 6

SOAK the dal in 500 ml (2 cups) water in a large saucepan for 2 hours. Wash the rice in a sieve under cold water until the water from the rice runs clear. Drain.

HEAT the ghee in a heavy-based saucepan over low heat and fry the cumin seeds, cloves and cinnamon for a few seconds. Increase the heat to medium, add the onion, garlic and ginger and cook until they soften and begin to brown.

ADD the rice and dal and toss to thoroughly coat in ghee. Add the garam masala, lemon juice, salt and 750 ml (3 cups) boiling water. Bring to the boil, then reduce the heat to very low, cover tightly and cook for 15 minutes. Remove from the heat and gently fluff up with a fork. Cover the pan with a clean cloth and leave for 10 minutes. Fluff up again and season with salt, to taste.

KHICHHARI

LAMB BIRYANI

THIS IS A RICE AND LAMB DISH IN WHICH BOTH INGREDIENTS ARE COOKED TOGETHER IN A SEALED CONTAINER. YOU CAN COOK THE LAMB WITHOUT BROWNING IT FIRST AND, IN FACT, THIS IS THE TRADITIONAL METHOD. HOWEVER, BROWNING THE MEAT ADDS EXTRA FLAVOUR.

Cook the meat and then put the rice and saffron mixture on top. Use a rope of dough to seal on the lid and keep in the flavours.

1 kg (2 lb 4 oz) boneless lamb leg or shoulder, cut into 3 cm (1¼ inch) cubes
8 cm (3 inch) piece of ginger, grated
2 garlic cloves, crushed
2 tablespoons garam masala (page 284)
½ teaspoon chilli powder
½ teaspoon ground turmeric
4 green chillies, finely chopped
20 g (²/₃ cup) chopped coriander (cilantro) leaves
15 g (¼ cup) chopped mint leaves
500 g (2½ cups) basmati rice
4 onions, thinly sliced
¼ teaspoon salt
125 ml (½ cup) oil
125 g (4½ oz) unsalted butter, melted
250 ml (1 cup) thick plain yoghurt (page 280)
½ teaspoon saffron strands, soaked in 2 tablespoons hot milk
3 tablespoons lemon juice

SEALING DOUGH
200 g (1⅓ cups) wholewheat flour
1 teaspoon salt

SERVES 6

MIX the lamb cubes in a bowl with the ginger, garlic, garam masala, chilli powder, turmeric, chilli, coriander and mint. Cover and marinate in the fridge overnight.

WASH the rice in a sieve under cold, running water until the water from the rice runs clear. Put the sliced onion in a sieve, sprinkle with the salt and leave for 10 minutes to drain off any liquid that oozes out. Rinse and pat dry.

HEAT the oil and butter in a large, heavy-based saucepan, add the onion and fry for about 10 minutes or until golden brown. Drain through a sieve, reserving the oil and butter.

REMOVE the lamb from the marinade, reserving the marinade, and fry in batches in a little of the oil and butter until the lamb is well browned all over. Transfer to a 'degchi' (thick-based pot) or heavy casserole and add the browned onion, any remaining marinade and the yoghurt, and cook everything over low heat for 30–40 minutes, or until the lamb is tender.

IN a separate saucepan, boil enough water to cover the rice. Add the rice to the pan. Return the water to the boil, cook the rice for 5 minutes, then drain well and spread the rice evenly over the meat. Pour 2 tablespoons of the leftover oil and ghee over the rice and drizzle with the saffron and milk.

TO MAKE the sealing dough, preheat the oven to 220°C (425°F/Gas 7). Make a dough by mixing the flour and salt with a little water. Roll the dough into a sausage shape and use to seal the lid onto the rim of the pot or casserole, pressing it along the rim where the lid meets the pot. Put the pot over high heat for 5 minutes to bring the contents to the boil, then transfer it to the oven for 40 minutes. Remove the pot and break the seal of dough.

YAKHNI PULAO

THIS RICE DISH IS PARTICULARLY DELICIOUS WHEN COOKED IN HOME-MADE STOCK (YAKHNI) BUT YOU CAN, OF COURSE, USE READY-MADE STOCK. YAKHNI PULAO IS DELICATELY FLAVOURED WITH WHOLE SPICES AND GOES WELL NOT ONLY WITH INDIAN DISHES, BUT WITH OTHER CASSEROLES.

225 g (8 oz) basmati rice
500 ml (2 cups) chicken stock
6 tablespoons ghee or oil
5 cardamom pods
5 cm (2 inch) cinnamon stick
6 cloves
8 black peppercorns
4 Indian bay leaves (cassia leaves)
1 onion, finely sliced

SERVES 4

WASH the rice in a sieve under cold running water until the water from the rice runs clear. Drain.

HEAT the stock to near boiling point in a saucepan.

MEANWHILE, heat 2 tablespoons of the ghee or oil over medium heat in a large, heavy-based saucepan. Add the cardamom, cinnamon, cloves, peppercorns and bay leaves and fry for 1 minute. Reduce the heat to low, add the rice and stir constantly for 1 minute. Add the heated stock and some salt to the rice and bring rapidly to the boil. Cover and simmer over low heat for 15 minutes. Leave the rice to stand for 10 minutes before uncovering. Lightly fluff up the rice before serving.

MEANWHILE, heat the remaining ghee or oil in a frying pan over low heat and fry the onion until soft. Increase the heat and fry until the onion is dark brown. Drain on paper towels, then use as garnish.

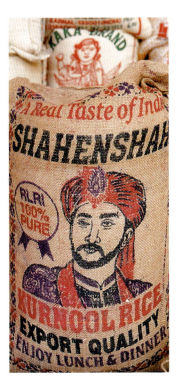

Rice is a staple across most of India. Hundreds of varieties exist, each with its own flavour, aroma and texture.

PRAWN PULAO

200 g (1 cup) basmati rice
300 g (10¹/2 oz) small prawns (shrimp)
3 tablespoons oil
1 onion, finely chopped
3 cm (1¹/4 inch) cinnamon stick
6 cardamom pods
5 cloves
4 Indian bay leaves (cassia leaves)
1 stalk lemon grass, finely chopped
4 garlic cloves, crushed
5 cm (2 inch) piece of ginger, grated
1/4 teaspoon ground turmeric

SERVES 4

WASH the rice in a sieve under cold running water until the water from the rice runs clear. Drain. Peel and devein the prawns, then wash thoroughly and pat dry with paper towels.

HEAT the oil in a karhai or heavy-based frying pan over low heat and fry the onion, cinnamon, cardamom, cloves, bay leaves and lemon grass until the onion is lightly browned. Stir in the garlic, ginger and turmeric. Add the prawns and stir until they turn pinkish. Add the rice and fry over medium heat for 2 minutes. Add 500 ml (2 cups) boiling water and some salt and bring to the boil. Reduce the heat and simmer for 15 minutes. Remove from the heat, cover tightly with a lid and leave for 10 minutes. Lightly fluff up the rice before serving.

PRAWN PULAO

Paddy fields in Kerala.

Fresh yoghurt is made and sold daily in India. It is left to set in earthenware pots which help to absorb any excess moisture.

YOGHURT RICE

THIS IS A POPULAR DISH TO PREPARE FOR TAKING ON JOURNEYS AS THE DISH IS SERVED COLD AND THE ACID IN THE YOGHURT ACTS AS A PRESERVATIVE. THE FLAVOURS WILL NOT BE AS STRONG IF YOU SERVE THE RICE STRAIGHT FROM THE FRIDGE, SO BRING IT BACK TO ROOM TEMPERATURE.

2 tablespoons urad dal
2 tablespoons chana dal
225 g (8 oz) basmati rice
2 tablespoons oil
$1/2$ teaspoon mustard seeds
12 curry leaves
3 dried chillies
$1/4$ teaspoon ground turmeric
pinch of asafoetida
500 ml (2 cups) thick plain yoghurt
   (page 280)

SERVES 4

SOAK the dals in 250 ml (1 cup) boiling water for 3 hours. Wash the rice in a sieve under cold running water until the water from the rice runs clear. Drain.

PUT the rice and 500 ml (2 cups) water in a saucepan and bring rapidly to the boil. Stir, cover, reduce the heat to a slow simmer and cook for 10 minutes. Leave for 15 minutes before fluffing up with a fork.

DRAIN the dals and pat dry with paper towels. For the final seasoning (tarka), heat the oil in a small saucepan over low heat, add the mustard seeds, cover and shake the pan until the seeds start to pop. Add the curry leaves, chillies and the dals and fry for 2 minutes, stirring occasionally. Stir in the turmeric and asafoetida.

PUT the yoghurt in a large bowl, pour the fried dal mixture into the yoghurt and mix thoroughly. Mix the rice into the spicy yoghurt. Season with salt, to taste. Cover and refrigerate. Serve cold, but before serving, stand the rice at room temperature for about 10 minutes. Serve as part of a meal. Yoghurt rice goes very well with meat dishes.

ANDHRA-STYLE CHICKEN PULAO

1.5 kg (3 lb 5 oz) chicken or
  chicken pieces
1 kg (5 cups) basmati rice
3 onions, sliced
1/2 teaspoon salt
125 ml (1/2 cup) oil
180 g (6 oz) ghee
4 cm (1 1/2 inch) cinnamon stick
2 cardamom pods
3 cloves
2 star anise
2 stalks of curry leaves
2 cm (3/4 inch) piece of ginger,
  grated
6 garlic cloves, crushed
4–6 green chillies, slit lengthwise
420 ml (1 2/3 cups) buttermilk
4 ripe tomatoes, diced
185 ml (3/4 cup) coconut milk
  (page 283)
1 litre (4 cups) chicken stock
1 lemon, cut into wedges

SERVES 8

IF USING a whole chicken, cut it into 16 pieces by removing both legs and cutting between the joint of the drumstick and thigh. Cut each of these in half through the bone with a cleaver or poultry shears (make sure there are no bone shards). Cut down either side of the backbone and remove the backbone. Turn the chicken over and cut through the cartilage down the centre of the breastbone. Cut each breast into 3 pieces and cut off the wings. Trim off the wing tips. Trim off any excess fat or skin from the pieces.

WASH the rice in a sieve under cold, running water until the water from the rice runs clear. Drain well. Put the sliced onion in a sieve, sprinkle with the salt and leave for 10 minutes to drain off any liquid that oozes out. Rinse and pat dry.

HEAT the oil and ghee over medium heat in a large, ovenproof 'degchi' (thick-based pot), or heavy casserole. Add the cinnamon, cardamom and cloves and heat until they begin to crackle. Reduce the heat to low and add the star anise and the curry leaves from one stem. Add the sliced onion and cook until golden brown. Add the ginger and garlic and cook until golden. Add the chicken, increase the heat to medium and fry until the pieces are browned on all sides. Add the slit chillies, the remaining curry leaves, the buttermilk and some salt. Cook for 12 minutes, or until the chicken is cooked through and the liquid is reduced by half. Add the diced tomato and the coconut milk. Cook until the tomato is tender, then add the stock and bring to the boil.

PREHEAT the oven to 220°C (425°F/Gas 7). Add the drained rice to the chicken and stir it in well. Check the seasoning, adjust if necessary, and cook for 10 minutes, or until nearly all the liquid is absorbed.

REMOVE the pot from the heat, cover it with a clean wet cloth, then a tight-fitting lid, and put it in the oven for 15 minutes, until the rice is cooked through. Serve hot with lemon wedges.

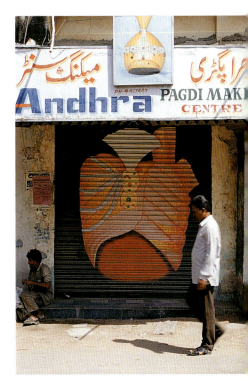

A shop which makes ceremonial headdresses in Hyderabad, Andhra Pradesh.

Sevian or vermicelli made from wheat flour are available as skeins of noodles or as bunches of straight lengths. Sometimes they are sold toasted.

SEVIAN KHEEMA

1 teaspoon cumin seeds
3 tablespoons ghee or oil
1 red onion, finely chopped
3 garlic cloves, crushed
2 cm (³/4 inch) piece of ginger, grated
225 g (8 oz) minced (ground) lamb or beef
1 teaspoon ground black pepper
225 g (8 oz) sevian, broken into small pieces
3 tablespoons lime or lemon juice

SERVES 4

PLACE a small frying pan over low heat, dry-roast the cumin until aromatic, then grind to a fine powder using a spice grinder or pestle and mortar.

HEAT 1 tablespoon ghee in a karhai or heavy-based frying pan and fry the onion, garlic and ginger for 3–4 minutes. Add the cumin, cook for 1 minute, then add the meat and cook for 8 minutes, or until the meat is dry, breaking up any lumps with the back of a fork. Season with the black pepper and salt, to taste, and remove from the pan.

HEAT the remaining ghee and fry the sevian for 1–2 minutes. Add the meat and fry for 1 minute. Add 170 ml (²/3 cup) water and cook until the sevian are tender, adding more water if necessary. The dish should be dry, so don't add too much at once. When cooked, sprinkle with the juice.

IDIYAPPAM

IDIYAPPAM

IN THIS DISH FROM KERALA, THE RICE NOODLES ARE OFTEN MADE AT HOME. HOWEVER, THIS IS QUITE LABOUR INTENSIVE SO WE HAVE USED RICE STICKS OR VERMICELLI AS A CONVENIENT SUBSTITUTE.

225 g (8 oz) rice sticks or vermicelli
4 tablespoons oil
50 g (¹/3 cup) cashew nuts
¹/2 onion, chopped
3 eggs
150 g (1 cup) fresh or frozen peas
10 curry leaves
2 carrots, grated
2 leeks, finely shredded
1 red capsicum (pepper), diced
2 tablespoons tomato sauce (ketchup)
1 tablespoon soy sauce
1 teaspoon salt

SERVES 4

SOAK the rice sticks in cold water for 30 minutes, then drain and put them in a saucepan of boiling water. Remove from the heat and leave in the pan for 3 minutes. Drain and refresh in cold water.

HEAT 1 tablespoon oil in a frying pan and fry the cashews until golden. Remove, add the onion to the pan, fry until dark golden, then drain on paper towels. Cook the eggs in boiling water for 10 minutes to hard-boil, then cool them immediately in cold water. When cold, peel them and cut into wedges. Cook the peas in boiling water until tender.

HEAT the remaining oil in a frying pan and briefly fry the curry leaves. Add the carrot, leek and red capsicum and stir for 1 minute. Add the tomato sauce, soy sauce, salt and rice sticks and mix, stirring constantly to prevent the rice sticks from sticking to the pan. Serve on a platter and garnish with the peas, cashews, fried onion and egg.

BREADS

CHAPATIS

CHAPATIS ARE THE MOST BASIC FORM OF UNLEAVENED BREAD. THEY SHOULD BE COOKED ON A HIGH

HEAT TO PREVENT THEM BECOMING TOUGH. YOU CAN USE EQUAL AMOUNTS OF WHOLEMEAL (WHOLE

WHEAT) AND MAIDA IF YOU CAN'T BUY CHAPATI FLOUR.

200 g (1 1/3 cups) atta (chapati flour)
1/2 teaspoon salt
100 g (3 1/2 oz) ghee or clarified
  butter

MAKES 8

SIFT the atta and salt into a bowl and make a well in the centre. Add about 170 ml (2/3 cup) tepid water, enough to mix to form a soft, pliable dough. Turn the dough out onto a floured work surface and knead for 5 minutes. Place in an oiled bowl, cover and allow to rest for 30 minutes.

PUT a tava or griddle, or a heavy-based frying pan over medium heat and leave it to heat up. Divide the dough into eight equal portions. Working with one portion at a time and keeping the rest covered, on a lightly floured surface roll out each portion to form a 15 cm (6 inch) diameter circle. Keep the rolled chapatis covered with a damp cloth while you roll them and cook them. Remove the excess surface flour on the chapati prior to cooking by holding the chapati in the palms of your hands and gently slapping it from one hand to the other. If you leave the flour on it may burn.

PLACE each chapati on the tava, leave it for 7–10 seconds to brown, then turn it over to brown on the other side. Depending on the hotness of the griddle, the second side should take about 15 seconds. Turn over the chapati again and, using a folded tea towel, apply gentle pressure to the chapati in several places to heat it and encourage it to puff up like a balloon. It is this puffing up process that gives the chapati its light texture. Smear the hot chapati with a little of the ghee or butter, and leave stacked and covered with a tea towel until all the chapatis are cooked.

Slap the chapati backwards and forwards to get rid of any excess flour. Press it with a tea towel to make it puff up as it cooks.

NAAN

PERHAPS THE MOST FAMOUS LEAVENED BREAD FROM NORTH INDIA, TRADITIONALLY THIS BREAD IS COOKED ON THE WALLS OF A TANDOOR (CLAY OVEN). IT IS NOT EASY TO RECREATE THE INTENSE HEAT IN A DOMESTIC OVEN SO THE TEXTURE IS SLIGHTLY DIFFERENT BUT THE TASTE IS DELICIOUS.

500 g (4 cups) maida or plain (all-purpose) flour

310 ml (1¼ cups) milk

2 teaspoons (7 g/¼ oz) easy-blend dried yeast or 15 g (½ oz) fresh yeast

2 teaspoons kalonji (nigella seeds), (optional)

½ teaspoon baking powder

½ teaspoon salt

1 egg, beaten

2 tablespoons oil or ghee

185 ml (¾ cup) thick plain yoghurt (page 280)

MAKES 10

SIFT the maida into a large bowl and make a well in the centre. Warm the milk over low heat in a saucepan until it is hand hot (the milk will feel the same temperature as your finger when you dip your finger into it). If you are using fresh yeast, mix it with a little milk and a pinch of maida and set it aside to activate and go frothy.

ADD the yeast, kalonji, baking powder and salt to the maida. In another bowl, mix the egg, oil and yoghurt. Pour into the maida with 250 ml (1 cup) of the milk and mix to form a soft dough. If the dough seems dry add the remaining milk. Turn out onto a floured work surface and knead for 5 minutes, or until smooth and elastic. Put in an oiled bowl, cover and leave in a warm place to double in size. This will take several hours.

PREHEAT the oven to 200°C (400°F/Gas 6). Place a roasting tin half-filled with water at the bottom of the oven. This provides moisture in the oven which prevents the naan from drying out too quickly.

PUNCH down the dough, knead it briefly and divide it into 10 portions. Using the tips of your fingers, spread out one portion of dough to the shape of a naan bread. They are traditionally tear-drop in shape, so pull the dough on one end. Put the naan on a greased baking tray. Bake on the top shelf for 7 minutes, then turn the naan over and cook for another 5 minutes. While the first naan is cooking, shape the next one. If your tray is big enough, you may be able to fit two naan at a time. Remove the cooked naan from the oven and cover with a cloth to keep it warm and soft.

REPEAT the cooking process until all the dough is used. You can only use the top shelf of the oven because the naan won't cook properly on the middle shelf. Refill the baking tray with boiling water when necessary.

Make sure that the naan dough is very soft but not sticky. Shape it by pulling it into the right shape with your hands.

PARATHAS

THIS FRIED UNLEAVENED BREAD IS OFTEN EATEN ON SPECIAL OCCASIONS. IT IS BEST COOKED ON A TAVA OR IRON GRIDDLE. YOU CAN USE EQUAL AMOUNTS OF WHOLEMEAL (WHOLE WHEAT) AND MAIDA IF YOU CAN'T BUY CHAPATI FLOUR.

200 g (1^1/$_3$ cups) atta (chapati flour)
^{1}/$_2$ teaspoon salt
1 tablespoon oil or ghee
oil or ghee for cooking
   and brushing

MAKES 6

SIFT the atta and the salt into a bowl and make a well in the centre. Add about 170 ml (^{2}/$_3$ cup) tepid water and the oil or ghee and mix to form a soft pliable dough. Turn the dough out onto a floured work surface and knead for 5 minutes, then place in an oiled bowl, cover and allow to rest for 30 minutes. Divide the dough into six equal portions.

ROLL each portion into a 15 cm (6 inch) diameter circle. Using a pastry brush, cover the surface of each paratha with a very thin coating of oil or ghee. Fold each into a semicircle and brush thinly with oil. Fold into quarters and roll out each quarter to roughly three times its original size. Cover the rolled-out parathas with a cloth and cook them one at a time.

PLACE a tava, griddle or a heavy-based frying pan over medium heat and leave it to heat up. Lightly brush the surface of the tava or griddle with oil. Remove the excess surface flour on each paratha prior to cooking by holding it in the palms of your hands and gently slapping it from one hand to the other. If you leave the flour on, it may burn.

PUT a paratha on the tava and cook for 1 minute. Turn it over and cook for another minute, or until the surface has brown flecks. This cooking process should be quick to ensure that the parathas remain soft. Repeat until all the parathas are cooked. Cover the cooked ones with a cloth.

PARATHAS must be served warm and can be reheated in a microwave oven, or wrapped in foil and heated in a conventional oven at 180°C (350°F/Gas 4) for 10 minutes.

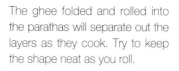

The ghee folded and rolled into the parathas will separate out the layers as they cook. Try to keep the shape neat as you roll.

POPPADOMS or padad are often made by small companies. The company shown here operates on a rooftop in Delhi, the perfect environment for drying the poppadoms in the hot sun. A dough *(left)* is made by kneading together besan flour, rice flour and water, along with a generous amount of dried chilli flakes for seasoning. The dough is then forced through an extruder *(centre left)* to make it smooth and to remove

BREADS

IN INDIA, ROTI IS THE GENERIC NAME FOR BREAD OR BREAD-LIKE ACCOMPANIMENTS. THERE IS A GREAT VARIETY AND THEY ARE BAKED, GRILLED (BROILED), ROASTED OR FRIED. THERE IS NO RULE REGARDING WHICH TYPE OF ROTI GOES WITH WHICH DISH.

Roti are popular all over India, especially in northern and central areas where wheat and grains are staples rather than rice. Although it is a common assumption that rice is part of every Indian meal, there are actually vast areas of India that don't have the right climate or terrain for rice growing. Therefore, these areas produce different grains and have a large repertoire of roti which commonly accompany meals.

In northern and central India, roti are eaten with every meal instead of rice. Throughout the rest of India, roti as well as rice are eaten with main meals every day. Roti function both as part of the meal and as a handy eating tool because they are used to scoop up the more liquid dishes including dal, or to pick up pieces of meat. Roti are also utilized as wrappers for grilled (broiled) meats, or as edible plates, with accompaniments piled on top, at roadside stalls.

COOKING ROTI

Roti made from wheat are generally cooked in one of four ways: on a tava (a flat, convex or concave griddle) without the use of fat, or on a tava using a little ghee or oil, or deep-fried in a karhai, or baked in a tandoor or oven. Each of the first three methods gives a different result using essentially the same unleavened dough. Sometimes, as for parathas, the dough is layered with ghee to give a more flaky texture. At other times, it may be covered as it cooks to create a softer texture. Baked roti are made from leavened dough.

KULCHAS are a speciality of Hyderabad. They are a bread which is baked in a wood-fired oven, rather like a tandoor, set in the floor of the bakery. The breads are baked and sold twice daily, once in the morning and once in the early afternoon. A leavened dough is made using maida and ghee. This is kneaded *(far left)*, then shaped by hand, either into a square *(left)* marked with a cross made of thumbprints in the

any excess moisture. As the dough emerges from the extruder, it is broken off into small balls, each big enough for one poppadom. The dough is rolled to a very thin disc by hand *(centre)*, each roller making only one or two quick passes over the dough. The discs of dough are then arranged on straw mats *(centre right and right)* and left in the hot sun until completely dry and brittle. They are then stacked in piles to be sold.

UNLEAVENED ROTI

Unleavened roti cooked on a tava include chapatis, rumali, and phulkas (a type of chapati which is made to puff up by briefly cooking it on hot coals) as well as roti flavoured with spinach. Those cooked with fat are parathas, either plain or stuffed with a range of fillings. The most common of the deep-fried bread is the puri, which ranges from the tiny mouthfuls (gol goppas) used to make chaat, such as pani puri, to bigger ones eaten with meals. Poppadoms are also a deep-fried accompaniment to meals, though unlike the softer roti they are made from a dough of ground pulses and form a very thin, crisp disc with a bubbled surface.

LEAVENED ROTI

Leavened breads rely on the intense, all-round heat of an oven or tandoor to make them rise and cook in minutes. The breads are stuck to the oven wall for a few minutes only. They include naan, kulcha and sheermal. Baked breads are common to areas such as the Punjab, Hyderabad and Kashmir where ovens or tandoors (often communal) are commonly used. These ovens have been present in the Indus valley in northern India since the 2nd century BC and were introduced by the Moghuls, though they are now very much associated with the Punjab. In other areas of India, baked breads are generally produced by restaurants as domestic kitchens do not have suitable ovens.

Other bread-like accompaniments include cakes and pancakes made of rice and gram batters, either steamed or cooked on griddles, such as idlis, appams and dosas.

FLOURS FOR ROTI

The flours most commonly used for rotis are maida, an all-purpose plain white flour, and atta, a mix of whole wheat and plain white flours. Other flours are made from pulses such as bengal gram or chickpeas (besan flour), mung beans (mung flour) and urad dal (urad flour) amongst others. These are used regionally, depending where they are grown.

dough, or a round bun-like disc marked with three vertical lines *(centre left, top and bottom)*. The shaped breads are then covered with a cloth and left to rise. Each bread is cooked by slapping it onto the red hot wall of the oven for a few minutes *(centre right)*. It is then removed using an iron rod *(right)* when the crust is crisp but the inside soft and doughy, before being eaten warm from the oven *(far right)*.

PURIS

PURIS AND PURI CRISPS ARE SIMPLE TO MAKE EVEN FOR A LARGE GROUP OF PEOPLE. THE DOUGH SHOULD BE PREPARED AHEAD OF TIME AND ALLOWED TO REST. THE OIL SHOULD BE HOT SO THE PURIS PUFF UP WELL, BUT NOT SO HOT THAT YOU BURN THE OUTSIDE AND UNDERCOOK THE INSIDE.

325 g (2²/₃ cups) maida or plain
 (all-purpose) flour
125 g (1 cup) fine semolina
oil for deep-frying

MAKES 12 LARGE OR
35 CRISPS

MIX the maida and semolina with 125 ml (¹/₂ cup) water into a dough and knead well until firm. If necessary, add more flour to make it a really firm dough. Cover and leave for 1 hour.

TO MAKE puri, knead the dough again, then divide into 12 balls. Roll each dough ball out to 1 mm (¹/₁₂ inch) thick (not too thin), making a circle about 10 cm (4 inches) in diameter.

FILL a karhai or heavy-based saucepan one-third full with oil and heat to 180°C/350°F. Test the temperature by putting a small piece of the dough into the oil. If the dough rises to the surface in a couple of seconds, the oil is ready. Put a puri into the hot oil, then about 5 seconds after it rises to the surface, gently push it down, using the back of a spoon, to keep it submerged in the hot oil until it puffs up—this will also take about 5 seconds. Turn over and cook until the other side is lightly browned. Remove from the oil and drain on a wire rack. This whole frying process should take 15–20 seconds for each puri. Continue until all the puris are cooked.

TO MAKE puri crisps, roll out the kneaded dough to 1 mm (¹/₁₂ inch) thick (not too thin), cut out 4 cm (1¹/₂ inch) diameter circles with a pastry cutter and set them aside on a tray.

FILL a karhai or heavy-based saucepan one-third full with oil and heat until a small ball of dough will rise to the surface in a few seconds. Deep-fry the puri crisps in batches until golden and puffed. Drain on paper towels. If you have any remaining pastry, cut it into pieces and deep-fry to make irregular-shaped crisps.

Roll out the puris until they are quite thin so that as they fry and puff up they split into two very light layers.

Make sure that the spinach is evenly distributed throughout the dough. Cover the roti with a lid to keep it soft as it cooks.

SAAG ROTI

A SIMPLE ROTI WITH A SPINACH BASE IS NOT ONLY INTERESTING AND TASTY, BUT NUTRITIOUS AS WELL. MAKE IT WITH SOME CHOPPED BROWNED ONION FOR AN AROMATIC ALTERNATIVE. YOU CAN USE EQUAL AMOUNTS OF WHOLEMEAL (WHOLE WHEAT) AND MAIDA IF YOU CAN'T BUY CHAPATI FLOUR.

200 g (7 oz) English spinach leaves, stalks removed
500 g (3$\frac{1}{3}$ cups) atta (chapati flour)
1 teaspoon salt
1 teaspoon ghee or oil
ghee or oil for cooking

MAKES 20

COOK the spinach briefly in a little simmering water until it is just wilted, then refresh in cold water. Drain thoroughly, then finely chop. Squeeze out any extra water by putting the spinach between two plates and pushing them together.

SIFT the atta and salt into a bowl and make a well in the centre. Add the spinach, ghee and about 250 ml (1 cup) tepid water and mix to form a soft, pliable dough. Turn out the dough onto a floured work surface and knead for 5 minutes. Place in an oiled bowl, cover and allow to rest for 30 minutes.

DIVIDE the dough into 20 balls. Working with one portion at a time and keeping the rest covered, on a lightly floured surface evenly roll out each portion to a 12 cm (5 inch) circle about 1 mm ($\frac{1}{12}$ inch) thick.

HEAT a tava, griddle or heavy-based frying pan until hot, oil it lightly with ghee or oil and cook one roti at a time. Cook each on one side, covered with a saucepan lid (this will help keep them soft), for about 1 minute. Turn it over, cover again and cook the other side for 2 minutes. Check the roti a few times to make sure it doesn't overcook. The roti will blister a little and brown in some places. Remove the roti and keep it warm under a tea towel. Cook the remaining roti.

STUFFED PARATHAS

STUFFED PARATHAS ARE VERY MUCH A FESTIVE FOOD. AFTER STUFFING THEM, ROLL THEM OUT CAREFULLY SO THE FILLING DOESN'T OOZE OUT. IF YOU CAN'T GET HOLD OF CHAPATI FLOUR YOU CAN USE EQUAL AMOUNTS OF WHOLEMEAL (WHOLE WHEAT) AND MAIDA.

400 g (2²/₃ cups) atta (chapati flour)
1 teaspoon salt
4 tablespoons oil or ghee
200 g (7 oz) potatoes, unpeeled
¹/₄ teaspoon mustard seeds
¹/₂ onion, finely chopped
pinch of ground turmeric
pinch of asafoetida
ghee or oil for shallow-frying
extra ghee or oil for brushing
  on the dough

MAKES 14

SIFT the atta and salt into a bowl and make a well in the centre. Add 2 tablespoons of the oil or ghee and about 310 ml (1¹/₄ cups) tepid water and mix to a soft, pliable dough. Turn out onto a floured surface, knead for 5 minutes, then place in an oiled bowl. Cover and allow to rest for 30 minutes.

SIMMER the potatoes for 15–20 minutes or until cooked. Cool slightly, then peel and mash. Heat the remaining oil or ghee in a saucepan over medium heat, add the mustard seeds, cover and shake the pan until the seeds start to pop. Add the onion and fry for 1 minute. Stir in the turmeric and asafoetida. Mix in the potato and cook over low heat for 1–2 minutes, or until the mixture leaves the side of the pan. Season with salt, to taste, and leave to cool.

DIVIDE the dough into 14 portions and roll each into a 15 cm (6 inch) circle. Spread 1 teaspoon of the potato filling evenly over one half of each circle of dough and fold into a semicircle. Rub oil on half the surface area, then fold over into quarters. Roll out until doubled in size. Cover the parathas with a cloth, then cook them one at a time.

HEAT a tava, griddle or a heavy-based frying pan over medium heat. Brush the surface of the tava or griddle with oil. Remove the excess flour on each paratha prior to cooking by holding it in the palms of your hands and gently slapping it from one hand to the other. If you leave the flour on it may burn.

COOK each paratha for 2–3 minutes, then turn over and cook for 1 minute, or until the surface has brown flecks. Cooking should be quick to ensure the parathas remain soft. Cover the cooked parathas with a cloth. Parathas must be served warm. They can be reheated in a microwave, or wrapped in foil and heated in a conventional oven at 180°C (350°F/Gas 4) for 10 minutes.

Fold the filling into the parathas and then gently roll them out so that the filling doesn't ooze out.

Pour the idli mixture into the steamer. It should be runny enough to find its own level and cook to a neat shape.

QUICK IDLIS

IDLIS

220 g (8 oz) urad dal
100 g (1/2 cup) rice flour (rava-idli)
1 teaspoon fenugreek seeds
1 teaspoon salt

MAKES 20

PUT the dal in a bowl, cover with water and soak for at least 4 hours, or overnight.

DRAIN the dal, then grind in a food processor or blender with a little water, to form a fine paste.

COMBINE the rice flour, fenugreek seeds and salt in a large bowl and mix in enough water to make a thick, pourable batter. Mix the batters together. Cover with a cloth and leave in a warm place for 8 hours, until the batter ferments and bubbles. The batter will double in volume.

POUR the mixture into a greased idli mould, filling the cups almost full. Cover and steam the idlis over simmering water for 10–15 minutes, until they are firm and puffed. Traditionally, the idlis are eaten with sambhar (page 53) or with podi (page 242), or as an accompaniment for dishes that have plenty of sauce.

QUICK IDLIS

50 g (1 3/4 oz) chana dal
2 cm (3/4 inch) piece of ginger, finely chopped
310 g (1 1/4 cups) thick plain yoghurt (page 280)
2 tablespoons oil
1 teaspoon black mustard seeds
10 curry leaves
1 green chilli, seeded and finely chopped
300 g (2 1/2 cups) fine semolina
25 g (1 oz) grated coconut (page 283)
1/4 teaspoon baking soda
2 teaspoons salt

MAKES 16

PUT the dal in a bowl, cover with water and soak for at least 4 hours, or overnight. Drain and blend with the ginger, yoghurt and 170 ml (2/3 cup) water in a food processor or blender, to form a loose paste.

HEAT the oil in a frying pan, add the mustard seeds, cover and shake the pan until the seeds start to pop. Add the curry leaves and chilli and fry for 1 minute. Add the semolina and grated coconut and stir for about 2 minutes, or until they start to brown.

MIX both the mixtures together and stir in the baking soda and salt. Leave for about 1 hour, until the mixture thickens and becomes fluffy. Add enough water, about 625 ml (2 1/2 cups), to make a thick, pourable batter. Pour the mixture into a greased idli mould, filling the cups almost full.

COVER and steam the idlis over simmering water for 10 minutes, or until they are firm and puffed.

DOSAS

THESE ARE LARGE, SPONGY, RICE PANCAKES WITH A CRISP SURFACE. THEY ARE TRADITIONALLY EATEN WITH SAMBHAR FOR BREAKFAST. FOR THE BEST RESULT, RICE FLOUR THAT IS SPECIALLY MADE FOR MAKING DOSAS SHOULD BE SOUGHT OUT AS IT IS GROUND TO THE RIGHT CONSISTENCY.

110 g (4 oz) urad dal
1 teaspoon salt
300 g (1³/₄ cups) rice flour
oil for cooking

MAKES 20

PUT the dal in a bowl and cover with water. Soak for at least 4 hours or overnight.

DRAIN, then grind the dal with the salt and a little water in a food processor, blender or pestle and mortar to form a fine paste. Mix the paste with the rice flour, add 1 litre (4 cups) water and mix well. Cover with a cloth and leave in a warm place for 8 hours, or until the batter ferments and bubbles. The batter will double in volume.

HEAT a tava or a non-stick frying pan over medium heat and leave to heat up. Don't overheat it—the heat should always be medium. Lightly brush the surface of the tava or frying pan with oil. Stir the batter and pour a ladleful into the middle of the griddle and quickly spread it out with the back of the ladle or a palette knife, to form a thin pancake. Don't worry if the dosa is not perfect, they are very hard to get exactly right. Drizzle a little oil or ghee around the edge to help it crisp up. Cook until small holes appear on the surface and the edges start to curl. Turn over with a spatula and cook the other side. (The first dosa is often a disaster but it will season the pan for the following ones.)

REPEAT with the remaining mixture, oiling the pan between each dosa. Roll the dosas into big tubes and keep warm. Dosas are often filled with potato masala filling (page 245) and served with sambhar (page 53) and chutneys, or with curries.

Spread the dosa batter out as thinly as you can. This will take a little practice. Drizzle the edge with oil to help it crisp up.

ACCOMPANIMENTS

Jaggery comes in different varieties and broken into varying sized lumps.

MANGO CHUTNEY

MANGO SALAD

THIS IS A DELICIOUS SALAD TO BE SERVED WITH ANY MEAL. TO CHOOSE RIPE MANGOES, CHECK THAT THEY ARE ONLY SLIGHTLY SOFT WHEN YOU TOUCH THEM, THEN SMELL THEM TO SEE WHETHER THEY HAVE THAT WONDERFUL MANGO AROMA.

300 g (10$^{1/2}$ oz) grated coconut (page 283)
2 dried chillies, seeded and chopped
1 tablespoon grated jaggery or soft brown sugar
300 g (10$^{1/2}$ oz) ripe mango flesh, cubed
1 tablespoon oil
$^{1/2}$ teaspoon coriander seeds
$^{1/2}$ teaspoon black mustard seeds
6 curry leaves

SERVES 4

PUT the coconut, chilli and jaggery in a blender and add enough water to make a thick, coarse paste. If you don't have a blender, crush everything together in a pestle and mortar, adding a little water as you go.

TRANSFER the paste to a bowl and toss the mango through. Season with salt, to taste, then refrigerate. Heat the oil in a small frying pan over low heat and add the coriander, mustard seeds and curry leaves. Cover and shake the pan until the seeds start to pop. Pour the oil and seeds over the mango mixture and stir.

MANGO CHUTNEY

THIS IS A WONDERFUL MANGO CHUTNEY THAT IS NOT TOO HOT AND IS VERY SIMPLE TO MAKE. IT IS ONE THAT IS FAMILIAR TO MOST PEOPLE AND GOES WITH ALMOST EVERYTHING. SWEET CHUTNEY BRINGS A CONTRASTING FLAVOUR TO SAVOURY DISHES AND ALSO GOES WELL WITH POPPADOMS.

1 tablespoon oil
2 garlic cloves, crushed
1 teaspoon grated ginger
2 cinnamon sticks
4 cloves
$^{1/2}$ teaspoon chilli powder
1 kg (2 lb 4 oz) fresh or frozen ripe mango flesh, roughly chopped
375 ml (1$^{1/2}$ cups) clear vinegar
230 g (1 cup) caster (superfine) sugar

MAKES 500 ML (2 CUPS)

HEAT the oil in a heavy-based saucepan over medium heat, add the garlic and ginger and fry for 1 minute. Add the remaining ingredients and bring to the boil.

REDUCE the heat to low and cook for 1 hour, or until the mango is thick and pulpy, like jam. It should fall in sheets off the spoon when it is ready. Add salt, to taste, and more chilli if you wish. Remove the whole spices.

POUR the chutney into hot sterilized jars (wash the jars in boiling water and dry them thoroughly in a warm oven). Seal the jars and allow to cool completely. Store in a cool place, or in the fridge after opening.

LACCHA

THIS SPECIALITY FROM DELHI IS A TOMATO AND ONION ACCOMPANIMENT THAT IS ALMOST LIKE A SALAD. IT IS EASY TO PREPARE AND GOES PARTICULARLY WELL WITH TANDOORI MEATS AND BREADS SUCH AS CHAPATIS, PURIS OR NAAN.

1 red onion, finely sliced into rings
1/2 teaspoon salt
1/2 teaspoon cumin seeds
1/4 teaspoon chilli powder
2 tomatoes, thinly sliced
450 g (1 lb) cucumbers, peeled
  and thinly sliced
3 tablespoons lemon juice

SERVES 6

MIX the onion with the salt and leave in a sieve or colander to drain for 10 minutes. Rinse under cold water, then drain and put in a bowl.

PLACE a small frying pan over low heat and dry-roast the cumin seeds until aromatic. Grind the roasted seeds to a fine powder using a spice grinder or pestle and mortar. Add the cumin and chilli powder to the onion and mix well.

ARRANGE the tomato slices on a plate and top with a layer of cucumber, then onion. Sprinkle with the lemon juice and season with salt and black pepper, to taste.

Cucumbers in India come with both green and yellow skins.

RAITA

A RAITA IS SIMILAR TO A PACHADI WHICH IS POPULAR IN SOUTHERN INDIA. BOTH HAVE A YOGHURT OR CURD BASE WITH VARYING VEGETABLES OR FRUITS ADDED. A YOGHURT DISH IS SERVED WITH ALMOST EVERY INDIAN MEAL AS A CONTRAST TO HOT OR SPICY DISHES.

450 g (1 lb) cucumbers, grated
1 large, ripe tomato, finely chopped
310 ml (11/4 cups) thick plain
  yoghurt (page 280)
1/2 tablespoon oil
1 teaspoon black mustard seeds
1 tablespoon coriander (cilantro)
  leaves (optional)

SERVES 4

PUT the cucumber and tomato in a sieve for 20 minutes to drain off any excess liquid. Mix them in a bowl with the yoghurt and season with salt, to taste.

FOR the final seasoning (tarka), heat the oil in a small saucepan over medium heat, add the mustard seeds, then cover and shake the pan until the seeds start to pop. Pour the seeds and oil over the yoghurt. Serve sprinkled with the coriander leaves if you wish.

RAITA

RADISH SALAD

USE THE SMALLEST RADISHES THAT YOU CAN FIND FOR THIS SALAD. COMBINING THE RADISHES WITH PEANUTS GIVES A CRUNCHY TEXTURE AND HOT FLAVOUR. IT SERVES AS A FRESH-TASTING ACCOMPANIMENT TO MOST COOKED DISHES.

200 g (7 oz) small radishes
1 tablespoon oil
1/4 teaspoon cumin seeds
1/4 teaspoon black mustard seeds
pinch of asafoetida
1/4 teaspoon ground turmeric
1/4 teaspoon salt
1 tablespoon lemon juice
100 g (2/3 cup) roasted peanuts,
  roughly chopped

SERVES 4

WASH the radishes and top and tail them. Cut each radish into four or eight pieces.

HEAT the oil in a small saucepan over medium heat, add the cumin and mustard seeds, then cover and shake the pan until the seeds start to pop.

ADD the asafoetida, turmeric and salt to the pan, then remove from the heat, add the lemon juice and leave to cool. Just before serving, arrange the radishes and the peanuts in a bowl, pour the dressing over the top and mix thoroughly.

CARROT SALAD

CARROT SALAD

CARROT SALADS ARE POPULAR THROUGHOUT INDIA. IN THIS ONE, THE SPICES ARE HEATED IN THE OIL IN ORDER FOR THEIR FLAVOUR TO PERMEATE THE DRESSING. THIS SALAD GETS MORE FLAVOURSOME IF IT IS ALLOWED TO STAND FOR HALF AN HOUR BEFORE SERVING.

1 tablespoon oil
1/4 teaspoon black mustard seeds
1/4 teaspoon cumin seeds
pinch of ground turmeric
1/4 teaspoon salt
1/4 teaspoon caster (superfine)
  sugar
1 1/2 tablespoons lemon juice
500 g (1 lb 2 oz) carrots, finely
  grated
coriander (cilantro) leaves

SERVES 4

HEAT the oil in a small saucepan over medium heat, add the mustard and cumin seeds, then cover and shake the pan until the seeds start to pop.

ADD the turmeric, salt and sugar to the pan, then remove the pan from the heat and leave the spices to cool for 5 minutes. Mix in the lemon juice, then toss the carrot through. Cover and leave for 30 minutes. Garnish with coriander leaves just before serving.

CHURRI

THIS IS A VERY REFRESHING SIDE DISH WHICH IS TRADITIONALLY USED AS AN ACCOMPANIMENT TO BIRYANI BUT IT IS VERSATILE AND CAN BE SERVED WITH MOST DISHES. THE YOGHURT AND BUTTERMILK HAVE A COOLING EFFECT WHEN CHURRI IS EATEN WITH HOT OR SPICY DISHES.

1 teaspoon cumin seeds
10 g (1/2 cup) mint leaves, chopped
15 g (1/2 cup) coriander (cilantro) leaves, roughly chopped
2 cm (3/4 inch) piece of ginger, roughly chopped
2 green chillies, roughly chopped
310 ml (1 1/4 cups) thick plain yoghurt (page 280)
310 ml (1 1/4 cups) buttermilk
1 onion, thinly sliced

SERVES 4

PLACE a small frying pan over low heat and dry-roast the cumin seeds until aromatic. Grind the seeds to a fine powder in a spice grinder or pestle and mortar.

CHOP the mint, coriander, ginger and chilli to a fine paste in a blender, or chop together finely with a knife. Add the yoghurt and buttermilk and a pinch of salt to the mixture and blend until all the ingredients are well mixed. Check the seasoning, adjust if necessary, then mix in the sliced onion and the ground cumin, reserving a little cumin to sprinkle on top.

The Charminar, Hyderabad.

CARROT PACHADI

THIS DELIGHTFUL CARROT SIDE DISH IS SIMILAR TO RAITA, PACHADI BEING THE SOUTHERN INDIAN TERM FOR A YOGHURT-BASED ACCOMPANIMENT. THIS GOES PARTICULARLY WELL WITH BIRYANI AND PULAO BUT IS SUITABLE FOR SERVING WITH MANY OTHER DISHES AS THE YOGHURT IS SOOTHING.

1 tablespoon oil
1 teaspoon black mustard seeds
2–3 dried chillies
1/4 teaspoon asafoetida
1 stalk of curry leaves
625 ml (2 1/2 cups) thick plain yoghurt (page 280)
4 carrots, finely grated
coriander (cilantro) leaves

SERVES 4

HEAT the oil in a small saucepan over medium heat, add the mustard seeds and chillies, then cover and shake the pan until the seeds start to pop. Remove from the heat and immediately stir in the asafoetida and curry leaves.

WHISK the yoghurt to remove any lumps, then mix in the grated carrot. Mix in the mustard seeds, chillies, asafoetida and curry leaves along with the oil, then season with salt, to taste. Garnish with coriander leaves.

CARROT PACHADI

KOSAMBRI

KOSAMBRI ARE SALAD-LIKE DISHES FROM MYSORE. THIS ONE USES A COMBINATION OF CARROTS OR RADISHES AND DAL BUT THERE ARE MANY VARIATIONS. THIS IS AN EXCELLENT COMBINATION OF INGREDIENTS AND CAN BE SERVED ALONGSIDE MOST INDIAN DISHES.

50 g (1/2 cup) moong dal
200 g (7 oz) carrots or white radish
25 g (1 oz) grated coconut (page 283)
25 g (3/4 cup) coriander (cilantro) leaves
1/2 tablespoon oil
1/2 teaspoon yellow mustard seeds
2 dried chillies
2 tablespoons lemon juice

SERVES 4

SOAK the dal in plenty of boiling water for 3 hours, then drain.

FINELY GRATE the carrot or radish and combine with the dal, coconut and coriander leaves in a salad bowl. Heat the oil in a small saucepan over medium heat, add the mustard seeds, then cover and shake the pan until the seeds start to pop. Add the chillies, remove from the heat and add the lemon juice. When cold, pour over the remaining ingredients and toss well. Season with salt, to taste.

EGGPLANT SAMBAL

EGGPLANT, OR AUBERGINE, IS ALSO KNOWN BY ITS INDIAN NAME BRINJAL. FOR THIS RECIPE, IT IS PREFERABLE TO USE THE LONG, THIN, ASIAN EGGPLANTS. USE THE SAMBAL AS AN ACCOMPANIMENT OR EAT IT AS A DIP WITH PIECES OF INDIAN BREAD.

EGGPLANT SAMBAL

2 medium (about 500 g/1 lb 2 oz) eggplants (aubergines)
1/2 tablespoon oil
1/2 teaspoon ground turmeric
3 tablespoons lime juice
2 red chillies, seeded and finely diced
1 small red onion, finely diced
4 tablespoons thick plain yoghurt (page 280)
coriander (cilantro) leaves

SERVES 4

PREHEAT the oven to 200°C (400°F/Gas 6). Slice each eggplant in half and brush the cut halves with the oil and ground turmeric. Place the eggplants in a roasting tin and roast them for 30 minutes, or until they are browned all over and very soft.

SCOOP the eggplant pulp into a bowl. Mash the pulp with the lime juice, chilli and onion, reserving some chilli and onion for garnish. Season with salt, to taste, then fold in the yoghurt. Garnish with the coriander leaves and remaining onion and chilli.

POUSSIN PICKLE

THIS RECIPE USES SPATCHCOCKS (POUSSIN OR BABY CHICKENS) AS THEY ARE AVAILABLE ALL YEAR ROUND. HOWEVER, IN NORTHERN INDIA, WHEN THE GAME SEASON IS UNDER WAY, PARTRIDGE WOULD BE USED. THE PICKLE IS AN IDEAL ACCOMPANIMENT TO MOST DISHES OR CAN BE EATEN WITH BREADS.

2 x 900 g (2 lb) spatchcocks (poussin) or 1 partridge
6 garlic cloves, roughly chopped
5 cm (2 inch) piece of ginger, roughly chopped
420 ml (1²/₃ cups) mustard oil or oil
2 Indian bay leaves (cassia leaves)
12 dried chillies
20 black peppercorns
1 teaspoon kalonji (nigella seeds)
3 teaspoons coriander seeds
1 teaspoon cumin seeds
2 teaspoons yellow mustard seeds
¹/₄ teaspoon ground turmeric
1 teaspoon garam masala (page 284)
pinch of asafoetida
1 tablespoon salt
100 g (3¹/₂ oz) jaggery or soft brown sugar
420 ml (1²/₃ cups) dark vinegar

MAKES 1 LITRE (4 CUPS)

CUT each spatchcock or partridge into six pieces by removing both legs and cutting between the joint of the drumstick and thigh. Cut down one side of each backbone, leaving it attached to one side. Turn each poussin or partridge over and cut through the cartilage down the centre of each breastbone. Trim off all the wing tips. Trim off any excess fat or skin.

CHOP the garlic and ginger in a food processor until finely chopped, or grate the ginger and crush the garlic and mix them together. Heat the mustard oil in a heavy-based saucepan over medium heat until smoking. Reduce the heat to low, then add the garlic and ginger mixture, bay leaves, dried chillies, peppercorns, kalonji, coriander, cumin and mustard seeds, turmeric, garam masala and asafoetida to the pan. Gently shake the pan until the seeds start to sizzle and pop. Add the spatchcock pieces and salt, stir well and fry over medium heat for 20 minutes, stirring occasionally until the spatchcocks are browned all over and cooked through. Remove the spatchcock pieces from the pan with a slotted spoon and place in a bowl. Leave the pan of spiced oil to cool.

PUT the jaggery and vinegar in a saucepan and bring to the boil, reduce the heat and cook over medium heat for 10–15 minutes, until the jaggery has completely dissolved and the vinegar has reduced by a third. Leave to cool.

WHEN the vinegar has cooled, mix it with the cooled oil, stir in the spatchcock pieces and mix well. Store the pickle in special ceramic pickling pots or sterilized jars (wash the jars in boiling water and dry in a warm oven). Marinate for 3–5 days, shaking the bottle carefully at least twice daily so that the poussin can absorb all the flavours. It will now be ready for serving. Store in a cool place, or in the fridge after opening.

Pickles (achar) and chutneys (chatnis) are popular all over India. Shops and stalls usually sell a bewildering variety.

PINEAPPLE CHUTNEY

THIS QUICK AND SIMPLE FRESH PINEAPPLE CHUTNEY CAN BE ENJOYED AS PART OF ANY MAIN MEAL INCLUDING MEAT AND POULTRY OR FISH AND SEAFOOD DISHES. THE ACIDITY OF THE PINEAPPLE WILL CUT THROUGH ANY RICH DISHES AND MAKE A REFRESHING CONTRAST.

2 small or 1 large pineapple, slightly green
1 teaspoon salt
1 red onion, thinly sliced into half rings
4 red chillies, seeded and finely chopped
4 garlic cloves, finely chopped
2 teaspoons ginger juice (page 280)
30 g (1/4 cup) icing (confectioners') sugar, or to taste
6 tablespoons lime juice, or to taste

SERVES 6

PEEL the pineapple by cutting down the outside in strips. Remove any remaining eyes, then slice the pineapple lengthwise and remove the tough central core.

RUB the pineapple with the salt and leave it to sit for a few minutes in a colander to draw out some of the juices. Rinse, then chop into small chunks and drain well on paper towels.

MIX all the ingredients together in a bowl, adding enough sugar, lime juice, pepper and salt to achieve a balanced flavour. Chill and serve.

PODI

PODI

PODI IS A COARSE POWDER USED AS A DIP OR AS A SEASONING. EAT IT WITH IDLI OR USE IT AS A SCATTER SEASONING FOR STEAMED VEGETABLES OR SALADS. THIS WILL MAKE ENOUGH TO LAST A LONG TIME SO STORE IT IN A JAR AND USE IT AS YOU NEED IT (YOU CAN MAKE HALF IF YOU WISH).

110 g (4 oz) urad dal
100 g (3 1/2 oz) chana dal
10 g (1/4 oz) dried chillies
75 g (1/2 cup) sesame seeds
1/2 teaspoon sugar
1/2 teaspoon salt
1 tablespoon ghee

MAKES 220 G (8 OZ)

PLACE a small frying pan over low heat and dry-roast the urad dal, stirring constantly until brown. Remove from the pan and repeat with the chana dal, dried chillies and sesame seeds. Grind the roasted mixture to a powder with the sugar and salt, using a spice grinder or pestle and mortar. Cool completely and store in a jar or an airtight container.

WHEN ready to serve, heat the ghee in a frying pan and add 2 teaspoons of podi per person. Toss together until well mixed.

POTATO MASALA

THIS FILLING IS TRADITIONALLY ROLLED IN DOSAS TO MAKE MASALA DOSA, WHICH IS SERVED FOR BREAKFAST OR AS A SNACK IN SOUTHERN INDIA. HOWEVER, IT ALSO MAKES AN EXCELLENT SPICY POTATO SIDE DISH.

2 tablespoons oil
1 teaspoon black mustard seeds
10 curry leaves
1/4 teaspoon ground turmeric
1 cm (1/2 inch) piece of ginger, grated
2 green chillies, finely chopped
2 onions, chopped
500 g (1 lb 2 oz) waxy potatoes, cut into 2 cm (3/4 inch) cubes
1 tablespoon tamarind purée (page 280)

SERVES 4

HEAT the oil in a heavy-based frying pan, add the mustard seeds, cover and when they start to pop add the curry leaves, turmeric, ginger, chilli and onion and cook, uncovered, until the onion is soft.

ADD the potato cubes and 250 ml (1 cup) water to the pan, bring to the boil, cover and cook until the potato is tender and almost breaking up. If there is any liquid left in the pan, simmer, uncovered, until it evaporates. If the potato isn't cooked and there is no liquid left, add a little more and continue to cook. Add the tamarind and season with salt, to taste.

PAPAYA MUSTARD PICKLE

THIS IS A WONDERFUL PICKLE SUITABLE FOR SERVING WITH ROAST LAMB RAAN OR WITH PIECES OF ROTI AND A QUICK DAL CURRY OR SAMBAR. MAKE SURE YOU USE A GREEN PAPAYA AND NOT A RIPE ONE, OTHERWISE THE FLESH WILL DISINTEGRATE WHEN YOU COOK IT.

PAPAYA MUSTARD PICKLE

5 red chillies, seeded and chopped
1 large red onion, chopped
6 cm (2 1/2 inch) piece of ginger, grated
3 garlic cloves, chopped
60 g (2 1/4 oz) black mustard seeds
500 ml (2 cups) clear vinegar
1 tablespoon oil
3 green chillies, seeded and chopped
200 g (7 oz) sugar
1/4 teaspoon salt
1/4 teaspoon ground turmeric
500 g (1 lb 2 oz) green papaya, cut into 1 cm (1/2 inch) cubes

MAKES 1 LITRE (4 CUPS)

CHOP the red chilli, onion, ginger, garlic, mustard seeds and 125 ml (1/2 cup) vinegar in a food processor or pestle and mortar to form a paste. The mustard seeds will not break up completely.

HEAT the oil in a large heavy-based saucepan and cook the paste and remaining vinegar until aromatic and reduced. Add the green chilli and sugar and stir until the sugar is dissolved. Add the salt, turmeric and papaya and simmer for 2 minutes, making sure the papaya stays firm.

POUR the pickle into sterilized jars (wash the jars in boiling water and dry in a warm oven) and leave to cool completely. Store in a cool place, or in the fridge after opening.

Shelled tamarind husk and pulp.

SWEET TOMATO CHUTNEY

THIS IS AN EASY STORE-CUPBOARD CHUTNEY. IT IS AN ESPECIALLY HANDY RECIPE IF YOU HAVE AN ABUNDANCE OF VERY RIPE TOMATOES (YOU WILL NEED ABOUT 800 G/1 LB 12 OZ PEELED FRESH TOMATOES). IF YOU CAN'T FIND CLEAR VINEGAR AT INDIAN FOOD SHOPS, USE WHITE VINEGAR.

8 garlic cloves, roughly chopped
5 cm (2 inch) piece of ginger,
 roughly chopped
2 x 400 g (14 oz) tins chopped
 tomatoes
310 ml (1 1/4 cups) clear vinegar
350 g (12 oz) jaggery or soft brown
 sugar
2 tablespoons sultanas
2 teaspoons salt
3/4 teaspoon cayenne pepper
chilli powder (optional)

MAKES 500 ML (2 CUPS)

COMBINE the garlic, ginger and half the tomatoes in a blender or food processor and blend until smooth. If you don't have a blender, crush the garlic, grate the ginger and push the tomatoes through a sieve before mixing them all together.

PUT the remaining tomatoes, the vinegar, sugar, sultanas and salt in a large, heavy-based saucepan. Bring to the boil and add the garlic and ginger mixture. Reduce the heat and simmer gently for 1 1/2–1 3/4 hours, stirring occasionally, until the mixture is thick enough to fall off a spoon in sheets. Make sure the mixture doesn't catch on the base.

ADD the cayenne pepper. For a hotter chutney, add a little chilli powder. Leave to cool, then pour into sterilized jars (wash the jars in boiling water and dry them in a warm oven). Store in a cool place, or in the fridge after opening.

TAMARIND AND RAISIN
CHUTNEY

TAMARIND AND RAISIN CHUTNEY

2 teaspoons fennel seeds
250 ml (1 cup) tamarind purée
 (page 280)
50 g (1/4 cup) pitted dates,
 chopped
30 g (1/4 cup) raisins
1 teaspoon chilli powder
180 g (6 oz) jaggery or soft brown
 sugar
1 tablespoon oil
1/2 teaspoon black mustard seeds
6 green chillies, slit in half and
 seeded but left whole

MAKES 250 ML (1 CUP)

PLACE a small frying pan over low heat and dry-roast the fennel seeds, stirring constantly until aromatic. Grind the seeds to a fine powder using a spice grinder or pestle and mortar. Mix the ground fennel with the tamarind, dates, raisins, chilli powder, jaggery and a pinch of salt.

HEAT the oil in a large, heavy-based saucepan over medium heat, add the mustard seeds, then cover and shake the pan until they start to pop. Add the date mixture and chillies, bring to the boil and cook for about 3 minutes, until the mixture starts to thicken. Reduce the heat and simmer for 40 minutes until the chutney is thick enough to fall off a spoon in sheets. Cool, then put in a sterilized jar (wash the jar in boiling water and dry in a warm oven). Store in a cool place. Refrigerate after opening.

LEMON PICKLE

PICKLES ARE VERY MUCH A PART OF AN INDIAN MEAL. ALTHOUGH THERE ARE MANY VARIETIES OF COMMERCIALLY MANUFACTURED PICKLES AVAILABLE, A HOME-MADE ONE IS FAR SUPERIOR. CHOOSE THIN-SKINNED LEMONS FOR THIS IF YOU CAN. YOU CAN ALSO USE INDIAN LIMES FOR THIS RECIPE.

Boiling the lemons will soften both the rind and flesh. Skim off any scum that appears on the surface of the water.

500 g (1 lb 2 oz) thin-skinned lemons
1/2 teaspoon ground turmeric
2 tablespoons salt
1/2 teaspoon fenugreek seeds
1 teaspoon yellow mustard seeds
1/2 tablespoon chilli powder
2 tablespoons oil

MAKES 500 ML (2 CUPS)

WASH the lemons, place them in a saucepan with 500 ml (2 cups) water and the turmeric and bring slowly to the boil, skimming off any scum which rises to the top. Boil for 8 minutes, then remove from the heat and drain well.

CUT each lemon into eight sections and remove any pips. By this time, the lemon flesh will have turned to a pulp. Sprinkle the lemons with the salt and pack them into a 500 ml (2 cup) glass jar which has been sterilized (wash the jar in boiling water and dry in a warm oven). Put the lid on tightly and keep the lemons in the jar for 1 week, turning the jar over every day. If the lid of the jar is too narrow to balance upside-down, store the jar on its side and roll it over every day instead.

PLACE a small frying pan over low heat and dry-roast the fenugreek and mustard seeds until aromatic and starting to pop, shaking the pan occasionally to prevent them burning. Grind the roasted seeds to a fine powder using a spice grinder or pestle and mortar.

TIP the lemons into a bowl and mix in the ground spices and the chilli powder. Clean the jar and sterilize it again. Put the lemons and any juices back into the jar and pour the oil over the top to act as an air barrier and stop the top layer from discolouring. Store in a cool place, or in the fridge after opening.

A coconut farm in Kerala.

A grinding stone is used in India instead of a pestle and mortar. The grinding stone is rubbed back and forth over ingredients.

FRESH COCONUT CHUTNEY

CHUTNEY MADE WITH FRESH COCONUT IS SERVED WITH IDLIS AND DOSAS FOR BREAKFAST, OR AS A SNACK. THE CURRY LEAVES AND TAMARIND GIVE A DISTINCTIVE INDIAN FLAVOUR.

1 teaspoon chana dal
1 teaspoon urad dal
1/2 fresh coconut, grated
2 green chillies, seeded and finely chopped
1/2 teaspoon salt
1 tablespoon oil
1 teaspoon black mustard seeds
5 curry leaves
1 teaspoon tamarind purée (page 280)

SERVES 4

SOAK the dals in cold water for 2 hours, then drain well.

PUT the grated coconut, chilli and salt in a food processor and blend to a fine paste. If you don't have a food processor, either finely chop everything together with a knife or pound them in a pestle and mortar.

HEAT the oil in a small saucepan and add the mustard seeds and dals, then cover and shake the pan until they start to pop. Add the curry leaves and fry for 1 minute, or until the dal browns. Add these ingredients to the coconut with the tamarind and mix well.

MINT AND CORIANDER CHUTNEY

MINT AND CORIANDER CHUTNEY

THIS REFRESHING MINT AND CORIANDER (CILANTRO) CHUTNEY IS PERFECT FOR SERVING WITH NIMKI, SAMOSAS OR SINGHARAS. HOWEVER, IT CAN BE SERVED WITH JUST ABOUT ANY INDIAN MEAL.

30 g (1 1/2 cups) mint leaves
30 g (1 cup) coriander (cilantro) leaves
1 green chilli
1 tablespoon tamarind purée (page 280)
1/2 teaspoon salt
1 1/2 teaspoons sugar
3 tablespoons thick plain yoghurt (page 280), (optional)

SERVES 4

WASH the mint and coriander leaves. Discard any tough stalks but keep the young soft ones for flavour. Blend all the ingredients together in a blender or food processor, or chop everything finely and pound it together in a pestle and mortar. Taste the chutney and add more salt if necessary. If you want a creamier, milder chutney, stir in the yoghurt.

SWEETS & DRINKS

The Writers building, Kolkata (Calcutta).

ROSSOGOLLAS

KOLKATA (CALCUTTA) IS THE CITY WHERE THE BEST BENGALI SWEETS CAN BE FOUND. ROSSOGOLLAS OR RASGULLAS ARE SWEETENED MILK BALLS IN SYRUP, SAID TO HAVE BEEN INVENTED BY AN OLD FIRM, K.C. DAS, WHICH SPECIALIZES IN SWEETS. MAKE THE CHENNA BEFORE YOU START.

Make a dent in each ball and fill it with nuts before smoothing the balls into shape. Gently poach them in the sugar syrup.

1 quantity chenna (page 279)
3 tablespoons chopped nuts
  (optional)

SYRUP
1 kg (4½ cups) sugar
3 tablespoons milk
rosewater (optional)

SERVES 6

DIVIDE the chenna dough into 30 portions and roll each into a ball. If you are using the nuts, make a hollow in each ball, add a few chopped nuts to the centre, then re-roll as a ball.

MAKE a thin syrup by combining the sugar with 1.5 litres (6 cups) water in a heavy-based saucepan and simmering the mixture over low heat until it is slightly thickened. The syrup should feel sticky and greasy. Add the milk to the boiling syrup to clarify it—this will force any scum to rise to the surface. Skim off the scum with a spoon.

DROP the rossogollas into the clean boiling syrup, reduce the heat and simmer for 10 minutes, or until they float. Sprinkle a little water on the boiling syrup every 2 minutes to stop it reducing too much and foaming. When the rossogollas are cooked, they will float on the surface.

REMOVE from the heat and leave to cool in the syrup. If you would like a rose flavour, add a few drops of rosewater. Keep the rossogollas refrigerated until required. Serve with a little of the syrup poured over them.

KARANJI

THESE MINI, COCONUT-FILLED, DEEP-FRIED SWEET PASTRIES ARE EATEN AS A SNACK AT AFTERNOON TEA TIME. BECAUSE THEY CAN BE STORED FOR ABOUT A WEEK, THEY ARE GOOD TO HAVE ON HAND FOR SERVING TO HUNGRY, UNEXPECTED VISITORS AT ANY TIME OF THE DAY.

215 g (1¾ cups) maida or plain (all-purpose) flour
4 tablespoons oil or ghee
oil for deep-frying

FILLING
10 cardamom pods
100 g (½ cup) sugar
5 cm (2 inch) cinnamon stick
150 g (5½ oz) grated coconut (page 283)

MAKES 30

SIFT the maida into a bowl. Add the oil or ghee and rub it in with your fingers until the mixture resembles breadcrumbs. Add 5 tablespoons lukewarm water, a little at a time, and, using a palette knife, blend the dough together. Turn out onto a floured surface and knead for 5 minutes, until smooth and pliable. Cover and leave at room temperature for 15 minutes. Don't refrigerate or the oil will congeal, making it difficult to roll.

TO MAKE the filling, remove the cardamom seeds from the pods and coarsely crush them in a pestle and mortar. In a heavy-based saucepan, combine the sugar, cinnamon and 185 ml (¾ cup) water. Heat gently until the sugar has dissolved. Bring to the boil, add the coconut, then stir over low heat until the liquid has evaporated and the mixture comes together. The mixture should not be bone dry. Remove from heat, add the cardamom and allow to cool.

ON a lightly floured surface, roll out one-third of the pastry to a 28 cm (11 inch) diameter circle. Using an 8 cm (3 inch) cutter, cut out 10 circles of pastry. Place ½ tablespoon of the filling in the centre of each circle, then moisten the edges with water. Seal into a semicircle and crimp the edge. Repeat until all the pastry and filling has been used. Cover until ready to fry.

FILL a karhai or deep, heavy-based saucepan one-third full with oil and heat. Add a small piece of pastry and if it rises to the surface in a couple of seconds the oil is ready for use. Put in a few karanjis at a time and fry for about 30–60 seconds, until lightly browned. Turn them over and brown them on the other side. Remove from the pan and place on a cooling rack for 5 minutes before draining on paper towels. When cold, store in an airtight container for up to a week.

Cut circles from the pastry with a cutter and then fill them with the coconut mixture. Seal firmly so they don't leak when cooked.

KULFI

YOUNG AND OLD TAKE GREAT DELIGHT IN THESE FLAVOURED ICES WHICH ARE SOLD IN INDIA AT ROADSIDE STALLS. THEY ARE NOT GENERALLY MADE IN HOUSEHOLDS AS THEY ARE TIME-CONSUMING.

2 litres (8 cups) milk
10 cardamom pods, lightly crushed
6 tablespoons sugar
15 g (1/2 oz) almonds, blanched
  and finely chopped
15 g (1/2 oz) unsalted pistachio
  nuts, skinned and finely chopped
edible silver leaf (varak), (optional)

MAKES 12

PUT the milk and cardamom pods in a heavy-based saucepan and bring to the boil. Reduce the heat to low and simmer, stirring frequently, for about 2 hours, until the milk has reduced to a third of the original amount, about 750 ml (3 cups). Whenever a thin skin forms on top, stir it back in.

ADD the sugar to the pan, simmer for 5 minutes, then strain into a shallow plastic freezer box. Add the almonds and half the pistachios, then cool. Put twelve 80 ml (1/3 cup) kulfi moulds or dariole moulds in the freezer to chill.

PLACE the kulfi mixture in the freezer and every 20 minutes, using electric beaters or a fork, give the ice cream a good stir to break up the ice crystals. When the mixture is quite stiff, divide it among the moulds and freeze until hardened completely. Dip the moulds in hot water and turn out the kulfi. Sprinkle with the remaining pistachios and decorate with a piece of silver leaf.

Kulfi are flavoured ices made in specially shaped moulds. When the mixture has hardened, fill the conical moulds, then freeze.

CARROT HALVA

THIS IS A VERY SIMPLE INDIAN SWEET. THE ONLY SECRET TO MAKING IT LOOK AUTHENTIC IS TO USE REALLY BRIGHT-ORANGE CARROTS TO GIVE A GOOD COLOUR. CARROT HALVA IS TRADITIONALLY MADE IN THE WINTER MONTHS AND IS BEST EATEN HOT WITH A DOLLOP OF CREAM.

CARROT HALVA

1 kg (2 lb 4 oz) carrots, grated
1 litre (4 cups) milk
100 g (3 1/2 oz) ghee
230 g (1 cup) caster (superfine)
  sugar
80 g (2/3 cup) raisins
1 teaspoon cardamom seeds,
  finely ground
50 g (1/2 cup) slivered almonds
ground cardamom

SERVES 8

PUT the grated carrot and milk in a heavy-based saucepan over low heat and bring to a simmer. Cook, stirring until the carrot is tender and the milk evaporates. This must be done slowly or the mixture will burn. Add the ghee and cook until the carrot starts to brown.

ADD the sugar and cook until the mixture is thick and dry. Add the raisins, cardamom and almonds. Serve hot in small bowls, with double cream or ice cream, and sprinkle with a little ground cardamom.

DIVALI is the Hindu festival of light when hundreds of oil lamps are lit and fireworks are let off in the streets. It is also particularly associated with sweets. The festival takes place in October or November, on the 15th day of Kartika in the Hindu calendar and lasts for 5 days. During the run-up to Divali thousands of kilos of sweets are made by the halvais (sweet-makers) of India. Extra workers are drafted in to help, temporary stalls are

SWEETS

A FONDNESS FOR SWEETS (MITHAI) IS COMMON THROUGHOUT INDIA. UNLIKE IN THE WEST THERE IS NO DISTINCTION BETWEEN SWEETS AND DESSERTS. BOTH ARE SOLD AT SWEET SHOPS AND NEITHER IS COMMONLY EATEN AT THE END OF A MEAL. INSTEAD, MITHAI REPRESENT A FORM OF GREETING, ARE USED AS RELIGIOUS OFFERINGS AND ARE SYMBOLIC OF HOSPITALITY.

Mithai vary regionally and common sweets such as barfi and laddu are available everywhere. Many places have a sweet speciality. In areas such as Bengal, the sweet capital of India, towns and small villages have their own particular varieties.

TYPES OF SWEETS

Sweets generally fit into categories based on their main ingredient, their shape, or the method of production.

BARFI are types of fudge. Their name comes from the Persian word for snow and in their original form they were probably all white. Barfi are based on khoya, a milk product, and are very sweet. Those with ground nuts or flour in them have a grainier texture than the plain milk (dhoodh) versions.

SANDESH, based on chenna mixed with sugar, are one of the finest Indian sweets. The name means 'news' and the sweets were originally sent to friends by messenger as a means of enquiring after them. Sandesh can be made in a variety of textures and flavours and are often pressed into decorative moulds. As a speciality of Bengal, sandesh are shaped into forms such as conch shells or fish, which are representative of that area.

HALVA have a thick, pudding-like texture and are based on ingredients such as semolina, grated carrot, besan flour and pulses. Sweet-makers in India are called 'halvais'.

ROSSOGOLLAS were the invention of Nobin Chandra Das in 1868. They are Kolkata's (Calcutta) most famous sweet. They are now made by the Das family at their factory in the city. First, paneer is made by separating milk into curds and whey and draining off the whey. The paneer is then pushed through an extruder to get rid of any excess moisture. Sugar is added to make chenna and the mixture is rolled into balls by hand.

set up and sweet production goes into overdrive. Every corner of every shop is utilized, including the basement and roof. Sweets are lavishly decorated using gold and silver leaf, nuts, dried fruit and saffron. Trays, each holding a different variety of sweet, are piled high. The sweets are sold by weight or packaged into fancy gift boxes. Sweets are bought as gifts for friends and relatives and also to use as religious offerings.

LADDU are named for their ball shape rather than their ingredients. They are made with a besan flour or coarse flour dough which is pressed into patties, deep-fried, then crumbled and shaped into balls with sugar, ghee, spices and nuts. There are many variations, some of which are made with puffed rice mixed with sugar and often nuts.

DEEP-FRIED sweets are fried in oil and then soaked in sugar syrup such as jalebi and imarti (loops of orange dough).

MILK-BASED sweets and desserts range from Bengali specialities such as rossogollas and kheer (rice pudding) to southern dishes such as payasam (sago or sevian puddings).

MILK-BASED SWEETS

Milk is often used in sweet-making. It is either boiled for prolonged periods until it thickens, or is converted to a type of fresh cheese (paneer) by coagulating it with lemon juice.

RABRI or RABADI is milk at a quarter of its original volume, eaten as a thick, creamy pudding, or as a sauce for sweets such as ras malai.

KHOYA, a fudgy solid mass, is milk at an eighth of its original volume. It is the main ingredient in many milk-based sweets.

CHENNA is paneer sweetened with sugar and is the ingredient on which rossogolla and sandesh are based.

MALAI is the Hindi word for cream. Malai varies in thickness.

DECORATIONS

Indian sweets are required not only to taste good but also to look fabulous. They are often coloured with pink, yellow or green, studded with nuts or sultanas, or covered with a gossamer-fine layer of gold or silver leaf (varak). Though everyday sweets are not as fancy, those sold around festival times are made more elaborate with extra decorations.

FLAVOURINGS

Saffron, cardamom, rose essence, kewra (pandanus), khus (fragrant grass), coconut, pistachio and almond are the most common flavours. Unrefined sugars such as gur or jaggery also add flavour and are often preferred to refined sugar.

The balls vary in size depending on whether they are to be sold loose (larger) or tinned (smaller). The rossogollas are cooked in large vats of simmering sugar syrup, each vat heated by a special system based on steam. When the rossogollas are spongy and cooked through they are either left to cool in the syrup or put straight into tins. The factory uses 1000 to 1500 litres of fresh milk every day for its sweet-making.

CASHEW NUT BARFI

500 g (1 lb 2 oz) cashew nuts
6 cardamom pods
200 g (2 cups) powdered milk
2 tablespoons ghee or butter
1/4 teaspoon ground cloves
230 g (1 cup) caster (superfine)
    sugar
2 sheets edible silver leaf (varak),
    (optional)

SERVES 12

PLACE a small frying pan over low heat and dry-roast the cashew nuts until browned all over. Cool and chop in a food processor or with a knife. Remove the cardamom seeds from the pods and crush them in a spice grinder or pestle and mortar. Line a 26 x 17 cm (10 1/2 x 7 inch) baking tin with baking paper.

COMBINE the milk powder and cashew nuts in a large bowl and rub in the ghee until completely mixed in. Stir in the cardamom and cloves.

COMBINE the sugar and 250 ml (1 cup) water in a heavy-based saucepan and heat over low heat until the sugar melts. Bring to the boil and simmer for 5–7 minutes to make a sugar syrup. Quickly stir the sugar syrup into the cashew mixture—if you leave it too long it will stiffen—and spread the mixture into the baking tin. Smooth with a buttered spatula. Place the silver leaf on top by inverting the sheets onto the surface and peeling off the paper backing. Leave to cool, then slice into diamond shapes. Serve cold.

Carefully lay sheets of silver on the barfi and pull off the backing paper. If you touch the silver with your hands it will stick to them.

PAYASAM

PAYASAM

100 g (1/2 cup) sago
2 tablespoons ghee
80 g (1/2 cup) chopped or slivered
    almonds
125 g (1 cup) sultanas
50 g (1 3/4 oz) sevian, broken into
    3 cm (1 1/4 inch) pieces
1 litre (4 cups) milk
185 g (1 cup) soft brown sugar
3 tablespoons golden syrup
1 teaspoon ground cardamom
1/4 teaspoon ground cloves
1 teaspoon rosewater (optional)
2 tablespoons grated coconut
    (page 283)

SERVES 6

COOK the sago in 1 litre (4 cups) simmering water, stirring occasionally, for 20–25 minutes, until the sago is clear, then drain. Rinse and drain the sago again.

HEAT the ghee in a heavy-based frying pan over low heat, brown the nuts and sultanas and remove from the pan. Fry the sevian in the same pan until light brown. Add most of the milk and simmer the sevian until soft, stirring as it cooks. Add the sago and remaining milk. Stir with a fork, add the sugar and golden syrup and simmer, stirring constantly.

ADD a little milk if necessary as the payasam thickens, then add the cardamom, cloves and rosewater and stir to a pourable consistency. Add two-thirds of the nuts and sultanas and stir. Serve immediately or chill. Garnish with the coconut and remaining nuts and sultanas.

GULAB JAMUN

LITERALLY TRANSLATED TO MEAN ROSE-FLAVOURED PLUM, GULAB JAMUN IS AN EXTREMELY POPULAR

INDIAN SWEET MADE BY SOAKING FRIED BALLS OF CHENNA IN SYRUP. A PINCH OF GROUND CARDAMOM

CAN BE ADDED TO THE DOUGH FOR EXTRA FLAVOUR.

SYRUP
440 g (2 cups) sugar
4–5 drops rosewater

GULAB JAMUN
100 g (1 cup) low-fat powdered
  milk
2 tablespoons self-raising flour
2 teaspoons fine semolina
2 tablespoons ghee
4 tablespoons milk, to mix
24 pistachio nuts (optional)
oil for deep-frying

MAKES 24

TO MAKE the syrup, put the sugar in a large heavy-based saucepan with 850 ml (3$\frac{1}{3}$ cups) water. Stir over low heat to dissolve the sugar. Increase the heat and boil for 3 minutes. Stir in the rosewater and remove from the heat.

TO MAKE the gulab jamun, combine the powdered milk, flour, semolina and ghee in a bowl. Add enough milk to make a soft dough, mix until smooth, then divide into 24 portions. If using the pistachio nuts, press each piece of dough in the centre to make a hole, fill with a pistachio, then roll into a ball. If not using pistachios, just roll each piece into a ball.

FILL a karhai or deep saucepan one-third full with oil. Heat the oil to 150°C/300°F (a cube of bread will brown in 30 seconds) and fry the balls over low heat until golden brown all over. Remove with a slotted spoon and transfer to the syrup. When all the balls are in the syrup, bring the syrup to boiling point, then remove from the heat. Cool and serve the gulab jamun at room temperature.

Roll the gulab jamun into smooth balls. When they have fried to a deep golden brown, add them to the flavoured sugar syrup.

SHRIKHAND

THIS IS YET ANOTHER MILK-BASED RECIPE. IT IS TRADITIONALLY MADE BY STRAINING YOGHURT AND

FLAVOURING IT WITH SAFFRON AND CARDAMOM TO GIVE A THICK, RICH, CREAMY DESSERT.

1/2 teaspoon saffron strands
3 cardamom pods
250 ml (1 cup) thick plain yoghurt
  (page 280)
3 tablespoons caster (superfine)
  sugar
a few toasted flaked almonds

SERVES 4

SOAK the saffron in 1 teaspoon boiling water. Remove the cardamom seeds from the pods and coarsely crush them in a spice grinder or pestle and mortar.

PUT the yoghurt, sugar, cardamom and saffron in a bowl and beat until well mixed. Divide among four bowls and refrigerate before serving. Serve with toasted almonds sprinkled on top.

SHRIKHAND

APRICOTS IN CARDAMOM SYRUP

A KASHMIRI SPECIALITY BEST MADE FROM DRIED KASHMIRI APRICOTS WHICH HAVE LOTS OF FLAVOUR. THE SILVER LEAF MAKES THIS A SPECIAL DESSERT BUT DOES NOT HAVE TO BE USED. IT CAN BE SERVED WITH THICK CREAM OR YOGHURT TO TEMPER THE SWEETNESS.

300 g (1²/₃ cups) dried apricots
3 tablespoons caster (superfine) sugar
3 tablespoons slivered, blanched almonds
1 cm (¹/₂ inch) piece of ginger, sliced
4 cardamom pods
1 cinnamon stick
4 pieces edible silver leaf (varak), (optional)

SERVES 4

SOAK the apricots in 750 ml (3 cups) water in a large saucepan for 4 hours, or until plumped up.

ADD the sugar, almonds, ginger, cardamom and cinnamon to the apricots and bring slowly to the boil, stirring until the sugar has dissolved. Reduce the heat to a simmer and cook until the liquid has reduced by half and formed a thick syrup. Pour into a bowl, then refrigerate.

SERVE in small bowls with a piece of silver leaf for decoration. To do this, invert the piece of backing paper over each bowl. As soon as the silver leaf touches the apricots it will come away from the backing and stick to them.

KHEER

THIS IS THE INDIAN VERSION OF RICE PUDDING AND IS MADE ON THE STOVETOP INSTEAD OF IN THE OVEN. IT IS EXOTICALLY DELICIOUS, RICH AND CREAMY, WITH THE CARDAMOM AND ALMONDS GIVING IT A DISTINCTIVE TEXTURE AND FLAVOUR.

KHEER

150 g (³/₄ cup) basmati rice
20 cardamom pods
2.5 litres (10 cups) milk
30 g (¹/₃ cup) flaked almonds
165 g (³/₄ cup) sugar
30 g (¹/₄ cup) sultanas

SERVES 6

WASH the rice, then soak for 30 minutes in cold water. Drain well. Remove the seeds from the cardamom pods and lightly crush them in a spice grinder or pestle and mortar.

BRING the milk to the boil in a large heavy-based saucepan and add the rice and cardamom. Reduce the heat and simmer for 1¹/₂–2 hours, or until the rice has a creamy consistency. Stir occasionally to stop the rice sticking to the pan.

DRY-FRY the almonds in a frying pan for a few minutes over medium heat. Add the sugar, almonds and sultanas to the rice, reserving some almonds and sultanas. Mix, then divide among bowls. Serve warm, garnished with almonds and sultanas.

An advertisement for dairy products.

SALT LASSI

LASSIS ARE A VERY POPULAR DRINK IN INDIA. THEY ARE MADE BY BLENDING YOGHURT WITH A FLAVOURING WHICH CAN BE EITHER SALTY OR SWEET. BOTH THESE VERSIONS ARE COOLING, REFRESHING AND PERFECT TO DRINK WITH A CURRY.

1 teaspoon cumin seeds
625 ml (2^1/$_2$ cups) thick plain
   yoghurt (page 280)
^{1}/$_2$ teaspoon salt

SERVES 4

PLACE a small frying pan over low heat and dry-roast the cumin seeds until browned and aromatic.

BLEND the roasted cumin seeds (reserve a few for garnish) with the yoghurt, salt and 310 ml (1^1/$_4$ cups) water, either by hand or in a blender, and serve in tall glasses. If you would like the lassi a little colder, add about eight ice cubes to the blender, or stir them into the blended lassi. Garnish with the reserved cumin seeds.

MANGO LASSI

500 g (1 lb 2 oz) ripe mango
250 ml (1 cup) chilled milk
250 ml (1 cup) thick plain yoghurt
   (page 280)

SERVES 4

CHOP the mango to a pulp with a knife or in a blender, add a pinch of salt and push through a nylon sieve with the back of a spoon. Discard any fibres. The remaining syrup should be thick but should not contain any stringy bits of pulp. Refrigerate until cold.

BLEND the mango with the milk and yoghurt, either by hand or in a blender. If you would like the lassi a little colder, add about eight ice cubes to the blender, or stir them into the blended lassi.

IF YOU want to use green unripe mangoes, cook them with 220 g (1 cup) sugar and a little water and add 500 ml (2 cups) milk to the lassi, instead of yoghurt and milk.

MANGO LASSI

ALMOND SARBAT

250 g (2¹/₂ cups) freshly ground
    almonds
1 kg (4¹/₂ cups) sugar
12 cardamom pods
almond essence, to taste
5–6 drops rosewater (optional)

MAKES 250 ML (1 CUP)

PUT the almonds, sugar and 250 ml (1 cup) water in a large, heavy-based saucepan and cook over low heat, stirring constantly until the sugar dissolves. Grind the cardamom with 1 tablespoon water in a pestle and mortar or spice grinder. Add to the almond syrup. Stir the mixture, removing any scum from the top. Cook until the syrup thickens. Remove from the heat, strain through a sieve lined with muslin, and leave to cool.

ADD the almond essence and rosewater, if using, and serve in long glasses, with water, over lots of crushed ice.

Brightly coloured bangles on sale in the market in Hyderabad.

FALOODA

SWEET DRINKS, INDIAN MUSLIM IN ORIGIN, ARE OFTEN DRUNK DURING THE MONTH-LONG RAMADAN FAST. IN THIS ROSEWATER DRINK, THE SUGAR IS AN ENERGY SOURCE THAT IS HIGHLY RECOMMENDED WHILE FASTING. FALOODA CAN ALSO BE MADE WITH FALOODA NOODLES INSTEAD OF THE AGAR JELLY.

ROSE SYRUP
220 g (1 cup) sugar
2 teaspoons rosewater,
    or to taste
pink food colouring

FALOODA
2 teaspoons agar-agar
yellow food colouring
30 g (1 oz) basil seeds
1 tablespoon icing (confectioners')
    sugar
1 litre (4 cups) milk, chilled
6 tablespoons ice cream
    or thick (double/heavy) cream
pistachios, chopped (optional)
almonds, chopped (optional)
mint leaves (optional)

SERVES 6

TO MAKE the rose syrup, put the sugar and 250 ml (1 cup) water in a large, heavy-based saucepan, bring to the boil and boil for 2 minutes. Add rosewater, to taste, and enough colouring to make a pink syrup. Cool.

TO PREPARE the falooda, dissolve the agar-agar in 250 ml (1 cup) boiling water in a small saucepan. Cook over medium heat, stirring constantly for 15 minutes. Add a little yellow food colouring. Pour into a large, flat dish and refrigerate until set. Turn out onto a board and slice into thin strips (thin enough to be sucked up a straw).

SOAK the basil seeds in a little water for 1 hour, then drain. Stir the icing sugar into the milk.

TO PREPARE six glasses of falooda, pour 2 tablespoons rose syrup into each large glass. Add a helping of falooda and 2–3 teaspoons basil seeds to each and top with the sweetened, chilled milk and 1 tablespoon cream or ice cream. Garnish with nuts and mint leaves if you wish.

FALOODA

MASALA CHAI

2 cm (³/4 inch) piece of ginger
5 cm (2 inch) cinnamon stick
4 peppercorns
3 cloves
3 cardamom pods
1 tablespoon black Indian tea
250 ml (1 cup) milk
3 tablespoons sugar

SERVES 6

DRY-ROAST the ginger under a grill (broiler) for 1 minute on each side. Put the spices and ginger in a pestle and mortar or spice grinder and roughly crush them. Put the spices, tea and milk in a saucepan with 1 litre (4 cups) water and bring to the boil. Leave for 3 minutes, then add the sugar.

STRAIN off the dregs (the easiest way is to put the whole lot through a coffee plunger or very fine strainer), then pour the tea from one jug to another in a steady stream. You need to hold the jugs far apart and repeat the process until the tea begins to froth. Serve while still hot, in glasses.

MASALA COFFEE

MASALA COFFEE

THIS IS THE KERALAN CAPPUCCINO, A TRADITIONAL WAY OF MAKING COFFEE, SEEN ON EVERY STREET CORNER. THE COFFEE-MAKER, OFTEN CLAD IN A CHECKED SARONG, IS THE FOCUS OF THE VILLAGE AFTER WORK AND COFFEE IS A MUST FOR STIMULATING TALK AS THE WORLD PASSES BY.

500 ml (2 cups) milk
2 tablespoons sugar
2 cm (³/4 inch) piece of ginger
2 tablespoons freshly ground
   Keralan or other coffee
5 cardamom seeds, pounded
1 cinnamon stick
cocoa powder

SERVES 4

PUT the milk and sugar in a heavy-based saucepan, bring to the boil over low heat and keep at a low simmer.

DRY-ROAST the ginger under a grill (broiler) for 1 minute on each side, then pound it a little in a pestle and mortar to crush it and release the juices. Add to the milk with the coffee, cardamom and cinnamon. Cover and allow the flavourings to steep in the heat for 3 minutes.

STRAIN off the dregs (the easiest way is to put the whole lot through a coffee plunger or very fine strainer), then pour the coffee from one jug to another in a steady stream. You need to hold the jugs far apart and repeat the process until the coffee begins to froth. Serve while still hot, garnished with a sprinkling of cocoa.

BASICS

Rinse the rice very thoroughly under cold running water until the water running through it is completely clear.

RICE

BASMATI IS A FRAGRANT, LONG-GRAIN RICE THAT GETS ITS UNIQUE FLAVOUR FROM THE SOIL IN WHICH IT IS GROWN. WE HAVE COOKED IT BY THE ABSORPTION METHOD BUT, IF YOU PREFER, YOU CAN ADD THE RICE TO A SAUCEPAN OF BOILING WATER AND BOIL THE RICE UNTIL READY.

400 g (2 cups) basmati rice

SERVES 6

RINSE the rice under cold running water until the water running away is clear, then drain well.

PUT the rice in a heavy-based saucepan and add enough water to come about 5 cm (2 inches) above the surface of the pan. (If you stick your index finger into the rice so it rests on the bottom of the pan, the water will come up to the second joint.) Add 1 teaspoon of salt and bring the water quickly to the boil. When it boils, cover and reduce the heat to a simmer.

COOK for 15 minutes or until the rice is just tender, then remove the saucepan from the heat and rest the rice for 10 minutes without removing the lid. Fluff the rice with a fork before serving.

BOILED ROSEMATTER OR PATNI RICE

ROSEMATTER IS EATEN IN SOUTHERN INDIA AND PATNI IN CENTRAL AND WESTERN INDIA. BOTH LOOK RED AND SPECKLED BECAUSE THE RICE HAS BEEN PRECOOKED IN ITS HUSK, LEAVING SOME BRAN AND HUSK STUCK TO THE GRAIN. COOK THEM AS WE HAVE, RATHER THAN BY THE ABSORPTION METHOD.

400 g (2 cups) rosematter or patni rice

SERVES 6

RINSE the rice under cold running water until the water running away is clear, then drain well.

BRING a large, heavy-based saucepan of water to the boil and add 1 teaspoon of salt. When the water is at a rolling boil, add the rice and bring back to the boil. Keep at a steady boil for 20 minutes, then test a grain to see if it is cooked. Drain the rice and serve.

ROSEMATTER RICE

PANEER

INDIAN CHEESE, CALLED PANEER OR CHENNA WHEN COMBINED WITH SUGAR, IS AN UNRIPENED CHEESE MADE BY COAGULATING MILK WITH LEMON JUICE, THEN LEAVING TO DRAIN TO ALLOW THE CURDS AND WHEY TO SEPARATE. IT IS THEN PRESSED INTO BLOCKS.

3 litres (12 cups) milk
6 tablespoons strained lemon juice, or vinegar

FOR THE CHENNA
1 teaspoon caster (superfine) sugar
1 teaspoon maida or plain (all-purpose) flour

MAKES 550 G (1 LB 4 OZ)

TO MAKE the paneer, pour the milk into a large heavy-based saucepan. Bring to the boil, stirring with a wooden spoon so that the milk doesn't stick to the base of the pan. Reduce the heat and stir in the lemon juice, then heat over low heat for a few more seconds before turning the heat off as large bits of curd start to form. Shake the pan slowly to allow the curds to form and release the yellow whey.

IF the curds are slow to form, put the pan over low heat again for a few seconds. This helps with the coagulation.

LINE a colander with muslin or cheesecloth so that it overlaps the sides. Pour off the whey, collecting the curds gently in the colander. Gently pull up the corners of the cheesecloth so that it hangs like a bag, twist the cloth so that the whey is released, then hold the "bag" under running water to wash off the remaining whey, twisting some more to remove the excess liquid.

LEAVE the bag to hang from your tap for several hours so the weight of the curds releases more liquid and the cheese compacts. To remove more liquid, press the bag under a heavy weight, such as a tray with some tinned food piled on top, for about 1 hour. This will form a firm block of paneer. When the block is firm enough to cut into cubes, the paneer is ready for use.

TO MAKE chenna, remove the cheese from the bag and knead the paneer well with the palms of your hands until it is very smooth. Combine the paneer with the sugar and maida, kneading the sugar in until it is fully incorporated.

Once curds have formed, drain everything through a muslin-lined sieve. Squeeze out any excess liquid and drain for several hours.

TAMARIND PUREE

150 g (5¹/₂ oz) tamarind block,
broken into small pieces

MAKES 310 ML (1¹/₄ CUPS)

PUT the tamarind in a bowl, pour in 250 ml (1 cup) very hot water and soak for 3 hours or until the tamarind is soft. (If you are in a hurry, simmer the tamarind in the water for 15 minutes. Although this is efficient, it doesn't give as good a result.) Mash the tamarind thoroughly with a fork.

PUT the mixture through a sieve and extract as much of the pulp as possible by pushing it against the sieve with the back of a spoon. Put the tamarind in the sieve back in the bowl with another 125 ml (¹/₂ cup) hot water and mash again. Strain again. Discard the fibres left in the sieve. The purée can be frozen in 1 tablespoon portions and defrosted as needed.

TAMARIND PUREE

GINGER JUICE

5 cm (2 inch) piece of ginger

MAKES 2 TABLESPOONS

POUND the ginger in a pestle and mortar, or grate with a fine grater into a bowl. Put the ginger into a piece of muslin, twist it up tightly and squeeze out all the juice.

YOGHURT

YOGHURT OR CURDS ARE EATEN WITH OR IN NEARLY EVERY INDIAN MEAL IN SOME FORM OR OTHER.

YOGHURT ACTS AS A TENDERIZER IN MARINADES, THICKENS SAUCES AND MAKES REFRESHING DRINKS.

625 ml (2¹/₂ cups) milk
2 tablespoons thick plain yoghurt

MAKES 625 ML (2¹/₂ CUPS)

BRING the milk to the boil in a heavy-based saucepan, then allow to cool to lukewarm. Stir in the yoghurt, cover and leave in a warm place for about 8 hours, or overnight. The yoghurt should be thick. If it is too runny, the milk was probably too hot for the starter yoghurt; if it is too milky, the yoghurt was probably not left in a warm enough place to ferment. From each batch, use 2 tablespoons to make the next batch.

WHEN the yoghurt is set, put it in a sieve lined with a piece of muslin and leave to drain overnight. This will give a thick yoghurt which does not contain too much moisture.

GINGER JUICE

GRATED COCONUT

GRATED COCONUT IS BEST WHEN IT IS FRESH. DRIED OR DESICCATED COCONUT CAN ALSO BE USED BUT IT NEEDS TO BE SOAKED, THEN CHOPPED MORE FINELY OR GROUND TO A PASTE, OTHERWISE IT WILL BE FIBROUS. IF YOU CAN BUY A PROPER COCONUT GRATER, YOUR LIFE WILL BE MUCH EASIER.

1 coconut

MAKES 300 G (10¹/₂ OZ)

DRAIN the coconut by punching a hole in two of the dark, coloured eyes. Drain out the liquid and use it as a refreshing drink. Holding the coconut in one hand, tap around the circumference firmly with a hammer or pestle. This should cause the coconut to split open evenly. If the coconut doesn't crack easily, put it in a 150°C (300°F/Gas 2) oven for 15 minutes. This may cause it to crack as it cools. If it doesn't, it will crack easily when hit with a hammer.

IF YOU would like to use a coconut grater (hiramne), the easiest ones to use are the ones that you sit on at one end, then scrape out the coconut from each half on the serrated edge, catching it in a large bowl. If you don't have a coconut grater, prise the flesh out of the shell, trim off the hard, brown, outer skin and grate either by hand on a box grater or chop in a food processor. Grated coconut can be frozen in small portions until it is needed.

Crack the coconut by tapping it around the circumference with a heavy object. It will open neatly.

COCONUT MILK AND COCONUT CREAM

COCONUT MILK IS NOT THE LIQUID WHICH IS FOUND INSIDE THE COCONUT, WHICH IS THE JUICE OR WATER, BUT IS MADE BY SOAKING THE GRATED COCONUT FLESH IN WATER AND THEN SQUEEZING IT. THE FIRST SOAKING AND SQUEEZING GIVES A THICKER MILK, SOMETIMES CALLED CREAM.

1 quantity grated coconut

MAKES 125 ML (¹/₂ CUP) COCONUT CREAM AND 250 ML (1 CUP) COCONUT MILK

MIX the grated coconut with 125 ml (¹/₂ cup) hot water and leave to steep for 5 minutes. Pour the mixture through a sieve lined with muslin, then gather the muslin into a ball to squeeze out any extra liquid. This will make a thick coconut milk.

REPEAT the process with another 250 ml (1 cup) water to make thinner coconut milk.

COCONUT MILK AND COCONUT CREAM

PANCH PHORON

PANCH PHORON IS A FIVE-SPICE MIX USED TO FLAVOUR VEGETABLES AND PULSES. THE MIX IS FRIED

AT THE BEGINNING OF A DISH, OR FRIED AND ADDED AS A FINAL SEASONING (TARKA).

1 teaspoon cumin seeds
1 teaspoon fennel seeds
1 teaspoon fenugreek seeds
1 teaspoon brown mustard seeds
1 teaspoon kalonji (nigella seeds)

GRIND all the spices to a fine powder in a spice grinder, a pestle and mortar, or with a grinding stone. Store in a small airtight container until you need it.

MAKES 1 TABLESPOON

PANCH PHORON

GARAM MASALA

GARAM MASALA MEANS 'WARMING SPICE MIX'. IT CAN BE A MIXTURE OF WHOLE OR GROUND SPICES.

RECIPES ARE NUMEROUS BUT THEY ARE ALL AROMATIC, RATHER THAN 'HOT' MIXES.

8 cardamom pods
2 Indian bay leaves (cassia leaves)
1 teaspoon black peppercorns
2 teaspoons cumin seeds
2 teaspoons coriander seeds
5 cm (2 inch) cinnamon stick
1 teaspoon cloves

REMOVE the seeds from the cardamom pods. Break the bay leaves into small pieces. Put them in a spice grinder or pestle and mortar with the remaining spices and grind to a fine powder. Store in a small airtight container until needed.

MAKES 3 TABLESPOONS

GARAM MASALA

CHAAT MASALA

CHAAT MASALA IS A SALTY, TANGY SEASONING USED IN POPULAR SNACKS SUCH AS BHEL PURI. IT CAN

BE TOSSED THROUGH DRY SNACK MIXES OR SPRINKLED ONTO FRUIT AND VEGETABLES AS A SEASONING.

4 tablespoons coriander seeds
2 tablespoons cumin seeds
1 teaspoon ajowan
3 tablespoons black salt
1 tablespoon amchoor powder
2 dried chillies
1 teaspoon black peppercorns
1 teaspoon pomegranate seeds

PLACE a small frying pan over low heat and dry-roast the coriander seeds until aromatic. Remove from the pan and dry-roast the cumin seeds, then separately, the ajowan. Grind the roasted mixture to a fine powder with the other ingredients, using a spice grinder or pestle and mortar. Store in an airtight container.

MAKES 10 TABLESPOONS

THE TWO main tea-producing areas in India are Assam *(left page)* and the Nilgiris *(right page)*. In Assam, the tea gardens are situated along a flat valley and the bushes are interspersed with shade trees. In the Nilgiris, they are on the rolling foothills. However, both areas have a high rainfall, a prerequisite for growing tea. Tea is picked by hand, with only the bud and top leaves being plucked. One section of the

TEA

TEA FROM CHINA WAS SO IMPORTANT TO EUROPE BY THE 18TH CENTURY THAT WHEN TRADE IN TEA STOPPED DURING THE OPIUM WARS, THE BRITISH DECIDED TO GROW CHINESE TEA IN INDIA. THEY THEN FOUND A NATIVE TEA ALREADY GROWING IN ASSAM.

The first tea garden in India was established in 1835 and India quickly became the world's biggest producer of tea and a nation of tea drinkers. Tea is made from the fresh leaves of the *Camellia sinensis or Camellia assamica* tree native to both south-west China and Assam in the far north-east of

India. The leaves can be processed in different ways. Green tea is dried before fermentation and black tea is fermented before drying. In India, black tea (chai) is the most common.

MAKING TEA

The process of turning fresh green tea leaves into black tea is called 'making'. Making tea by either the CTC or the Orthodox method refers to the way the leaves are cut or rolled. CTC means 'crush or cut, tear, curl'—the leaves are fed through a cutter before they are fermented and dried. This gives a fine, granular tea. Orthodox refers to the method of rolling the leaves (only the best are used) on a rolling table to give whole leaf or broken leaf tea. Both methods break down the veins in the leaves and start the fermentation process. Orthodox tea is considered to have superior flavour and CTC tea to have more strength. The two are often blended to give a strength and flavour balance.

garden is worked on at a time to make sure that the tea bushes are kept to the same height. A stick is laid out along the bush and the leaves above it are picked. The tea is collected three times a day. The leaves are tipped out of their baskets, briefly sorted through to get rid of any twigs, then weighed at the collection points throughout the garden. The leaves are then delivered to the factory to be made into tea.

TEA-PRODUCING AREAS IN INDIA

ASSAM lies beneath the foothills of the Himalayas. Assam tea is produced seasonally in first and second flushes. The second flush produces 'tippy' tea which means the black tea has plenty of young gold tips. Assam tea is known as 'orange' tea due to its brown and gold colour. Assam teas are full-bodied, with a strong, rich taste which tends to linger in the mouth.

THE NILGIRIS these hills form part of the Western Ghats in the south of India. Tea produced here has a bright colour and astringent quality and is picked at all times of the year.

DARJEELING, a rich tea produced in the foothills of the Himalayas, has a 'muscatel' flavour. Sometimes described as the champagne of teas, it is produced in limited quantities. Darjeeling tea is often sold as tea from a single garden.

OTHER AREAS in India where tea is grown include the Dooars in Bengal, and the Kangara valley in Himachal Pradesh where green tea is produced.

INDIA produces about 500 million kilograms of tea a year. Half of this is exported and the rest is drunk in India. Chai is made by boiling tea with milk and sugar to make a strong, sweet brew.

GLOSSARY OF INDIAN FOOD AND COOKING

agar-agar Also known as China grass, this is a setting agent made from certain types of seaweed. It is sold as strips, sheets, flakes or powder, dissolves in boiling water, and unlike gelatine will set at room temperature. Available from supermarkets, health food shops and Indian food shops.

ajowan (ajwain) A spice that looks like miniature cumin seeds and has a similar aroma but stronger flavour. Use sparingly.

amaranth (marsa) A leafy green, or green and dark red vegetable. It has a peppery flavour and can be substituted with spinach in recipes. Available at Indian food shops.

amchoor/amchur powder (khatai) A fine beige powder made by drying green mangoes. It is used as a souring agent or meat tenderizer in Indian cooking. It is an essential flavour in chaat masala (page 284). Available at Indian food shops.

asafoetida (hing) This yellowish powder or lump of resin is made from the dried latex of a type of fennel. Asafoetida has an extremely pungent smell which has earned it the name 'devil's dung'. It is used to make pulses and legumes more digestible and Hindu Brahmins and Jains use it instead of garlic and onions which are forbidden to them. Asafoetida is always fried to calm its aroma. It comes in small airtight containers and is available from Indian food shops.

atta Sometimes called chapati flour, this is made from finely ground whole durum wheat. Some have a proportion of white flour added, labelled as 80/20 or 60/40. Atta is much finer and softer than wholemeal flour so if you can't find it, use half wholemeal and half maida or plain (all-purpose) flour.

banana flower (kere kafool/mocha) This is the purple, teardrop-shaped flower of the banana plant.The purple leaves and pale yellow buds which grow between them are discarded. Only the inner pale core is eaten. This needs to be blanched in boiling water to remove any bitterness. Wear rubber gloves to prepare banana flower as it has a gummy substance, which can stain your fingers. Available from Indian food shops.

banana leaves Large green leaves which can be used as a wrapping (dip in boiling water to soften them) for foods, or as a plate to eat off. Young leaves are preferable. Available from Indian food shops.

basil seeds (subja) These tiny black seeds of a type of wild Indian basil are soaked in water until they swell. When soaked, they are surrounded by clear jelly. They have no flavour and are used for texture in drinks like falooda (page 271). Buy at Indian food shops.

besan flour Also known as gram flour, this is a yellow flour made from ground Bengal gram or chickpeas. It has a nutty flavour and is used as a thickener in curries, as well as in batters, dumplings, sweets and breads.

bitter melon Also known as bitter gourd, karela or warty melon, this looks like a pale cucumber with a warty skin. The flesh is bitter and needs to be blanched or degorged, then married with strong flavours.

black-eyed beans (lobhia) Also called black-eyed peas, these are actually dried cow peas and are also known as chowli dal when split. They are buff-coloured beans with a small dark eye on one side. They need to be soaked overnight or pre-cooked before use. Avoid dark or wrinkled beans as they are old.

black salt (kala namak) A rock salt mined in central India. Available as black or dark brown lumps, or ground to a pinkish grey powder. Unlike white salt, it has a tangy, smoky flavour. Buy at Indian food shops.

buttermilk (chaas) The mildly sour liquid left when milk is churned to butter. Commercial buttermilk is made from fermented skim milk and is not 'live' as real buttermilk would be.

cardamom (elaichi) Dry green pods full of sticky, tiny brown or black seeds which have a sweet flavour and pungent aroma. If you need ground cardamom, open the pods and grind the seeds. Ready-ground cardamom quickly loses flavour. Use pods whole or crushed. Brown cardamom has a peppery flavour not suitable for sweet dishes.

cayenne pepper A very hot red chilli powder made from sun-dried red chillies.

chaat masala Seasoning used for various snacks known as chaat (which means 'to lick' in Hindi). The spice blend uses a variety of flavourings including asafoetida, amchoor, black salt, cumin, cayenne, ajowan and pepper. (See page 284.)

chana dal (gram lentils) These are husked, split, polished, yellow Bengal gram, the most common type of gram lentil in India. They are often cooked with a pinch of asafoetida to make them more easy to digest.

chenna Sweetened Indian cheese, used in sweet dishes. Found in the refrigerated section in supermarkets and Indian food shops. To make your own, see page 279.

chickpeas (chana) Chickpeas come white (kabuli/kubli) or black (kala). The white chickpeas are actually a tan colour and the black ones are dark brown. Usually sold whole, but also sold split, dried chickpeas need to be soaked for 8 hours in cold water before use. They will double in size. Tinned ones can be used but need to be added at the end of the cooking time as they are already very soft.

chillies (lal mirch/hari mirch) Red and green chillies are widely used in Indian cuisine. Recipes generally give a colour, rather than a variety. Many varieties are grown in India and are used in a regional or seasonal context. Kashmiri chillies are dark red and mild, Goan chillies are short and stubby and mundu chillies are round. Small dhani (bird's eye chillies) are the hottest.

chillies, dried (sabat lal mirch) Dried whole chillies of various shapes, sizes and heat levels. Sometimes soaked to soften them. Remove the seeds if they are very hot.

chilli flakes Dried, coarsely ground chillies with the seeds included; usually hot.

chilli powder A wide variety of chillies are dried and crushed to make chilli powders. Some, such as Kashmiri chilli powder and paprika, are used for colour, whereas others like cayenne are used for heat. Don't use chilli powder indiscriminately. The amount used can be varied, to taste, so start with a small amount and determine how hot it is.

cloves (laung) The dried, unopened flower buds of the clove tree. Brown and nail-shaped, they have a pungent flavour, so use in moderation. Use whole or ground.

coconut (nariyal) The fruit of a coconut palm. The inner nut is encased in a husk which has to be removed. The hard shell can then be drained of juice and cracked open to extract the white meat. Coconut meat is jellyish in younger nuts and harder in older ones. Dried coconut meat is known as copra. The method for cracking coconuts is shown on page 283.

coconut cream This is made by soaking freshly grated coconut in boiling water and then squeezing out a thick, sweet coconut-flavoured liquid. It is available tinned. To make your own coconut cream, see page 283.

coconut milk A thinner version of coconut cream, made as above but with more water or from a second pressing. Available tinned. To make your own, see page 283.

coconut milk powder A powdered form of coconut which when mixed with water makes coconut milk or cream. Sold in supermarkets or Indian food shops.

coriander (hara dhaniya) Fresh coriander (cilantro) leaves are used in recipes and as a colourful garnish. Buy healthy bunches of green leaves. Avoid any which are yellowing.

coriander (dhaniya) seeds The round seeds of the coriander plant. The seeds have a spicy aroma, are widely used in Indian cooking and are common in spice mixes such as garam masala. To intensify the flavour, dry-roast the seeds until aromatic, before crushing them. Best freshly ground for each dish. Available whole or ground.

creamed coconut A solid block of coconut cream which needs to be reconstituted with water, or can be added straight to a dish to give a strong coconut flavour. Slice pieces off the block as required.

cumin (jeera) seeds The green or ochre, elongated ridged seeds of a plant of the parsley family. It has a peppery, slightly bitter flavour and is very aromatic.To intensify the flavour, dry-roast the seeds before crushing them. Best freshly ground for each dish. Available whole or ground. Kala jeera are a black variety.

curry leaves (kadhi patta/meetha neem) Smallish green aromatic leaves of a tree native to India and Sri Lanka. These give a distinctive flavour to south Indian dishes. They are usually fried and added to the dish or used as a garnish at the end.

dal (dhal) is used to describe not only an ingredient but a dish made from it. In India, dal relates to any type of dried split pea, bean or lentil. The cooking times vary as do the texture and flavour. A dal dish can be a thin soup or more like a stew. All dal should be rinsed before use.

degchi A cooking pot, often brass lined with tin, which has no handle. It has a thick base and straight sides like a saucepan.

drumsticks (sahjan) Long, dark green, ridged fibrous pods from the horseradish tree. Drumsticks, so called because of their rigidity, need to be cut into lengths before being cooked. The inner pulp, the only part eaten, is scooped out with a spoon or scraped out with your teeth. Buy uniformly slim pods. Sold in Indian food shops.

fennel (saunph) seeds The dried seeds of a Mediterranean plant, fennel seeds are oval, greenish yellow, with ridges running along them, and look like large cumin. Used as an aromatic and a digestive. To intensify the flavour, dry-roast the seeds before crushing them. Available whole or ground. Best freshly ground.

fenugreek (methi) seeds Not a true seed, but a dried legume. Ochre in colour and almost square, with a groove down one side, fenugreek has a curry aroma (it is a major ingredient in commercial curry powders) and is best dry-roasted for a few seconds before use. Don't brown them too much or they will be bitter.

garam masala A northern Indian spice mix which means 'warming spice mix', it mostly contains coriander, cumin, cardamom, black pepper, cloves, cinnamon and nutmeg. There are many versions and you can buy ready-ground mixes or make your own (page 284). Garam masala is usually added to meat dishes as a final seasoning.

ghee A highly clarified butter made from cow or water buffalo milk. Ghee can be heated to a high temperature without burning and has an aromatic flavour. Vegetable ghees are also available but don't have the same aromatic qualities. You can substitute clarified butter, or make your own ghee by melting unsalted butter in a saucepan, bringing to a simmer and cooking for about 30 minutes to evaporate out any water. Skim any scum off the surface, then drain the ghee off, leaving the white sediment behind. Leave to cool.

ginger (adrak) The rhizome of a tropical plant which is sometimes referred to as a 'root'. It is sold in 'hands'. Fresh young ginger should have a smooth, pinkish beige skin and be firm and juicy. As it ages, the skin toughens and the flesh becomes more fibrous. Avoid old ginger which is wrinkled as it will be tough. Choose pieces you can snap easily. Ginger is measured in centimetre or inch pieces and this means pieces with an average-sized width. Variations in size will not adversely affect the flavour of the dish. Ginger is also available dried and ground.

green banana (kela) Cooking banana, also known as plantain, which looks like a large, unripe green banana.

green unripe mango (kacha am) A variety of mango widely used for cooking in Asian countries. Available from Indian food shops.

hilsa (elish) A much-prized fish, this is a type of shad with sweet flesh and lots of tiny bones. Hilsa are caught when they enter fresh water to spawn. Large herrings or firm white fish can be used instead.

Indian bay leaves (tej patta) These are the dried leaves of the cassia tree. They look somewhat like dried European bay leaves but they have a cinnamon flavour. They are used mainly in Bengali cuisine and cuisine of the north of India and are available from Indian food shops.

jaggery (gur) Made from sugar cane, this is a raw sugar with a caramel flavour and alcoholic aroma. Jaggery, which is sold in lumps, is slightly sticky and varies in colour depending on the juice from which it is made. Jaggery can also refer to palm sugar. Soft brown sugar can be used as a substitute.

kalonji (nigella seeds) Small teardrop-shaped black seeds with an onion flavour, used both as a spice in northern India and as a decoration for breads such as naan. It is used in panch phoron (page 284).

karhai/kadhai A deep wok-shaped cooking dish. Heavy cast iron ones are best for talawa (deep-frying) and carbon steel ones for bhoona (frying). There are decorative ones which are best for serving, not cooking.

Kashmiri chilli powder Made from ground red Kashmiri chillies which have a deep red colour but little heat. A mild, dark red chilli powder can be substituted.

kokum The dried purple fruit of the gamboge tree which is used in southern Indian, Gujarati and Maharashtran cuisine to impart an acid fruity flavour. Kokum looks like dried pieces of purple/black rind and is quite sticky. It can be bought from Indian food shops and is sometimes called cocumful. A smoked version which is called kodampodli is also available. Kokum needs to be briefly soaked before use.

maida Plain white flour used for making naan and other Indian recipes. Plain (all-purpose) flour is a suitable substitute.

masoor dal (red lentils) When whole (known as matki or bagali) these are dark brown or green. When split, they are salmon in colour. The split ones are the most common as they cook more easily and do not usually need soaking as the whole ones do.

methi (fenugreek leaves) The leaves of young fenugreek plants, these are used as a vegetable and treated much like spinach. They have a mildly bitter flavour. Strip the leaves off the stalks as the stalks are often tough. English spinach leaves can be used but will not give the same flavour. Available fresh or dried, from Indian food shops.

moong dal Split and skinned mung beans, which are pale yellow. The dal does not always need to be soaked. Whole mung beans (sabat moong), also called green gram, must be soaked before use.

mustard oil (sarson ka tel) Made from pressed brown mustard seeds, this is a strongly flavoured oil which is used in Bengali and Punjabi cooking. The oil is usually preheated to smoking point and then cooled to temper its strong aroma.

mustard seeds (rai) Yellow, brown and black mustard seeds are used in Indian cooking, especially in Bengal. Brown and black are interchangeable. The seeds are either added to hot oil to pop, to make them taste nutty rather than hot, or are ground to a paste before use in which case they are still hot. Split mustard seeds are called mustard dal.

oil (tel) Several types of oil are used in Indian cuisine, depending on where the dish comes from. An Indian pantry should contain several oils for different uses. Cold-pressed or refined peanut (groundnut) oil is used in northern and central India and is a good all-purpose oil (use only the refined version for deep-frying). Sesame oil made from raw sesame seeds is used in the South, and mustard oil in the Punjab and Bengal. These oils impart flavour to the dishes in which they are used. Coconut oil is also used in the South where coconut is a major flavouring. It fries well but is very high in saturated fats.

okra (bhindi) Also known as ladies' fingers, these are green, fuzzy, tapered pods with ridges running down them. When cut they give off a mucilaginous substance which disappears during cooking.

panch phoron (panch phora) Meaning five spices, this mix is used in Bengali and Bangladeshi cuisine. It contains fennel, brown mustard, kalonji, fenugreek, and cumin seeds in equal amounts. It can be used whole or ground. (See page 284.)

paneer A fresh cheese made by coagulating milk with lemon juice and leaving it to drain. Paneer is usually pressed into a block and can be found in the refrigerated section in supermarkets and Indian food shops. To make your own, see page 279.

paprika (deghi mirch) A reddish orange powder made from ground capsicums (peppers) grown in Kashmir. Usually sweet rather than hot, paprika is used for colour. It needs to be fried before use. Spanish or Hungarian paprika can be substituted.

pine nuts Small cream-coloured seeds from Neosia pine cones which grow in the Himalayas. In Kashmir, they are a staple and are used both whole and ground. Any pine nut may be used.

pomegranate seeds (anardana) Sun-dried whole or ground sour pomegranate seeds, used to add a sour, tangy flavour to north Indian dishes. They are also used as a garnish. Available from Indian food shops.

pomfret (rupchanda, chamna) A silvery seawater fish with tiny black spots. Pomfret is expensive and hard to find outside India, although it is sometimes available frozen. Sole, flounder, leatherjacket or John Dory fillets can be substituted.

poppadom (papadam, papad, appalam) These are quite thin wafers made from a paste of lentil (gram) flours, rice flour or even tapioca or sago flour, which is rolled out very thin and then sun-dried. Poppadoms come in different sizes and flavours. Northern Indian ones often have chilli flakes or spices added. To fry poppadoms, heat about 2.5 cm (1 inch) oil in a frying pan until very hot, add the poppadoms one at a time and press them down into the oil with a spatula until they expand and lighten in colour. To flame-roast them, hold a poppadom in some tongs above a gas flame until it expands in size, curls and gets flecked with bubbles (toast both sides). Fried poppadoms will stay crisp for about two hours.

poppy seeds (khus khus) In India, white poppy seeds are used rather than the European black or grey ones. They are used either whole or ground. The ground poppy seeds are used to thicken dishes like korma. Whole ones are often roasted and used in spice mixes. Don't use black poppy seeds as a thickener or the colour of your dish will be greyish.

puffed rice (moori, mamra, kurmura) Rather like popcorn, puffed rice is made by exploding dried rice out of its husks by dropping the grains onto hot sand. It is used in snacks such as bhel puri, or rolled in jaggery to make sweets. Available from Indian food shops.

rice (chaaval) Rice grain types and sizes vary across India. Much of the rice which is eaten is grown locally and it is nearly always white and polished. Popular long-grained rices include basmati, a particularly fragrant rice used for special occasions (it is expensive); patna, with a more rounded grain, is eaten in the North; and gobindavog is used in Bengal. Rices with some husk left on, which gives them some red colouration, include red patni, grown in central and western India, and rosematter, grown in southern India. You can use whichever variety you like best.

rice flour (chaaval ka atta) Finely ground rice which is used for making dosas. A coarser grind called idli-rava is used for idlis. Buy at Indian food shops.

rice sticks (rice vermicelli, chaaval ke sev) Made from rice flour, these noodles are very thin. They are used for sweets or savoury snacks and need to be softened in boiling water. Other Asian rice vermicelli can be used as a substitute.

roasted chana dal Bengal gram which have been roasted so they puff up and get a porous, crunchy texture. Used in snacks. Buy in bags from Indian food shops.

rohu A black, silvery carp with one central bone and firm flesh. It cuts into steaks very well. Any firm-fleshed fish can be substituted.

rosewater (ruh gulab/gulab jal) Made from rose essence and water, this is used to perfume sweets, desserts and drinks. It has aroma but no flavour. Use sparingly.

saag A generic term for leafy greens.

saffron strands (kesar/zaffran) The dried stigmas of a crocus flower. The strands give an intense yellow colour and musky aroma. Only a few are needed for each dish. Indian saffron grows in Kashmir. It needs to be soaked in liquid before use.

sago (sabudhana) Small dried balls of sago palm sap which are used for milky desserts and savoury dishes. Cooked sago is transparent and soft with a silky texture.

semolina (sooj, rava) A fine, coarse or medium grain made from processed wheat with the wheat germ removed. It swells when cooked to give a creamy, textured effect. Used for sweets and upama.

sev Very fine noodles, used in bhel puri, made from besan flour. Sold at Indian food shops.

sevian These are very fine noodles made from wheat flour. They have a biscuity flavour. Sold at Indian food shops.

silver leaf (varak) Very thin, edible sheets of silver. They have no flavour or aroma and come in boxes or books between sheets of tissue paper. Always apply the silver to the food from the backing sheet and then pull off the backing sheet. If you touch the foil it will stick to you. Silver leaf does not go on in an even layer because it is so fragile.

split peas (matar dal) Split dried peas which need to be soaked before they are cooked and have a slightly chewy texture. Green and yellow ones are available.

tamarind (imli) A souring agent made from the pods of the tamarind tree. Sold either as a block of pulp, fibrous husk and seeds, as cleaned pulp, or as ready-prepared tamarind purée or concentrate. If using the pulp, see page 280 to make your own purée.

tandoori food colouring A bright red powder which is used to colour tandoori dishes. Add to tandoori pastes to colour them.

tarka A seasoning process, either the first or last step, used in Indian cookery. Spices and aromatics are fried in oil to flavour the oil, then the oil is stirred into the dish, most commonly at the end of cooking.

tava A specially shaped hotplate used in India to cook breads. Some are flat, others are slightly convex or concave. Keep oiled to stop them going rusty. Non-stick ones are also available.

toor dal (toovar dal) Also called yellow lentils, these come oiled and plain. Oiled ones look slightly greasy and need to be soaked in hot water to remove the oil. Soak the dal for a few hours before cooking.

turmeric (haldi) Dried turmeric, sold whole or ground, is a deep yellow colour. It has a slightly bitter flavour and a pungent aroma. Turmeric is used for both colour and flavour.

urad dal The split variety (chilke urad) is a cream colour with black skin. The skinned variety is cream. Urad dal does not usually need to be soaked. The dal is used when making dosa and idli batters and it becomes glutinous and creamy when cooked.

vinegar (sirka) Made from fermented alcohol, vinegars based on sugar cane molasses (dark) and coconut (clear) are used, mainly in Parsi, Anglo-Indian and Goan food. If unavailable, substitute balsamic or white vinegar.

whole black gram (sabat urad) This whole urad dal has a black skin. Usually it has to be soaked or precooked before use.

yoghurt (dahi, doi) Yoghurt in India is made with whole milk and is a thick, set yoghurt. If you use commercial yoghurt, you may need to drain it in muslin first to remove any excess liquid. See page 280 for home-made yoghurt instructions.

INDEX

BIBLIOGRAPHY

Achaya, K.T. *A Historical Dictionary of Indian Food.* Oxford University Press, 1998.

Baljekar, Mridula. *Secrets from an Indian Kitchen.* Pavilion Books Limited, 2000.

Banerjee, Satarupa. *Book Of Indian Sweets.* Rupa and Co, 1994.

Bharadwaj, Monisha. *The Indian Kitchen.* Kyle Cathie Limited, 1996.

Bladholm, Linda. *The Indian Grocery Store Demystified.* Renaissance Books, 2000.

Bradnock, Robert and Roma. *Footprint India Handbook.* Footprint Handbooks, 1999

Davidson, Alan. *The Oxford Companion to Food.* Oxford University Press, 1999.

Gupta, Minakshie Das and Bunny, Jaya, Chaliha. *The Calcutta Cook Book.* Penguin Books, 1995.

Jaffrey, Madhur. *A Taste of India.* Pavillion Books Limited, 2000.

Kaimla, Maya. *Savouring the Spice Coast of India.* HarperCollins, 2000.

Kingman, Rani. *A Taste of Madras.* Interlink Books, 1996.

Lonely Planet. *India.* Lonely Planet Publications. Pty Ltd, 1999

Marks, Copeland. *The Varied Kitchens of India. Cuisines of the Anglo-Indians of Calcutta, Bengalis, Jews of Calcutta, Kashmiris, Parsis, and Tibetans of Darjeeling.* M. Evans and Company, Inc., 1986.

The Rough Guide. *India.* Rough Guides Ltd, 1999

Sinclair, Charles. *International Dictionary of Food and Cooking.* Peter Collin Publishing Ltd, 1998.

Singh, Dharamjit. *Indian Cookery.* Penguin Books, 1970.

Solomon, Charmaine. *Encyclopedia of Asian Food.* William Heinemann, 1996.

Stobbart, Tom. *The Cook's Encyclopedia.* Grub Street, 1998.

Veerasawmy, E. P. *Indian Cookery.* Arco Publications, 1964.

Westrip, Joyce. P. *An ABC of Indian Food.* Prospect Books, 1996.

Wickramasinghe, Priya. *Leith's Indian and Sri Lankan Cookery.* Bloomsbury Publishing Plc, 1998.

THE FOOD OF INDIA

Published by Murdoch Books Pty Limited

ISBN 1 74045 472 3

Publishing Manager: Kay Halsey
Food Editor: Lulu Grimes
Design Concept and Cover Design: Marylouise Brammer
Designer: Susanne Geppert
Editors: Wendy Stephen, Justine Harding
Photographers: Jason Lowe (location); Alan Benson (recipes)
Stylist: Sarah de Nardi
Stylist's Assistants: Rekha Arnott, Julie Ray, Sonia Grieg
Recipes: Priya Wickramasinghe, Carol Selva Rajah
Additional Recipes: Kuvel Sundar Singh, Lisa Harvey, Margaret Grimes, Ajoy Joshi, Rekha Arnott, Radha Jayaram
Map: Rosanna Vecchio
Production: Megan Alsop

Publisher: Kay Scarlett
Chief Executive: Juliet Rogers

Murdoch Books Australia Pty Limited
Pier 8/9, 23 Hickson Road, Millers Point NSW 2000
Phone: + 61 (0) 2 8220 2000   Fax: + 61 (0) 2 8220 2558

Murdoch Books UK Limited
Erico House, 6th Floor North, 93–99 Upper Richmond Road
Putney, London SW15 2TG
Phone: + 44 (0) 20 8785 5995 Fax: + 44 (0) 20 8785 5985

IMPORTANT: Those who might be at risk from the effects of salmonella food poisoning
(the elderly, pregnant women, young children and those suffering from immune deficiency
diseases) should consult their GP with any concerns about eating raw eggs.

ACKNOWLEDGMENTS

The Publisher wishes to thank the following for all their help in making this book possible:

The Oberoi Group: Victoria Hobbs, Aleysha Allan; Taj Hotels and Palaces: TATA Tea Ltd: Mr S.M. Kidwai, Mr Shamsher
Singh Dogra, Kiran Desai; Spices Board of India: V. Jayashankar, Dr. P.S.S.Thampi. James Finlay: Mike Jones.
Ian Hemphill. Ajoy Joshi, Arun Ramrakha.

Kerala: Joerg Drechsel and Txuku Iriarte Solana, K.P.Francis, Joseph Jescil, Ram Prem, Saju, Sony, Stephen, Suresh,
Rajesh, Eldhose, Malabar House Residency, Kochi; Mr Lakshmanan, Ramkumar Menon, Mr Kalyanraman, Tata Spices
Centre, Kochi; Mr Angelos, Mr Balakrishan, Tata Tea Bag Unit, Kochi; George Netto, TATA Tea, Munnar; Mr Devanand,
Jacob, Spices Board of India, Kochi; Spice Village, Periyar; High Range Club, Munnar; Mylamdumpara Spice Research
Station. *Chennai:* Alex Baja, B. Balaji, Sanjeev Khan,Taj Coromandel, Chennai. *Hyderabad:* G. Pulla Reddy, Hyderabad;
Sanjukthaa Roy, Taj Krishna, Hyderabad. *Calcutta:* Rabindra Nath Das (late) and family, K.C. Das Private Ltd, Calcutta;
Ranvir Bhandari, Oberoi Grand, Calcutta. *Assam:* Mr and Mrs Prabal Choudhury, Mr and Mrs A. Bhattacharya, S. Rafique, A.
Dutta, Loni Borpatra Gohain, Chubwa Tea Estate; Mr and Mrs Bordoloi, A. Kapur, G. Bora, S. Das, R. Hazarika, Powai Tea
Estate, Assam. *Delhi:* Ashima Lal Sharma, Ramneek Lamba, Oberoi, New Delhi; Bengali Sweet House, Delhi; Haldiram,
Delhi. *Mumbai:* Anil Kaul, Oberoi Mumbai; V.R.Joglekar, Mumbai Port Trust.